Brexit, Boris, and the Media

EDITED BY
JOHN MAIR, TOR CLARK,
NEIL FOWLER, RAYMOND SNODDY
and
RICHARD TAIT

Published 2020 by Abramis academic publishing

www.abramis.co.uk

ISBN 978 1 84549 764 4

Typeset in Garamond

Abramis is an imprint of arima publishing.

arima publishing
ASK House, Northgate Avenue
Bury St Edmunds, Suffolk IP32 6BB
t: (+44) 01284 700321

www.arimapublishing.com

Contents

iv

Acknowledgements

This book is the result of three years of active debate and discussions among the five editors. Ever since we published *Brexit, Trump and the Media* in 2017 we knew we wanted to curate another book on Britain and Brexit. Until Boris Johnson came along as Prime Minister in July 2019 we did not have a real focus. That became even sharper with the December 12 election. Johnson and the Tories' thumping victory showed us something was stirring in the populace and we should try to analyse and explain it. We hope we have.

These books are not just the very hard work of the five editors but also the (unpaid) work of 40 authors. To them we owe a deep gratitude – as well as to our publisher Abramis for its work.

Our hope is that this work informs and explains.

John Mair, Oxford
Tor Clark, Leicester
Neil Fowler, Northumberland
Raymond Snoddy, London
Richard Tait, London

The editors

John Mair has taught journalism at the Universities of Coventry, Kent, Northampton, Brunel, Edinburgh Napier, Guyana and the Communication University of China. He has edited 22 'hackademic' volumes over the last ten years, on subjects ranging from trust in television, the health of investigative journalism, reporting the 'Arab Spring', to three volumes on the Leveson Inquiry. He and Richard Lance Keeble invented the sub-genre. John also created the Coventry Conversations, which attracted 350 media movers and shakers to Coventry University; the podcasts of those have been downloaded six million times worldwide. Since then, he has launched the Northampton Chronicles, Media Mondays at Napier and most recently the Harrow Conversations at Westminster University. In a previous life, he was an award-winning producer/director for the BBC, ITV and Channel 4, and a secondary school teacher.

Tor Clark is Associate Professor in Journalism and programme director of the BA Journalism at the University of Leicester, UK. After studying Politics and History at Lancaster University, he worked for the Northamptonshire Evening Telegraph, before becoming editor, first of the Harborough Mail in Leicestershire, and then of Britain's oldest newspaper, the Rutland & Stamford Mercury. Previously he was Principal Lecturer in Journalism at De Montfort University in Leicester, where he launched two Journalism degrees, one accredited by the NCTJ. He holds an MA in Mass Communication from the University of Leicester.

He is a regular commentator on politics and media for BBC Leicester and a Senior Fellow of the Higher Education Academy.

He dedicates his contribution to this book to the memory of his friend and colleague, Andy Plaice, 1965-2020, Senior Lecturer in Journalism at De Montfort University in Leicester, who was keen to read this book, but did not live long enough to see it completed.

Neil Fowler has been in journalism since graduation, starting life as trainee reporter on the Leicester Mercury. He went on to edit four regional dailies, including The Journal in the north east of England and The Western Mail in Wales. He was then publisher of The Toronto Sun in Canada before returning to the UK to edit Which? magazine. In 2010/11 he was the Guardian Research Fellow at Oxford University's Nuffield College where he investigated the decline and future of regional and local newspapers in the UK. From then until 2016 he helped organise the college's prestigious David Butler media and politics seminars. As well as being an occasional contributor to trade magazines he now acts as an adviser to organisations on their management and their external and internal communications and media policies and strategies.

Raymond Snoddy OBE, after studying at Queen's University in Belfast, worked on local and regional newspapers, before joining The Times in 1971. Five years later he moved to the Financial Times and reported on media issues before returning to The Times as media editor in 1995. At present, he is a freelance journalist writing for a range of publications. He presented NewsWatch on the BBC from its inception in 2004 until 2012. His other television work has included presenting Channel 4's award-winning series Hard News. In addition, Snoddy is the author of a biography of the media tycoon Michael Green and of *The Good, the Bad and the Ugly*, which looked at the UK national press in the 1990s. He was awarded an OBE for his services to journalism in 2000.

Richard Tait CBE is Professor of Journalism at the School of Journalism, Media and Culture, at Cardiff University. From 2003 to 2012, he was director of the school's Centre for Journalism. He was editor of Newsnight from 1985 to 1987, editor of Channel 4 News from 1987 to 1995 and editor-in-chief of ITN from 1995 to 2002. He was a BBC governor and chair of the governors' programme complaints committee from 2004 to 2006, and a BBC Trustee and chair of the Trust's editorial standards committee from 2006 to 2010. He is a fellow of the Society of Editors and the Royal Television Society, board member of the International News Safety Institute and an independent trustee of the Disasters Emergency Committee.

Introduction

All change for UK politics and journalism?

Despite the Government being run by a journalist, Boris Johnson and his team may be aiming to change the long-established relationship between journalists and politicians. But these uncertain times should be seized upon as an opportunity not a threat, says BBC *Today* programme host Nick Robinson, who has known the PM since university and covered his political rise

I've known Boris Johnson since we were students together, since we debated together, since we were hacks together. I made one big mistake for much of that time. It's a mistake some continue to make. I didn't take him seriously. All that changed when I bumped into Boris (as we were happy to call him then) walking through the House of Commons soon after he announced he was going to run for Parliament. "Why?" I asked him. Why turn his back on a glittering journalistic career, as editor of *The Spectator* and star columnist at the *Telegraph,* and on growing fame and fortune after starring on *Have I Got News for You* for the relative obscurity, powerlessness and low pay of a backbench MP. He replied without the faintest flicker of a smile: "What we do is all too easy, isn't it, Nick? We don't actually change anything, do we?" Many in the media have assumed Boris is not serious about very much other than power and, since he's 'one of us', he won't seek to challenge the journalistic culture. They couldn't be more wrong.

I relate this story as it is increasingly clear to me the Prime Minister is serious in his belief that the British media has to change or be changed. The events set out and analysed in this book – the events which all have Boris Johnson as their focus – have, I believe, convinced him that his old colleagues in the Guild of Hacks, Scribblers, Pundits and Allied Trades hold up a distorted mirror to the country and what we all see in that mirror holds the country back.

What we saw in the run up to Brexit, the elections that followed and are continuing to see now is a power struggle between politicians and journalists over control of the news agenda, the right to hold those in authority to account and allegations of alleged bias. It can hardly be described as new. In the 1770s Lord North had those who dared to print accounts of debates in the House of Commons thrown into prison. In 1926 Winston Churchill berated the BBC for being impartial between the fireman and the fire during the General Strike. So much has changed but so much has not changed at all

What is new is the structure, the shape and form of both our politics and the media. Politics is no longer dominated by parties, their HQs and the staff who run them. We live now in an era of personalities and their pop-up campaigns – Johnson and Vote Leave, Corbyn and Momentum, Farage and the Brexit Party, which proved parties could now rise and fall quicker than your average soufflé, but have much longer lasting effects.

This change has posed particular problems for broadcasters who are, let's never forget, obliged by law to be impartial. Once all that meant was a requirement to broadly balance voices from the two big parties. In the 2019 General Election it required the BBC, ITV and Sky to take legal advice about how they could stage TV debates taking into account the dominance of the SNP in one part of this still United Kingdom against the far from insignificant presence of the Liberal Democrats, Brexit Party and Greens in England, Wales and Scotland. To make matters much more headache-inducing, we broadcasters were harangued daily by champions for both Leave and Remain. Should Philip Hammond, the Chancellor who had campaigned for Remain but was now serving in a government committed to taking us out of the EU be treated as a Remainer or a Leaver? It may not surprise you to learn no agreement could ever be found on this or, indeed, much more besides between the two sides of an argument that had divided the country into angry, bawling and, all too often, abusive factions.

Politics had changed because the media had changed. A decade or more after people predicted the death of broadcast media as the dominant means of communication for politicians, we finally discovered it had actually happened. TV and radio continued to command huge audiences but YouTube, Facebook, Twitter, Instagram, Snap and all the rest of the social media platforms opened up the opportunity for politicians to broadcast without the assistance of the filter or the scrutiny of those pesky hacks, pundits and interrogators.

Long before the EU Referendum Boris Johnson had described my own organisation, the BBC, as 'statist, defeatist and biased'. During the election which secured his majority he refused to submit himself to an extended interview on BBC1 by Andrew Neil. The lesson he and his closest advisers learned from the row that followed was that they didn't have to follow the old rules. They could do it their own way and win.

Since the election a newly empowered 10 Downing Street has chosen to boycott Radio 4's *Today* programme and Piers Morgan on GMB, to divide the parliamentary lobby into an inner and outer circle and to exclude reporters from papers whose views it doesn't like. Some in the Prime Minister's circle now dream of creating a British equivalent of Fox News to hold up a different mirror to the nation. With the backing of Rupert Murdoch all it would take is a tweak to the law – would Conservative MPs resist? Would Labour? All this could come sooner than many think.

The question this book should and does raise is what lessons we in the media can learn from the success of Boris and Brexit. The wrong answer would be that it is time to man the barricades. We can and should make the case for journalism that scrutinises, challenges and holds to account. We can and should argue against the destruction of the British media model – which is admired throughout the world – to be replaced by the American alternative – raucous, partisan and, all too often, fact free.

However, we should also take this opportunity for self-reflection and self-examination. We need to ask why most pundits and poll-watchers didn't take victory for Boris, Brexit, or for that matter, Corbyn seriously enough. We should challenge more vigorously the bias that has blighted the mass media for decades – the bias in favour of the conventional wisdom of the day. We ought to find new ways of engaging with politicians and political ideas that extend beyond an interrogation or a 'grilling'. We should study and learn from the Boris 'Heineken effect' – his ability to reach the parts that others cannot reach. In short, we need see the new world as an opportunity and not just a threat.

The old saying goes that 'it takes one to know one'. Boris Johnson – columnist, editor, hack – has come to a view about what is wrong with the media from which he sprung. It is our challenge now to know and understand and learn from ourselves.

Note on the contributor

Nick Robinson presents BBC Radio 4's flagship *Today* programme and *Political Thinking*. Previously, in a career covering politics over 30 years, he was political editor of both BBC News and ITV News. His books about politics have included *Live From Downing Street: The Inside Story of Politics, Power and the Media* (2012) and *Election Notebook: The inside story of the battle over Britain's future and my personal battle to report it* (2015).

Brexit, the general election and the campaign

***

Exciting political times – but where does it leave us?

Tor Clark

By 2020 people in the UK had been riding a political rollercoaster for more than three years. That rollercoaster had had an unexpected start then climbed slowly to its highest point, before rushing down in the autumn of 2019, shaking us around bends and turning us upside down and inside out. It lurched to an unexpectedly decisive halt on the morning of December 13 and was wheeled away into its maintenance shed for five or ten years, depending on your outlook. Put another way, we have just lived through exceptional and unprecedent political times.

This has created much material for politicians, journalists and academics to pore over, contemporaneously and in retrospect. We are still only beginning to see the shape of the terrain we have just travelled and the vision of the future in not clear. Big questions need to be answered: Will Boris Johnson's northern and midland strategy deliver power to his Conservative Party for a generation or just a five-year parliament? Will the Labour Party understand the state of its predicament and elect a leader who can challenge Johnson's dominance? Can the Lib Dems re-establish themselves as the third party of UK politics? Will Scotland and/or Northern Ireland leave the UK? What will life be like outside the EU? And, perhaps most interesting of all, has a person's views on the UK's EU membership replaced their socio-economic class as the most useful indicator of their political preferences? What does all of it mean for the relationship between journalism and politics in the UK?

At the start of 2020, we don't know the answers to any of these questions, but the expertly-written chapters in this section will help readers start to assemble the evidence on which to base their judgements on the shape of UK politics to come.

The section opens with a brief account of the period from May 2015 to December 2019 which encapsulates the whole Brexit drama. This is intended to help provide wider political context for the expert chapters which follow.

Professor Sir John Curtice is the guru of UK political polling. His exit poll at 10pm on December 12 gave us the first indication of the political shocks we were about to see unfolding that night. But, as you would expect, Professor Curtice takes a much more nuanced view of the election and the period leading up to it in his chapter. His analysis of voters' Leave/Remain preferences in the run-up to the election shows a remarkably even split – indeed a slight Remain majority most of the time – so the result of the 2019 General Election was not a triumphant endorsement of Boris Johnson's Brexit policy, he argues: "Rather than reflecting where public opinion now stood on Brexit, the outcome of the election was a reflection of the very different ways in which Remain and Leave voters distributed their support."

David Cowling, former BBC political expert, is another wise head on all things electoral, having analysed every UK election, often for ITN or the BBC, since 1987. His analysis makes very uncomfortable reading for Labour supporters as he sets out starkly the huge efforts the party would have to make to regain power. The Tory path to consolidating its recently augmented power is not without its challenges, but could be very fruitful, Cowling concludes, arguing: "The Conservatives could gain political benefits if they make the effort to understand the hard-pressed communities they now represent better than did the London-centric Labour party which lost them. If the Conservatives… do not over-claim the likely outcomes, the sheer improbability of the Conservatives as rescuers could reap dividends that far outweigh the money involved."

David Deacon, Dominic Wring and their team at Loughborough University have over the years produced swift and insightful analysis of the reporting of UK elections. This time, joined by collaborators Cristian Vaccari and David Smith, who has recently moved a few miles down the road to Leicester, the Loughborough team throw more doubt on the idea that Britain categorically voted for Brexit in 2019. They conclude: "Boris Johnson's emphatic electoral victory when the results came through on December 13 means his 'oven ready' Brexit deal did in the end get microwaved. But the extent to which journalists adequately dissected the ingredients of this together with the other alternatives on the menu is a matter of concern."

Two seasoned political editors, whose careers take them back through the Thatcher era, offer insightful and interesting analysis of recent events, with the benefit of their years of political analysis. Elinor Goodman, political editor of Channel 4 News, from 1988 to 2005, thinks Boris Johnson should enjoy his honeymoon because strict tests will await him down the political road. She uses her long political hinterland to assess his challenges and opportunities. "Having fought as a populist Johnson has got to show he is prepared to deal with the causes of his new supporters' resentment, even if it means upsetting the more liberal-minded, cosmopolitan seats in the south. But he wants to do this without becoming a fully-fledged populist government like Trump's which he insists – to the disbelief of his critics – is not his model. Popular pragmatism, as opposed to naked populism, is how one of his aides describes his approach."

Michael White sat alongside Elinor Goodman in the front seat of UK political history when he was political editor of *The Guardian* between 1990 and 2016. He too has seen that history unfold and now comments on it in his regular column in the *New European*, but having witnessed so much political history, he has a bleak take on the political present: "The tone of the dis-spiriting 2019 election seemed uglier than before, the willingness of the parties to cut corners greater and the electorate's indifference to such behaviour more egregious. That did seem new."

Vyv Simson, a veteran television journalist and documentary-maker, thinks Brexit and the election which followed demonstrated real problems in journalism's depiction of a fractured and fracturing nation, particularly the broadcast media. He writes: "It's the national broadcast journalists who must face the truly damning indictment. They seem to me to have become blinded to the basics of their trade. They have become overwhelmed by the need for TV in particular to entertain. They have allowed their bosses to marginalise true current affairs programming and seem to be more interested in empty chairing or highlighting blocks of melting ice than in actually finding and reporting a story."

And finally, attempting to bring perspective to the big issues brought to the surface by Brexit and the conduct of the 2019 General Election, former *Guardian* editor Alan Rusbridger, now chair of the Reuters Institute for the Study of Journalism, has a worrying verdict: "So, as Trump has discovered, the liars, myth-makers and manipulators are in the ascendancy – and however valiantly individual journalists attempt to hold them to account (and many, especially at a local level, have tried magnificently) the dice are loaded against them."

Journalism has had a rough ride through Brexit and the 2019 General Election. It has faced huge challenges from politicians and their spinners, whose devotion to what we used to call the truth seems to have suffered in recent years, with the result that the public's faith in journalism to accurately mediate politics is in question as never before. There is much criticism of journalism in the many pages which follow and very clear analysis of the many challenges ahead but also examples of where excellent journalism is doing its job for the public. Uncertainty lies ahead in the relationship between journalism and politics, but the optimists amongst us will hope now the rollercoaster has come to a halt, a degree of political perspective will allow for a more measured political ride.

The Brexit timeline

2019 will go down as one of the most remarkable years ever in UK politics as a central issue divided parties and people more deeply than any issue in living memory. Throughout most of the year it seemed Brexit would not, could not be resolved, but then with just days left of the year, suddenly it was. Tor Clark charts the Brexit journey

Brexit has been the most intractable divide in UK politics for generations, dividing not just political parties, but families and communities. Indeed it can be argued it has fundamentally reshaped the traditional divides of British politics in just a handful of years and the fallout from that divide will shape our nation's future for years to come. To understand how we ended up with Brexit and Boris, we need to understand the political landscape of the period from 2015 to 2020.

The unexpected majority

Many people have spent the last few years cursing David Cameron. It was his concerns over management of his own Conservative Party which persuaded him to promise a referendum on Britain's membership of the European Union. Opinions vary as to whether this was necessary, for Cameron to appease the right wing of his own party, but two premises seem widely agreed upon; firstly the PM believed he would never have to deliver his promise because he would remain in coalition with Liberal Democrats, who could be relied on to veto it and secondly, in the unlikely event he had to hold a referendum on EU membership, he would easily win.

Interestingly, his trusty lieutenant and fellow architect of Tory revival, former Chancellor George Osborne, was always more sceptical. If Cameron had listened to his right-hand man, Osborne might now be running the country rather than a free newspaper.

So after five years of unexpectedly successful cohabitation with the Liberal Democrats, the Fixed Term Parliament Act meant a general election had to be held in May 2015, and to everyone's surprise – presumably including his own – Cameron won a small majority, and with it the obligation to deliver a referendum on EU membership.

Cameron, who had previously, and unconvincingly, in the past described himself as a Eurosceptic, vowed to renegotiate Britain's membership of the EU and then put his 'new deal' to the electorate in a national vote. Friends and foes alike point to his failure to really negotiate any significant change or, more sympathetically, to present is deal as a significant change, as the beginning of the end of his pro-European cause.

The EU Referendum looked like a hopeless mismatch to the watching media: Remain had most of the Conservative cabinet, every living past prime minister, all the leading Labour politicians, all the Liberal Democrats, Greens and Scottish Nationalists, top economists, the Bank of England, and of course, Gary Lineker. Leave offered a few renegade Tories, led by political maverick Boris Johnson and his nerdy fellow journalist chum Michael Gove, all being driven around in a big red bus sporting the most cravenly inaccurate political slogan of modern times. And on June 23, 2016, that ragtag army of soapbox populists won an historic victory, securing a 52 per cent victory, 17.4m votes in favour, 1.2m more than their Remain rivals.

A surprised Cameron inevitably fell on his sword, to be succeeded by his tough Home Secretary Theresa May, a strangely quiet Remainer during the referendum, who was nevertheless now bound to deliver the opposite outcome to the one she had nominally just campaigned for. Into her cabinet came maverick Johnson, out, at least temporarily, went the safe hands of Gove.

Mrs May had a slim parliamentary majority and a clear mandate. Opposite her sat an old-style unreconstructed left-winger Jeremy Corbyn, elected leader of the Labour Party a year earlier to the shock of the Blairite moderate heart of Labour's parliamentary party. He was busy alienating most of the Labour politicians anyone outside parliament had ever heard of after a decidedly lacklustre referendum campaign, which many have subsequently blamed for the defeat of Remain. The Liberal Democrats had been completely mauled in the 2015 election, ruthlessly targeted by their erstwhile coalition partners and punished by voters for going into that partnership, and reduced to just eight MPs.

Mrs May installed key Leavers in key Brexit-related posts, with Johnson as Foreign Secretary, David Davis returning to take charge of departure negotiations with the EU as Brexit Secretary and Liam Fox returning as International Trade Secretary. Her brief seemed about as clear as any electoral instruction ever had been – deliver Brexit. And with the referendum result so recent, she faced little political opposition.

The tortured premiership

So began, relatively positively, the tortured premiership of Theresa May, a woman who had worked hard all her political life and waited for this opportunity only to see all the potential of the most powerful position in the country soaked up and offset by the most toxic issue in recent politics, Brexit.

Mrs May's initial momentum was emphasised by the passing in March 2017 of Article 50, which laid out the process and timeline of the UK's orderly and negotiated exist from the EU, which according to its provisions, would take place two years later on March 29, 2019.

With everything in place, riding high in the polls and facing a seemingly weak and unpopular Labour leader, Mrs May then surprised all and took a huge gamble to improve the Conservative majority bequeathed to her by Cameron, by calling a snap election for June 2017.

In those few weeks Mrs May stumbled and bumbled her way from an unassailable lead to near disaster, finding out that her constant repetition of her 'Strong and Stable' slogan was not believed by the majority of voters, who chose to rob her of her majority and leave her needing to go cap in hand to the Northern Irish Democratic Unionist Party to ask their ten MPs to prop up her government.

Meanwhile, Jeremy Corbyn strengthened his position with a lively issues-based election campaign, which delivered his party a few extra seats and 40 per cent of the vote, a result which made him unchallengeable as Labour leader, which was to have disastrous consequences two years later.

Mrs May returned to 10 Downing Street chastened by her defeat and determined to make the most of the poor political hand she now held to get Brexit done as smoothly as possible. At this stage her government focused on negotiating a withdrawal agreement with the EU. There was no approach to other political parties to do a parliamentary deal to get a soft Brexit deal through the House of Commons.

Instead, it would seem Mrs May was banking on the alliance of the Conservative Party with the DUP to give her the parliamentary numbers to get Brexit approved, but discontent was brewing with her own right wing, notably the European Research Group, under Jacob Rees-Mogg and within the DUP, which was desperate to protect Ulster's links with the British mainland despite the Good Friday Agreement of 1998, which had ended 30 years of violence in Northern Ireland, demanding relations were maintained with the Republic of Ireland to the south. Whatever else was to beset the painful Brexit process, this issue looked intractable all along.

As Mrs May negotiated with Brussels and with her own cabinet, one-by-one she lost Brexiteers from her government – first David Davis, then Boris Johnson and others. Eventually, despite vocal objections from her own backbenches, she put her Brexit deal to the House of Commons in January 2019 – and lost by 432 votes to 202, the biggest government defeat in modern parliamentary history.

She tried again on March 12, 2019, with a smaller, but significant margin of defeat 391 votes to 242 and then with the clock ticking towards the intended March 29 deadline in 2019, had a third and final attempt at getting her EU Withdrawal Agreement approved on March 27, this time losing by the slimmest margin of 344 votes to 286. Britain was forced to ask the EU for an extension to Article 50 and to humiliatingly set up elections to a European Parliament, which a majority of voters had said they wanted no part of.

The ramifications of the European elections

If the three Withdrawal Agreement Bill defeats weren't enough to finish off Mrs May as Prime Minister, then her party's disastrous showing in the pointless 2019 European Elections was. Those elections, always spectacular but ultimately meaningless politically, saw Nigel Farage's freshly minted Brexit Party winning 32 per cent of the vote, the pro-European Liberal Democrats coming second with 20 per cent, while Labour were third with 14 per cent, the Greens fourth with 12 per cent and the Conservatives a humiliating fifth with only nine per cent of the vote – the party's worst ever showing in any significant election.

The European elections are never an indication of subsequent general election performance, and they are used as a major protest vote by the much smaller number of people who vote, but they are always used as a political weather vane and their impact lives on in many ways. These results had several important consequences.

Firstly the Conservatives were shocked rigid by the Brexit Party's success and it would seem many Tory MPs and party members decided its Brexit position needed to harden if it was the see off the challenge of the Brexit Party. This may have led to the election of EU Referendum Leave campaign leader as Tory leader and Prime Minister just a month later.

Labour was also chastened by the Brexit Party's success in some of its own key areas, but at the same time concerned about being beaten into third by the staunchly pro-European Liberal Democrats. The European election results were confusing for Labour in suggesting it firmed up its position to supporters of both sides of the Brexit argument. Perhaps this was the moment Labour thinkers realised it had become two parties both dressed in red – one a traditional northern and midlands-based working class 'Labour movement' party, the other an intellectually-based metropolitan socialist party.

It couldn't be both if it adopted a firm position on Brexit, yet it was terrified of losing either group, the traditional supporters to the Brexit Party and the liberal metropolitans to the Lib Dems or Greens – so Labour fudged its policy with the result than no-one either understood it or gave it any credibility.

The result was perhaps most disastrous to the Liberal Democrats. Their wily, experienced leader Vince Cable enjoyed leading his party to victory then stepped down to be succeeded by the enthusiastic 39-year-old Scottish MP Jo Swinson, who had been a minister in the Coalition years. Bolstered by the much-improved Euro elections performance, the Lib Dems over-played their Remain hand at their 2019 party conference in September, coming up with a policy of revoking Article 50, and thus overturning the 2016 referendum result, if they won a majority and formed a government in the coming election.

Until this point, momentum had been growing for a second referendum or People's Vote to test the 2016 result. As Sir John Curtice's chapter below clearly shows, opinion polls throughout most of this period had showed a narrow lead for Remain versus Leave of about 52:48 if another referendum had been held. The Lib Dems had been at the heart of that campaign and, as Professor Curtice's analysis shows, were taking votes from Labour because of how categoric their support for the UK staying in the EU was.

The party's vote to revoke produced two longer-term problems. Firstly, it looked ridiculous. The Lib Dems were never going to win an election outright. Even they knew that. It was a typical example of the hubris which occurs when political activists just talk to themselves.

The second problem with this dominant policy was that it was, ironically, illiberal. For a liberal party to advocate overturning a huge democratic decision, without putting that decision to another electoral test, fatally damaged the party's credibility even with otherwise sympathetic voters. Even committed Remainers thought if Brexit was to be reversed, as they wanted, that decision could only be made by a second referendum. No-one knows exactly how well the Lib Dems might have done if they had simply played the very safe card of leading the campaign for a People's Vote, but it seems likely they would have won more votes and seats.

Boris takes control

In July 2019 the Conservative Party overwhelmingly elected Boris Johnson, the arch-Brexiteer as its leader and thus Prime Minister. His pitch ever since his referendum victory had been to get Brexit done and this became his mantra, to be repeated enthusiastically, despite all evidence to the contrary at every opportunity.

He picked a new much more Brexity cabinet, shut down Parliament so it couldn't mess with his plans, insisted the UK would leave Europe on October 31 and was castigated by the Supreme Court for badly advising the Queen over his prorogation of Parliament, resulting in that decision being overturned and Parliament being forced to return by the end of that month instead.

The House of Commons took its revenge on Johnson, who was trying to threaten the EU with a no-deal Brexit, by voting to ban such a deal in law and tying the PM's hands. He was forced to agree to another extension of the UK's EU membership when Parliament would not allow the UK to crash out without a deal in October and was looking like the most wretched prime minister in history as he consistently failed to get any legislation through Parliament as MPs defected from his party, and those who didn't defect but didn't support him had the whip removed.

Then, seemingly out of the blue, Johnson secured a deal. He had a meeting with Irish prime minister Leo Varadkar at which the pair went for a walk without aides, had a chat and agreed they could make progress. The basis of that agreement was taken back to the EU and hammered out into an agreement, the major change of which appeared to be the abandoning of Mrs May's former allies the DUP, by settling on a trade border down the Irish Sea to protect the Good Friday Agreement – and thus the hard-won peace in Northern Ireland – by selling out the Unionist community's political representatives. Thus the intractable Northern Irish issue was 'solved' by Johnson at a stroke.

When the House of Commons approved Johnson's miraculous deal, which in most other senses was remarkably similar to Mrs May's, he gambled that a nation sick of Brexit using up all the oxygen in the room as a political issue for more than three years, would join him in voting to get it done. He secured a two-thirds majority in the House of Commons to circumnavigate the Fixed Term Parliament Act and set December 12 as the Christmas election date.

Labour's policy of negotiating a deal with the EU then holding a second referendum on that deal, but not necessarily supporting it in that referendum, confused and angered voters. Jeremy Corbyn's subsequent announcement he would be neutral in a second referendum only added to the confusion. It wasn't a viable policy and Labour spent the election trying to talk about anything but Brexit.

The Conservatives on the other hand wouldn't talk about anything else. They ruthlessly targeted the small-C conservative Labour seats in the north and midlands which had enthusiastically voted Leave and were frustrated that government had not followed their democratic instructions. Their plan worked and many traditional Labour working class constituencies, including many former mining seats, voted Conservative for the first time. It was a remarkable achievement and the Conservatives' 80-seat majority took almost everyone by surprise.

Boris Johnson's relentless optimism and his strategists' rigid adherence to the slogan Get Brexit Done, backed up by a host of lesser but populist policies won over voters who had never voted Tory before.

At the same time the Liberal Democrats' hubris robbed them of the opportunity to maximise the Remain vote for their candidates and Labour's Brexit confusion and a poor reception of its leader by voters condemned the party to its worst election result since 1935.

The Brexit argument *was* done. Britain would leave the EU and more than three years of the fiercest political debate and most divisive issue was over. The big question to consider as the dust settles from this political earthquake is whether Brexit will continue to cast its shadow in reshaped political loyalties or whether, after a short interlude, UK politics will return to its normal loyalties and dividing lines.

It is the great fear and fascination of UK politics that, as we survey the shattered landscape of Brexit and particularly 2019, we just don't know what the political future will look like.

Note on the contributor
Tor Clark is Associate Professor in Journalism and BA Journalism programme director at the University of Leicester. Previously he was editor of two UK regional newspapers. He has been a political journalist for more than 30 years and in that time has covered eight UK general elections, the last four for BBC Leicester. He is co-editor of this book.

A decisive vote to leave? A closer look at the 2019 General Election

How well did the outcome of the 2019 General Election reflect the public mood on Brexit? Did it indicate a clear majority were in favour leaving the EU or that voters were still deeply divided on the subject, asks polling expert Professor John Curtice

The outcome of the 2019 General Election was decisive. It gave the Conservatives an overall majority of 80 and thereby enabled the Prime Minister, Boris Johnson, to end nearly a year of 'dither and delay' and deliver the UK's withdrawal from the European Union just six weeks later. The outcome appeared to signify the British public had clearly swung in favour of the view a majority had already seemingly expressed in the EU Referendum in 2016, that is, that it was more important the country should be able to exercise its sovereignty and control its borders than participate in an institution which facilitated cross-border trade and collaboration in an increasingly globalised world (Curtice, 2017) – an outlook that might, perhaps, be characterised as putting 'Britain First'.

However, the outcome of an election is not necessarily a reliable guide to the balance of public opinion on any particular issue. There is no guarantee in an election that voters are basing their choice on where the parties stand on any individual subject. After all parties espouse a myriad of policies and proposals in their election manifestos. Different voters might focus on different promises and few are likely to agree with all of the proposals put forward by the party they choose to back. Even if a particular issue is of high importance to many voters, they may still find more than one party is close to their point of view on it and thus have to use additional criteria to decide which to back. Meanwhile, we should remember the parliamentary outcomes generated by the UK's first-past-the-post electoral system typically provide an exaggerated reflection of the electoral strength of whoever comes first. Indeed, no post-war British government has come even close to winning over half the popular vote.

In this chapter, we use evidence from opinion polls to examine more closely what the outcome of the 2019 election does and does not tell us about public attitudes towards the decision to leave the European Union. We begin by examining the evidence on where public attitudes towards the principle of leaving the EU stood some three years after the EU Referendum. We then assess attitudes towards the various ways in which it was suggested a final decision should be made on the issue, and how, in the light of that picture, the revised withdrawal deal the Government negotiated in early autumn 2019 and now wished to implement was regarded by voters. Thereafter we explain how the political parties positioned themselves in response to that attitudinal landscape – together with the outcome of elections to the European Parliament held in May 2019 – and thereby between them framed the choice put before voters in the election. Finally, against that backdrop, we then assess the extent to which how people voted in the general election reflected their view on Brexit and whether the outcome represents clear evidence that the country had shifted decisively in favour of leaving.

Attitudes towards Brexit

Two consistent findings emerged from polls conducted during 2019 of how people would vote if they were asked once again whether the UK should remain in or leave the EU. First, most of those who participated in the 2016 referendum said they would vote the same way again. Nevertheless, the polls also suggested there was now a small majority in favour of remaining in the EU rather than, as in the referendum, a majority for leaving.

How both things could be true becomes clear in Table 1. Based on the last half dozen polls to be conducted before the election was called, it shows how people said they would vote in another referendum, broken down by the choice people said they had made in the 2016 ballot. According to these polls, 86 per cent of those who voted Remain and 86 per cent of those who backed Leave in 2016 would vote the same way again. That would seem to suggest the outcome of a second ballot would be much the same as that of the initial contest. Nevertheless, these polls all suggested any second ballot would in fact result in a narrow reversal of the outcome in 2016; on average (once those who did not indicate a preference are left aside) 52 per cent said they would vote Remain and 48 per cent Leave. The explanation lies in the figures in the third column of our table, which reveal those who did not vote in 2016 but expressed a view as to how they would vote in another ballot were more than twice as likely to say they would vote Remain as indicated they would back Leave. Included in this group, of course, are those who had been too young to vote in 2016, though they far from comprise a majority of these voters.

Table 1. Second EU Referendum vote intention by vote in 2016 EU Referendum, October 2019

Vote Intention in Second Referendum	Vote in 2016 Referendum		
	Remain	Leave	Did Not Vote
	%	%	%
Remain	86	9	53
Leave	10	86	23
Don't Know etc	4	5	23

Source: Average of six polls conducted by BMG, Deltapoll, Kantar, Panelbase and Survation, 1-21.10.19

Of course, these figures do not represent any guarantee a majority would have voted in favour of staying in the EU if a second referendum had been held. Much would seemingly depend on the willingness of those who did not vote in 2016 to participate in a second ballot, as well as the relative effectiveness of the campaigning undertaken by those on the two sides of the argument. However, together with the fact that during 2019 a running average of polls of second referendum vote intention never shifted beyond the narrow range of 52:48 and 54:46 in favour of Remain (What UK Thinks, 2019), it is clear that, more than three years after the original ballot, the country was still more or less evenly divided on the subject and public attitudes towards the principle of remaining in or leaving the EU were proving to be remarkably stable.

Next steps

At the same time, Remain and Leave voters also appeared to have very different views about how Brexit should proceed (Curtice, 2019). This was illustrated by polling from Kantar, which on four occasions between April and September 2019 asked respondents whether they thought the UK should leave the EU without a deal, should leave on the basis of the withdrawal agreement Theresa May had made, should leave but on the basis of a softer deal which would involve staying in the single market and the customs union, or should reverse the decision to leave the EU by revoking Article 50. Among voters as a whole, the two most popular options were the two extremes of revoking Article 50 (backed on average by 33 per cent) and leaving without a deal (23 per cent). The two 'compromise' options of implementing a very soft Brexit (14 per cent) and leaving on the basis of the deal Mrs May had negotiated (9 per cent) were much less popular. The reason for this polarised pattern is that revoking Article 50 was by far the most strongly supported option among those who voted Remain, 67 per cent of whom backed that approach, while around a half of Leave voters (51 per cent) stated they thought the UK should leave without a deal. Building a bridge between the two sides in the Brexit debate would evidently not be easy.

However, despite the considerable level of support for leaving without a deal among Leave voters, the revised agreement reached between the UK and the EU at an EU Council meeting in the middle of October proved to be more popular than the one Mrs May had struck, primarily because of a relatively favourable reaction among those who had voted to leave the EU. Deltapoll, for example, asked their respondents on seven occasions between the conclusion of the agreement and polling day whether they supported or opposed the revised deal. True, these polls suggested voters as a whole were no more than evenly divided about its merits. On average, 33 per cent said they supported it, slightly more than the 31 per cent who indicated they were opposed, though the single most common response, offered by 36 per cent, was, 'Don't Know'. However, among those who voted Leave, just over half said they supported the deal (52 per cent), while only one in six (17 per cent) were opposed. Other companies obtained similar results, including Opinium who, in response to exactly the same question they had asked previously about Mrs May's deal, reported on average that 25 per cent of all voters thought Mr Johnson's deal was a good one for the UK, while 25 per cent reckoned it was a bad one – whereas the equivalent figures for Mrs May deal had been 13 per cent and 48 per cent respectively.

Meanwhile, when in October Kantar offered respondents the same options as they had done previously between April and September, but now including leaving with Mr Johnson's deal among the options rather than leaving with the one Mrs May had negotiated, 43 per cent of Leave voters said they would prefer to leave on the basis of the new deal, while support for leaving without a deal now stood at just 28 per cent. In contrast, most Remain voters (62 per cent) still wanted to revoke Article 50. In short, while far from being rapturously received, the Government's revised deal at least provided it with a better foundation from which to appeal for the support of those who did want to leave the EU, even if it was unlikely to provide a bridge from which it could hope to appeal to those on the other side of the Brexit debate.

Lessons from the European elections

The importance of building such a foundation had been brought home to the Government by the outcome of the European elections that were held in May 2019 as a result of the UK's failure to meet the original deadline for leaving the EU of March 29. The Conservatives won just nine per cent of the vote (in Great Britain), whereas the newly-formed Brexit Party, which advocated leaving the EU without a deal, came first with 32 per cent. More importantly, perhaps, polling of how people would vote in a general election conducted after the May ballot on average put the Conservatives on just 25 per cent across the country as a whole, and suggested the party was trailing the Brexit Party by 39 per cent to 34 per cent among those who had voted Leave. While attitudes towards Brexit itself might be remarkably stable, voters were evidently quite willing to change their minds about which party to back as a way of expressing their views. Not surprisingly, many in the Conservative party drew the conclusion from this outcome that the party would likely be in deep electoral trouble unless it delivered Brexit – and looked to Boris Johnson to do so.

The fallout from the European elections presented Labour with a similar challenge. It only managed to win 14 per cent of the vote, while it too was running at an average of little more than a quarter of the vote (26 per cent) in polls of general election vote intention. But while the party had, like the Conservatives, lost ground to the Brexit Party among those who had voted Leave, it also found the dominance it had hitherto enjoyed among Remain voters under challenge. At 35 per cent, the party's support among the opponents of Brexit was now only narrowly ahead of the 31 per cent enjoyed by the Liberal Democrats. After the European election, Labour tried to shore up its support among Remain voters by backing the idea that any proposal for leaving the EU (including any alternative any future Labour government might negotiate with the EU) should be put to second referendum – a proposition that, as we have already indicated, was favoured by around two-thirds of Remain supporters – while still trying to appeal to Leave voters by leaving open the question of what recommendation the party would make in any such ballot. In short, in contrast to the Conservatives and despite the polarised character of public opinion on Brexit, Labour entered the 2019 election still trying to bridge the Brexit divide.

In contrast the Liberal Democrats, who ever since shortly after the 2016 referendum had argued there should be a second ballot and out of which the party hoped a Remain majority would emerge, decided to take an even firmer anti-Brexit stance. The party indicated in September that in the event of the election of a majority Liberal Democrat government, that government would simply revoke Article 50 without holding another referendum, though the party would still be willing to back another ballot if it did not win any immediate general election. That stance proved controversial, but in fact polling on four occasions by BMG Research between July and October found that, at 39 per cent, the idea of revoking Article 50 was rather more popular among Remain voters than was holding another referendum (30 per cent).

An election is called

Thus, by the time the election was precipitated (thanks to a decision by the Liberal Democrats and the SNP to back the Government's call for a ballot in the hope it would resolve the Brexit impasse that had developed in the House of Commons), a clear dividing line had emerged on Brexit. On one side of the divide was the Conservative Party, which advocated leaving the EU on the basis of the revised deal Boris Johnson had negotiated, together with the Brexit Party, which was still inclined to the view the UK should leave the EU without a deal, but which in the event stood down its candidates in seats the Conservatives were defending. On the other side of the dividing line were the Liberal Democrats, the SNP, and the Greens, who were all not only willing to back a second referendum (the SNP having adopted that stance some 12 months previously), but also made it clear they would campaign in such a referendum in favour of Remain. They were joined by Labour, who we have seen now also supported a second ballot, albeit the party was not willing to state which side it would support. If voters wanted to use the election to express their apparently polarised views about Brexit, they were seemingly being given a clear opportunity to do so.

During the campaign voters proved to be volatile once again in their choice of party, despite the stability of their views about the principle of Brexit. However, it was a volatility clearly structured by Brexit. The advent of Boris Johnson as Prime Minister in July and his subsequent success in securing a revised deal with the EU had already seen a restoration of the Conservatives' fortunes – among those who had voted Leave. By the time the election was called the party's overall average standing in the polls had risen to 35 per cent, almost all of it on the back of a 21-point increase in its support among those who had voted Leave. Indeed, it now outpaced the Brexit Party by 55 per cent to 23 per cent among those who voted Leave. However, that squeeze on the Brexit Party vote continued apace during the election campaign, such that by the eve of polling day the polls were suggesting nearly seven in ten Leave voters (69 per cent) were set to vote for the Conservatives.

Labour, in contrast, had made little progress in restoring its fortunes during the summer and early autumn, and at the beginning of the campaign still faced stiff competition for the support of Remain voters from the Liberal Democrats. However, the election campaign saw the party reclaim some of the ground it had lost in that direction, and by the time the final opinion polls were published it was claiming the support of just under a half of Remain voters (49 per cent), whereas only one in five (20 per cent) were now backing the Liberal Democrats. In contrast, at five points or so, the party's progress among Leave voters during the campaign had been much more modest.

A Brexit election?

The election campaign therefore saw the Conservatives come to dominate the support of those who had voted Leave, while Labour, despite its more ambiguous stance, became clearly the single most popular party among Remain voters. But did this ensure the outcome of the 2019 election provided a clear indication of where the balance of public opinion lay on Brexit? Table 2 enables us to address that question by showing the outcome of the election in terms of votes both among voters as a whole and separately (according to a large post-election poll conducted by YouGov) among those who voted Remain and those who backed Leave. It also shows how the overall result of the 2019 election differed from that in 2017.

Table 2 Vote in 2019 Election and change since 2017 Election by EU Referendum vote, 2016

	All Voters		Remain Voters		Leave Voters	
	%	Change in % vote since 2017	%	Change in % vote since 2017	%	Change in % vote since 2017
Conservative	44.7	+1.2	19	-6	74	+9
Brexit Party*	2.1	+0.2	0	0	4	0
Labour	33.0	-8.0	49	-6	14	-10
Liberal Democrats	11.8	+4.2	21	+9	3	0
SNP/PC	4.4	+0.8	7	+2	2	0
Greens	2.8	+1.1	4	+2	2	+2
Other	1.1	+0.4	1	0	1	0

* Change since 2017 is as compared with Ukip. Source: BBC News; YouGov 9-13.6.17; 13-16.12.19

First of all, we can see most voters – though not all – voted for a party whose stance on Brexit was consistent with how they had voted in 2016. Moreover, the propensity to do so was more or less the same among both Remain and Leave voters. Thus, according to YouGov's poll, 78 per cent of Leave voters voted for one of the two parties in favour of Brexit, that is, the Conservatives or the Brexit Party, while just over four in five (81 per cent) of Remain supporters voted for one of the parties in favour of another referendum. Moreover, both figures represented an increase on the equivalent proportions in the 2017 election, when YouGov reckoned only 69 per cent of Leave voters voted for the Conservatives or Ukip, and 74 per cent of Remain voters backed one of the parties which by 2019 (but not necessarily in 2017) were in favour of a second referendum.

So, for most voters the election did prove to be an opportunity for them to express their views about Brexit. Indeed, more of them seemingly took that opportunity than had been the case two years previously. To that extent, the 2019 election did register what most voters thought about Brexit and, in so doing, confirmed the evidence of the polls that there was a sharp division between Remain and Leave voters about what should happen next in the Brexit process.

However, there is little sign here of a country that had moved decisively in favour of leaving the EU, as suggested by the outcome in terms of seats. Remain voters were just as likely to have voted for a pro-second referendum party as Leave supporters were to back a pro-Brexit one – a pattern which hardly suggests a significant change of heart among Remain supporters. Moreover, at 47 per cent the overall level of support for the two pro-Brexit parties was rather less than the 52 per cent secured by those parties in favour of putting the issue back to the people – much as we would expect given that at the end of the election polls of vote intention in another EU ballot put support for Remain at 53 per cent and Leave 47 per cent, little different from what we have seen was the position at the beginning of the election campaign.

Rather than reflecting where public opinion now stood on Brexit, the outcome of the election was a reflection of the very different ways in which Remain and Leave voters distributed their support. The Conservatives won the votes of nearly three-quarters of Leave voters, while Labour only secured the backing of a little less than half of Remain voters. Britain's first-past-the post system then turned this difference into a chasm. Instead of revealing a country which had decisively swung behind the 'Britain First' stance implied by the decision to leave the EU, Britain remained a country still deeply divided over the merits of that decision. What now remains to be seen is whether a government that still has no more than half of the country backing its stance on Brexit can persuade the other half that leaving the EU is not such a bad move after all.

References

Curtice, J. (2017), 'Why Leave won the UK's EU referendum', *Journal of Common Market Studies*, 55, S1, 19-37.

Curtice, J. (2019), 'Searching in Vain? The Hunt for a Brexit Compromise', Posted at https://whatukthinks.org/eu/searching-in-vain-the-hunt-for-a-brexit-compromise/

Whatukthinks (2019), 'EURef2 Poll of Polls'. Posted at https://whatukthinks.org/eu/opinion-polls/euref2-poll-of-polls-2/

Note on the contributor

John Curtice is Professor of Politics at Strathclyde University and Senior Research Fellow, NatCen Social Research and the 'UK in a Changing Europe' programme. He has written extensively about political attitudes, elections and voting behaviour in Britain, and is a regular media commentator on British and Scottish politics. He is also Chief Commentator at whatukthinks.org/eu, which provides a comprehensive collection of polling data on attitudes of relevance to the debate about the UK's relationship with the EU.

Labour in denial?

For once, the pollsters got the result dead right. But veteran UK elections analyst David Cowling thinks the Labour Party now needs to come to terms with the scale of its defeat.

In recent years, voting intention polling in Britain has been a dangerous sport. In the 2015 General Election the campaign polls pointed relentlessly to a hung parliament, yet the outcome was a majority Conservative Government. The performance of the polls in the 2016 EU Referendum was not as dire but nor did it deliver results that washed away the stain of 2015. In 2017, the campaign polls significantly understated the final Labour vote share.

The polling industry could therefore be forgiven for popping champagne corks when the 2019 election result became clear. All 78 polls published during the campaign had recorded Conservative leads and the average of final polls delivered by ten companies overstated the Conservative share by 1.4 per cent and understated the Labour and Lib Dem shares by 0.9 per cent and 0.1 per cent respectively. In the world of sampling that is as near perfection as you can hope for.

The Conservatives also had grounds for celebration, given the remarkable records the 2019 election result delivered for them. They achieved the largest-ever swing to a party in office in any election stretching back at least to the 1920s. Their net gain of 59 seats was the largest number won by a government party in any election since at least 1885. For a party that had been in government for over nine years, this was the third election in a row where they increased their share of the vote, something that has not happened since at least 1900. And even Margaret Thatcher, in her crushing 1983 election victory, was unable to capture Bishop Auckland, Bolsover, Durham North West, Redcar, Sedgefield, Wakefield and Workington – all of which now have Conservative MPs.

Why then were so many people astonished by the outcome? It seemed as if the result crept in like a burglar in the night as the nation slept. During the campaign two polling companies regularly asked respondents what they thought the most likely outcome of the election. In their final polls, Opinium (sampled 10-11

December) and Deltapoll (sampled 5-7 December) found 31 per cent and 28 per cent respectively who expected the result to be a Conservative majority. Perhaps the months preceding polling day hold one clue as to why so many were surprised. Time and again over that period questions had been raised about the suitability of the three main party leaders; their competence, integrity, trustworthiness and values had been criticised relentlessly. Many voters declared they were reduced to choosing the least awful from a bad bunch. Not exactly the classic ingredients for an historic victory. For a decade we had lived with either no single party majority government in Westminster or with a small overall majority that splintered apart in a crisis. 2019 appeared to offer no commanding figure capable of replacing life on a knife-edge with the smack of firm government. And yet that was precisely what the election delivered.

Volatile voters

It was also astonishing to have such a decisive vote amid the unprecedented voter volatility that now defines UK politics. In October 2019, the British Election Study which has been documenting voting behaviour at every general election since 1964, published some remarkable data. It appears that in 2015, some 43 per cent of voters supported a different party than in 2010; and that in 2017, 33 per cent changed their vote from 2015. Overall, across all three of the last elections 2010-17, 49 per cent of people did not vote for the same party each time. Underpinning these figures is another set of BES data that tracks the collapse in strength of party identification over past decades. In 1964, some 48 per cent of Conservative voters described their party identification as 'very strong'; the figure among Labour voters was 51 per cent. In 2017, the comparable figures were 14 per cent and 23 per cent respectively. It is not just opinion pollsters who struggle to find traces of order in such electoral turmoil.

Yet, despite all this, the Conservatives achieved an outstanding election victory. However, did the Conservatives win the 2019 election or did Labour lose it? The answer seems pretty clear: the Conservative vote share rose by 1.3 per cent compared with 2017 and Labour's fell by 8 per cent. None of which diminishes the remarkable Conservative performance but it should concentrate the attention of the main parties when they consider what the future holds for them.

The Lib Dems gambled the family silver on securing a great chunk of the 2016 Remain vote that would place them firmly back on track to become a key player in Westminster. That gamble did not pay off and we were left with the question: "If remaining in the EU was so central to the purpose of the Lib Dems, what is the point of them politically now that we have left?" The answer is not obvious. They could return their attention to domestic politics and hope to restore their fortunes over time. More tempting but, in my opinion, ultimately less politically rewarding, would be for them to wait until the inevitable difficulties and challenges of Brexit emerge and become the individual who always ends up annoying all sides with their perpetual cry of 'I told you so'.

'Winning the argument but losing the election'

Labour is faced with plenty of problems but its biggest is its refusal to acknowledge the causes of its failures. The result of the 2017 election was dire for Labour – a mere two per cent national swing to them from the Conservatives – when placed in the context of the appalling Conservative campaign performance. However, the outcome was immediately weaponised by Mr Corbyn's supporters so as to protect his position as party leader. No effort was made to investigate why Labour had lost its third election in a row: the party merely accelerated towards the brick wall that constituted its fourth. The accuracy of the 2019 campaign polls was a disaster for them. They relied on a repetition of the 2017 experience of polls understating their support but this secret weapon turned out to be a total dud. It took only a matter of minutes, following the broadcast of the exit poll, for Labour spinners to claim they had been defeated because the election campaign had been dominated by Brexit. We have the benefit of two surveys conducted on polling day among actual voters against which we can test this assertion. Opinium's on-the-day poll sampled 5,641 voters. All were asked why they had not voted for particular parties. The main reasons given by non-Labour voters for not voting Labour were 'leadership' 43 per cent, 'Brexit stance' 17 per cent. 'economic policies' 12 per cent. In the Ashcroft on the day poll, when their 13,000 respondents were invited to choose the most important issues that had decided how they voted, the top five selected were: the NHS 55 per cent; getting Brexit done 38 per cent; stopping Brexit 22 per cent; the economy 20 per cent; and the environment 16 per cent. And then Labour claimed to have 'won the argument but lost the election', an assertion most people would find difficult to accept when the party concerned had lost 2.6 million votes after making their argument. Labour will have great difficulty in winning the next election in any event but it only makes its challenge all the harder if it refuses to face up to why it lost the previous four.

Winning was the easiest bit

The challenges that lie ahead for the Conservatives are no less formidable than they were before polling day but now Boris Johnson has his own, decisive mandate to pursue his own solutions. His biggest challenge will be to consolidate the new composition of the Conservative parliamentary party delivered by the 2019 election. Choosing to make his first post-election speech in Sedgefield, a former mining seat in County Durham that had been Tony Blair's constituency and a Labour seat since 1935, which the Conservatives won with a 12.8 per cent swing this time, was astute. Winning so many heartland Labour seats for the first time was a truly astonishing achievement. Yet across much of England and Wales, the Conservatives proved more adept at sweeping up Labour seats than they did in seizing a significant share of the 2.6 million votes Labour lost compared with 2017. However, the Conservatives could gain political benefits if they make the effort to understand the hard-pressed communities they now represent better than did the London-centric Labour party which lost them. For many of these voters, life is tough and has been for years; they are sceptical about politicians who claim they can transform their lives and their communities quickly and at no cost to them as taxpayers. If the Conservatives do shift investment to these areas the problem remains that the lead-times for such investment to translate into positive results is long – certainly not designed to match electoral cycles. Yet, if they do not over-claim the likely outcomes, the sheer improbability of the Conservatives as rescuers could reap dividends that far outweigh the money involved.

Some would argue the Conservatives have the next general election in the bag already. The Labour Party needs to gain 124 seats at the next election just to secure a majority of two seats in the Commons. It will require a swing of around 12 per cent for them to achieve this – the same degree of swing Labour received in 1945 when there had not been an election for ten years and at the close of the Second World War. Just in order for Labour to become the largest party in a hung parliament requires the second biggest swing in post-war history. As if all this was not challenge enough, another is on its way. Present parliamentary constituency boundaries are based on electoral registers for the year 2000: two decades later there is certain to be a boundary review before the next election. If the present total of Westminster seats – 650 – is retained, then Labour could face the loss of around 20 from its 2019 election total of 202 seats, and this would simply increase the size of swing Labour will need to achieve if they are to secure even the smallest of majorities at the next election

It would be a foolish person who dismisses any prospect of change at the next election. We live in a time when old loyalties are fast evaporating. Who, even ten years ago, would have predicted that Canterbury would be a Labour seat and that Blyth Valley would be represented by a Conservative? The UK has decided to launch itself into a challenging environment outside the European Union and by the time of the next election the profound effects of that decision, for good or ill, will be apparent. But the electoral landscape created by the 2019 general election result will not be fundamentally re-shaped unless historic electoral shifts in party support occur, probably no later than four years from now.

Note on the contributor

David Cowling is a visiting senior research fellow at the policy institute at King's College, London. He was involved in the analysis of the polls in every UK general election from 1987 to 2017, first as ITN's political analyst and then as the BBC's Editor of Political Research.

Here, there, and everywhere? Brexit and mainstream news coverage during the 2019 General Election

The 2019 election was branded the 'Brexit election' even before campaigning started, but was that the case in the end? Detailed research of media coverage by David Deacon, Dominic Wring, David Smith and Cristian Vaccari reveals Brexit was indeed the dominant issue, but their analysis offers a much more complex verdict on the overall media coverage

In every election, rival parties seek to control the issue agenda. In 2019 this matter assumed even more critical importance. Boris Johnson and the Conservatives wanted the campaign dominated by Brexit, as did the Liberal Democrats, who believed their staunchly pro-Remain stance would garner electoral gains. By contrast Labour were keen for the election to be about a diverse range of other subjects, most notably the state of the economy, the future of the National Health Service and the precarity of the environment.

One step communication: party priorities on Twitter

These different issue priorities were demonstrated starkly in the official leader and party tweets posted during the latter stages of the 2019 campaign. Figure 1 compares the extent to which each of the main parties' tweets addressed the five main policy issues identified across their entire Twitter output for this period. The results show an extraordinary emphasis on Brexit in Conservative tweets, exceeding even the percentage found for the Brexit Party. The Liberal Democrats were not far behind. Labour's priorities were in marked contrast and confirmed their 'anything but Brexit' line. A similar contrast between the strategies of the Conservative and Labour parties had also been observed in the 2017 General Election (Vaccari, Smets and Heath, 2019), but in 2019 it was even more pronounced.

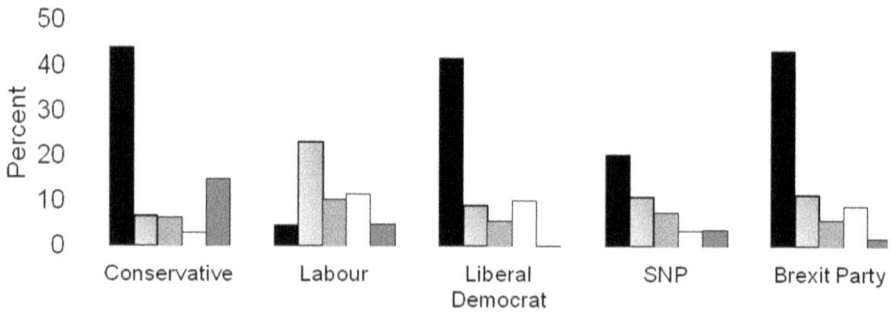

Figure 1: Main topics in official party tweets (18 November - 11 December 2019)

■Brexit □Health ▣Economy/business □Environment ■Taxation

Notes: Analysis conducted by Centre for Research in Communication and Culture, Loughborough University (Deacon et al. 2019). Counts only include tweets that addressed a substantive policy issue. Up to two topics could be counted per tweet. Percentages=appearance of topic/all topics*100

Two step communication: Brexit and the media election

The major national news organisations have always been critically important in defining the terms of any election and this remains the case despite the rise of social media. From the very start of the formal campaign, some editors seemed to enshrine their preconceptions in editorial straplines, with the *Daily Mail* and *The Sun* branding 2019 the 'Brexmas election' and Sky News adopting the onscreen logo 'The Brexit Election'. The latter proved controversial and prompted the Labour Party to complain to the official regulator that this breached impartiality rules as it framed the election narrowly and on terms favourable to Boris Johnson's core objective to 'Get Brexit Done'. Labour's complaint was rejected by Ofcom because 'Brexit is an important background contextual factor (and) what happens next in terms of the UK's relationship with the EU will be determined by the election result' (Bakhurst, 2019). Nevertheless, the matter still rankles with senior Labour party figures (e.g. McDonald, 2020)

These initial skirmishes and assumptions aside, did Brexit dominate media reporting of the 2019 campaign or did other issues emerge to disrupt the Government's preferred agenda? Furthermore, which elements of this multifaceted subject received most attention? As it has for every election since 1992, Loughborough University conducted a 'real time' content analysis of all weekday campaign coverage by the main evening TV news bulletins and in the front pages and prioritised editorial spaces of every national, paid-for daily newspaper (see Deacon et al., 2019)[1]. A key element of this audit involved monitoring the details as well as the extent of Brexit coverage during the campaign.

Table 1 shows Brexit was the most prominent substantive policy issue by a considerable margin. Its prominence was particularly striking in television news coverage, receiving two and a half times more coverage than 'Health/ health care'.

Table 1: The key issues in the 2019 General Election (7 November – 12 December 2019 inclusive)

	TV	Press	All
	%	%	%
Electoral process	31	32	31
Brexit/ EU	18	11	13
Business/ economy/ trade	6	9	8
Health/ health care	7	7	7
Standards/ scandals	6	8	7
Taxation	4	6	5
Minorities/ religion	4	5	4
Defence/ military/ security/ terrorism	2	4	4
Public services	4	3	3
Environment	4	2	3
Immigration/ border controls	2	2	2
Scotland/ Wales/ Northern Ireland	5	1	2
Social Security	1	2	2
Crime/ law and order	1	2	2
Education	1	1	1
All other issues	4	5	6

Note: percentages = (number of appearance of an issue/ all issues *100). Up to three issues could be coded per news item.

One step, two step: media priorities versus party priorities

This dominance of Brexit meant that media coverage corresponded more closely with the Conservatives' preferred agenda. Figures 2 & 3 measure the correlation between (a) each party's preferred agenda communicated via Twitter and (b) the topics discussed in TV and press reporting[2]. To interpret the diagrams: the further away each party's data point is from the centre of the radial plot, the closer the parallels between their issue priorities and the news agenda.

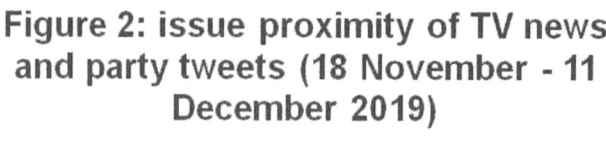

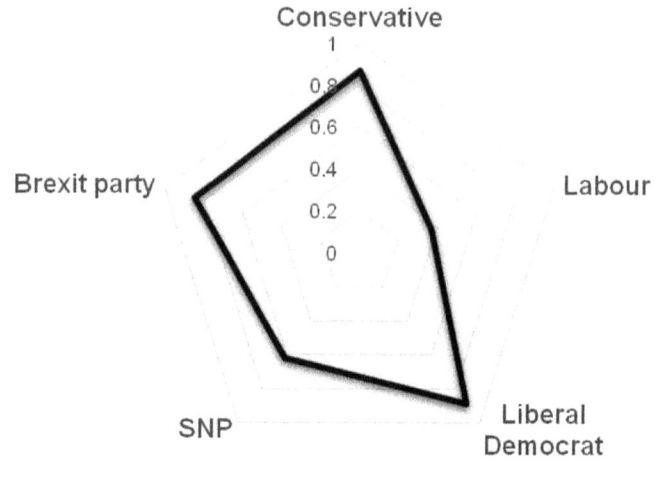

Figure 2: issue proximity of TV news and party tweets (18 November - 11 December 2019)

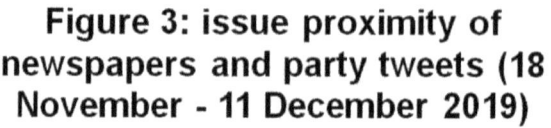

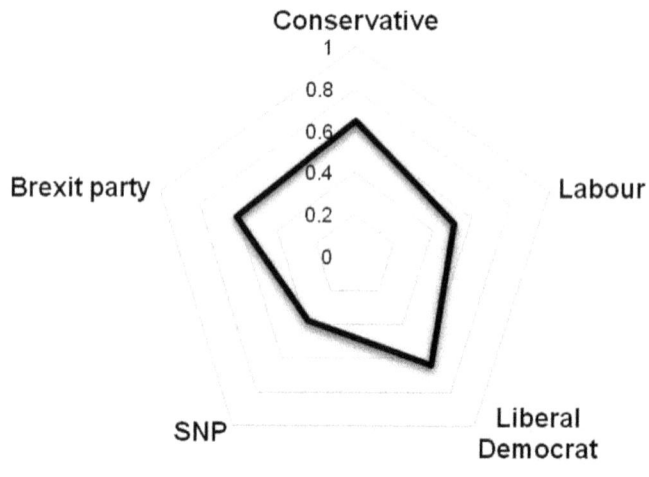

Figure 3: issue proximity of newspapers and party tweets (18 November - 11 December 2019)

The results for broadcast coverage show the clearest party differences, with Labour the most notable outlier. The greater priority given by the broadcasters to Brexit pulled the issue agenda away from the principal Opposition party. Newsspace on prime-time TV news is far more competitive and this limits the range of topics covered and thereby narrows and restricts the news agenda. The SNP were the next least aligned, largely as a result of the considerable emphasis they placed on the relations between the Scottish Parliament and Westminster and the possibility of a future referendum on Scottish independence in their twitter activity.

Patterns in press coverage might at first sight seem counterintuitive. In particular, the data do not show clear evidence of a similar or accentuated party advantage. As figure 4 shows, levels of press partisanship in the 2019 campaign far exceeded those identified in 2017, with Labour attracting double the levels of negative reporting from that campaign[3]. And yet this directional imbalance did not translate into a similarly marked issue imbalance in press coverage.

There are several reasons for this. The lower relative prominence of Brexit in press coverage meant the Conservatives' obsession with the topic and Labour's reticence to address the subject in their Twitter accounts effectively cancelled themselves out in this calculation. Elsewhere, the press demonstrated greater issue independence from any of the main parties' priorities. For example, the press gave more prominence to allegations about anti-Semitism in the Labour Party[4] and issues related to 'defence/ military/ terrorism/ security'. All of these were barely mentioned in the main parties' Twitter output. Overall, the SNP were the least aligned with the press in issue terms, which again was largely due to their considerable emphasis on Scottish independence and related matters. As Figure 1 shows, these issues barely registered in press coverage.

Figure 4: Press evaluations of Cons & Labour: 2017 and 2019 General Elections

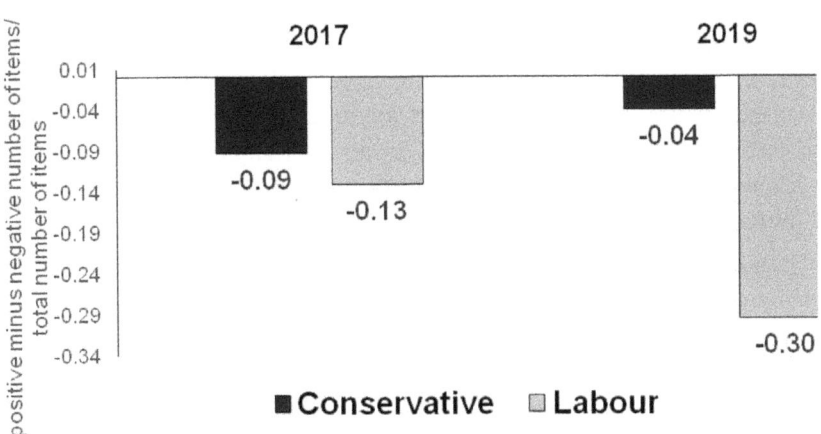

The dynamics of the 'Brexit' election

In charting the cumulative parameters of news coverage of the election, it is important not to lose sight of the underlying dynamics of this campaign. News interest in Brexit fluctuated markedly during the five weeks of the formal race. As Figure 5 shows, the topic dominated the first week, which was also the period when the Brexit Party commanded its greatest media presence. After that, the issue became less prominent, and by week 4 Brexit had subsequently fallen behind other major policy themes.

Figure 5: Top issues by week (press and TV)

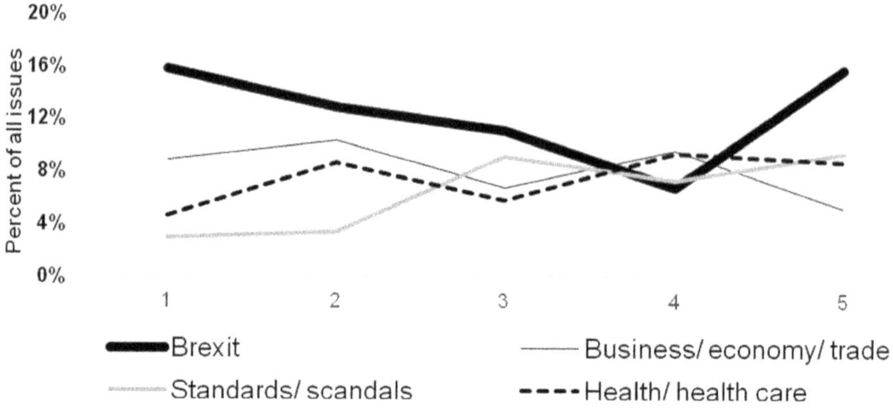

This decline in the penultimate week requires interpretation as it shows how Brexit had become a more latent element in news coverage terms. For example, several health/health care items during this week were linked to discussion of hypothetical post-Brexit trade deals. However, for such items to be coded as Brexit-related in our analysis there had to be a manifest and substantial reference made to the UK's withdrawal from the EU (eg coverage of future potential trading scenarios and their implications for public health provision were insufficient on their own to gain a 'Brexit' allocation in our study). This growth in more allusive referencing to Brexit shows how the issue had, by this stage of the campaign, become more of a contextual factor than a focal point for much electoral coverage: the topic was at once everywhere, yet nowhere. We were not alone in noting this. In an interview with *The Sun*'s political editor in the penultimate week of campaigning, Boris Johnson lamented:

> "I think what has happened in the course of the campaign is it has gone through various phases and people have slightly lost their focus on the political crisis that we face. Unless we get this thing done, unless we get Brexit done, this country cannot move forward (Newton Dunn, 2019)".

The final week, however, saw a marked reversion, with Brexit reasserting itself as the dominant policy issue in the press and TV news alike. This refocusing on the subject during the critical, and arguably crucial phase of the campaign consciously revisited the original reason the Prime Minister had called the election.

The newsworthiness of Brexit alternatives

Did the considerable, if fluctuating, amount of Brexit reporting provide deeper insights into the subject, particularly the implications of the UK exiting from the EU? The catch-all term 'Brexit' captures a myriad of policy and financial considerations as well as the rhetoric extolling the merits of Leave and Remain. Consequently, we examined the relative news prominence of the various alternative options on offer. Figure 5 underlines the success of Boris Johnson in promoting his much vaunted 'oven ready' withdrawal agreement during the campaign. Significantly this, unlike the other options, was the only one to receive overall positive coverage largely because of favourable reporting in the press. Some way behind Johnson's Brexit deal were the traditionally pro-EU stances supporting a second referendum or just plain Remain. Both received hostile press coverage. But more notable was the lack of interest in the other so-called 'softer' and 'harder' versions of Brexit that had previously been extensively discussed and debated in Parliament. The former position includes that embraced by Theresa May in her Chequers proposals and far softer versions, including the UK staying in the Customs Union and/or single market. And while these and other options are now off the agenda, a hard Brexit remains a possibility given the extensive negotiations ahead.

Even when Brexit was reported, there was a lack of policy focused analysis as to what implementation might mean. This stood in contrast to the detailed appraisals often applied to other manifesto commitments. For example, the Institute for Fiscal Studies gained considerable campaign coverage through its analysis of parties' spending pledges and projections. Fifty three percent of its appearances linked to taxation related coverage and 46 percent to business and economy coverage. Only eight percent were connected to Brexit[5].

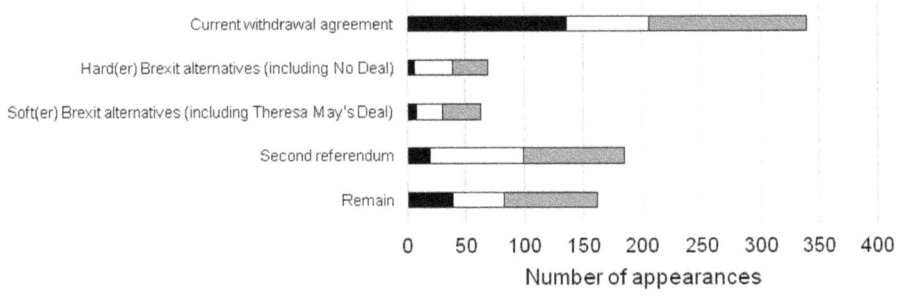

Figure 6: Brexit alternatives in election news coverage
(7 November - 11 December 2019)

Boris Johnson's emphatic electoral victory when the results came through on December 13 means his 'oven ready' Brexit deal did in the end get micro-waved. But the extent to which journalists adequately dissected the ingredients of this together with the other alternatives on the menu is a matter of concern.

Notes
[1] TV sample: weekday broadcasts of BBC1 10pm news, ITV News at Ten, Sky TV news 10pm, C5 news 6.30pm, C4 7pm news. Newspaper sample: weekday printed editions of the *Guardian, Financial Times, The Times, Daily Telegraph, The I, Daily Mail, Daily Express, The Sun, Daily Mirror* and *Star*.

[2] Correlation coefficients were calculated using Pearsons' r.

[3] To ensure standardisation of this comparison we divided the number of positive minus negative items by the total number of newspaper items in each campaign. This produced a decimal number between -1 and +1, where -1 = complete negativity, +1= complete positivity and 0 = complete balance of negativity/ positivity.

[4] As reflected in the results for the categories 'scandal/ standards' and 'minorities/ religion'.

[5] These percentages are separate and do not add up to 100.

References
Bakhurst, K. (2019) Letter from Group director of the Ofcom Content Media to Anjula Singh, Director of Communications for the Labour party, 20 November (https://www.ofcom.org.uk/__data/assets/pdf_file/0014/180113/letter-ofcom-labour-party-election-strapline.pdf accessed 9 January 2020).

Deacon, D., Smith, D., Wring, D., Goode, J., Vaccari, C., Downey, J. (2019) News Media coverage of the 2019 General Election, Report 5, Loughborough: Centre for Research in Communication and Culture (https://www.lboro.ac.uk/news-events/general-election/report-5/, accessed 25 January 2020).

McDonald, A. (2020) 'Labour's unfair treatment shows broadcasters need urgent democratic reforms', *Daily Mirror*, 9 January (https://www.mirror.co.uk/news/politics/labours-unfair-treatment-shows-broadcasters-21222653, accessed 10 January 2020).

Newton Dunn, T. (2019) 'Boris Johnson warns voters Jeremy Corbyn is a national security risk who will bow down to Britain's enemies', *The Sun*, 2 December (https://www.thesun.co.uk/news/10469823/boris-johnson-warns-jeremy-corbyn-bow-enemies/, accessed 28 January 2020).

Vaccari, C., Smets, K., & Heath, O. (2020). The United Kingdom 2017 election: polarisation in a split issue space. *West European Politics, 43*(3), 587-609.

Note on the contributors
David Deacon is Professor of Communication and Media Analysis, Centre for Research in Communication and Culture, Loughborough University.

Dominic Wring is Professor of Political Communication, Centre for Research in Communication and Culture, Loughborough University.

David Smith is Lecturer in Media and Communication, School of Media, Communication and Sociology, University of Leicester.

David Deacon, Dominic Wring, David Smith and Cristian Vaccari

Cristian Vaccari is Professor of Political Communication and co-Director of the Centre for Research in Communication and Culture, Loughborough University.

How to win in Guildford and Grimsby: the balancing act facing Boris

Boris Johnson's victory in the 2019 General Election has transformed the political map of the UK, with Conservative MPs in Labour heartland seats joining more traditional Tory constituencies with rather different priorities. Former Channel 4 News political editor Elinor Goodman thinks the Prime Minister will have to work hard to keep them all happy

Last September, shortly before Boris Johnson threw 21 Conservative MPs out of the party, for refusing to back a no-deal Brexit, he was warned by the then MP for Guildford, Anne Milton, that he could lose pro-Remain seats like hers. After she had said this several times in tones of rising desperation, he is variously reputed to have said 'Bugger Guildford' or more decorously: "OK, if Guildford is lost, it's lost."

In the event, the Conservatives held on to Guildford with a majority of around 3,000, though had Anne Milton herself not split the Remain vote by standing as an independent, the Liberal Democrats might have taken it. But the Prime Minister was prepared to gamble on winning more seats in Labour's traditional heartlands in the Leave voting north and midlands than he lost in the Conservatives' own traditional backyard commuter belt. The support of sensitive-souled Remainers was worth risking for the greater prize of winning over the Brexiteers.

There certainly were Conservative Remainers who felt the party had abandoned them and voted Conservative with their noses held. But fear of Jeremy Corbyn and his economic policies made them reluctant to vote Lib Dem. After all the hype at the start of the campaign, the Liberals only took Zac Goldsmith's seat in Richmond Park and St Albans from the Conservatives. Remain-voting Putney was Labour's one gain. The political map of Britain was transformed. And, along with it, the Conservative Party itself. According to the former Conservative leader, and European Reform Group member, Ian Duncan Smith, the Conservatives had become the Brexit party even before the election. Now there is absolutely no doubt about that. The pro-European wing has been purged as effectively as in any revolution. Instead of being the party of the Establishment, dedicated to protecting the institutions of state, it has become a party which gained power by attacking Parliament. It was worth the risk of losing Guildford to win Brexit seats like Grimsby.

Purge of Remainer Tories

The 21 rebels, including two former Chancellors, were replaced with candidates who were prepared to back the Prime Minister's deal – even if it means a hard exit. Other former Remainers, like Nicky Morgan, and Keith Simpson, who had held onto the whip were replaced with Brexiteers who had all signed on Conservative Central Office's dotted line. All that is left of the pro-European tendency which dominated the Tory Party under Ted Heath, and went on fighting for Europe from Mrs Thatcher's premiership right through to Theresa May's, are a rump of MPs like Damian Green and Greg Clark.

That does not mean Johnson won't face opposition from his own side during the negotiations on the future shape of trade relations with the EU. The opposition though is not likely to come from a solid block as it did when the European Research Group was whipping for Brexit. Instead the new Conservative MPs are more likely to take a pragmatic view of how particular decisions affect their constituencies. Ultimately though they owe their very existence at Westminster to Boris and Brexit. Some of the newcomers might have voted Remain in the referendum but the whips will tell them they signed away their right to rebel when they were nominated to stand as candidates even if the negotiations over a trade deal with Europe breaks down and Boris Johnson asks them to approve a no deal exit, albeit dressed up as an 'Australian deal'. Their local parties, even more militantly Eurosceptic than the new parliamentary party, will ensure they comply.

Should re-joining the European Union come on the agenda at some future date, it will be a battle for a future generation of Tory MPs to fight. All the Europhile rump can do now is harrumph, and point out the particular dangers of no deal Brexit to the seats which fell to the Brexit tide. So overwhelmingly have the Eurosceptics won the battle within the Tory party, that come 2021 the description 'Brexit Party' – be it used pejoratively by the Prime Minister's opponent to describe his new dawn Conservative Party, or Nigel Farage's party – could become irrelevant.

Permanent revolution?

The question is the extent to which other aspects of the revolution, engineered by Dominic Cummings, will remain permanent. To get such an overwhelming majority, Cummings used the same tactic he used for the Leave campaign at the referendum by casting the Conservatives as the insurgents against the cloth-eared liberal establishment. It was an extraordinary somersault for a party which traditionally stood for protecting institutions like Parliament and the rule of law and which, even under Mrs Thatcher, usually opted for incremental change. But the Tory party is famous for reinventing itself to win power. In its history it has been socially liberal, libertarian, protectionist and free market. According to Trollope 'no revolution stinks so foully in the nostrils of an English Tory as to be absolutely irreconcilable to him. When taken in the refreshing water of power any such pill can be swallowed'.

Even so perpetual revolution of the kind seemingly favoured by Dominic Cummings may meet resistance from MPs more concerned about the practical delivery of better services to their constituents than attacking the Supreme Court or remaking Whitehall. As a tactic for getting elected the party may have gone along with it, but as a strategy for government some may fret. Even Boris Johnson himself may weary of it. But that doesn't mean going back to the *status quo ante*. He turned the Conservatives into the Heineken party precisely because he pulled off the trick of persuading voters sick of the old parties that his was a new government, unsullied by – and not responsible for – the austerity which had left their towns lagging behind in the first place. It won't be enough just to increase the money going into regenerating their high streets and may be tempting Marks and Spencer back (see Peter Kellner's fascinating analysis of the correlation between towns that had lost their M&S store and Leave voting). Nor will devolving power north be a panacea in itself: it could just be dismissed as another layer of bureaucracy without real money behind it. The idea of moving the Lords to York could well turn out to be one of those ideas floated to demonstrate a commitment to the north which impresses nobody.

Having fought as a populist Johnson has got to show he is prepared to deal with the causes of his new supporters' resentment, even if it means upsetting the more liberal-minded, cosmopolitan seats in the south. But he wants to do this without becoming a fully-fledged populist government like Trump's which he insists – to the disbelief of his critics – is not his model. Popular pragmatism, as opposed to naked populism, is how one of his aides describes his approach.

One test of this could be the detail of the points-based immigration system he has promised to introduce. Even within those towns which have lost their traditional industries there will be tensions between employers who depend on foreign labour and local people who believe immigrants have stolen their jobs and destroyed their communities. Control for them means restoring their communities to places they recognise.

The return of One Nation Conservatism?

Boris Johnson constantly boasted during the campaign that he had an 'oven ready' solution to Brexit. But his domestic policies are far less well prepared. He repeatedly claimed he would govern as a One Nation Conservative. But that is a phrase which over the 150-odd years since Disraeli first used it has been open to numerous different interpretations. For Disraeli himself, it was a kind of paternalism, combined with self-interest, under which the ruling class had an obligation to help the lower classes to provide social stability, and avoid revolution. For his successor Lord Salisbury it meant uniting the nation, rather than the classes, which could be a bit ironic in this Parliament if the Government ends up accepting a border down the Irish Sea between Britain and the island of Ireland, let alone presiding over the breakaway of Scotland. Post-war, it reverted to nearer its original paternalistic interpretation to support the welfare state but Mrs Thatcher used it as philosophical justification for selling council houses. Michael Heseltine on the other hand deployed it to advocate European integration and economic intervention.

Boris Johnson seems to want to combine all these strands in a highly elastic philosophy. He told his cabinet he sees himself as a kind of 'Brexity Hezza'. This presumably means he will negotiate for as much deviation as possible from European trade rules, while domestically favouring a bigger role for Government intervention and more state spending. On infrastructure, the bail-out of Flybe. which connects cities in the southwest and the north, was an early indication of this. Another clue is his mantra of 'levelling up', presumably meant to show that better-off areas won't suffer as a result of helping the only industrial towns – a reasonable goal as long as the economy is growing but very difficult to achieve if it slows right down.

The 2019 Conservative manifesto leaves him plenty of flexibility. According to one of its authors, Rachel Wolf, quoted in *The Economist*, it was aimed particularly at people who shared Conservative values on things like crime and punishment but who relied on public services. Hence the promise to increase borrowing and invest in the National Health Service. Stripped of the commitment to Brexit, it could have come out of the Tony Blair playbook, and he could well govern as a mirror image of Blair, steering to the centre right instead of the centre left. Thus on the day the Government was demonstrating a centrist faith in infrastructure spending by announcing the go ahead for HS2 plus £5bn for buses, it also burnished its right-wing credentials on social policy by pushing ahead with the deportation of criminals to Jamaica in defiance of a court ruling.

Because of scale of his victory, Boris Johnson will have enormous authority in the parliamentary party for the foreseeable future, though, as the protests about his decision to link up the Chinese telecoms giant, Huawei, showed, the Conservative party is not suddenly going to change its rebellious stripes. Going ahead with the High Speed Rail link will certainly provoke a big rebellion, as well as tensions with Dominic Cummings who thinks it's a waste of money. But he is not going to deal with the constant sniping over Europe that ultimately destroyed his immediate predecessors. Having won the argument over Brexit, members of the European Reform Group may now find themselves far less popular with the media, and even written off as swivel-eyes obsessives in the way the Eurosceptic 'bastards' were under John Major. But the Eurosceptic/Europhile divisions within cabinet could metamorphose into splits between the fiscal conservatives, who may feel very queasy about the scale of debt needed to meet expectations, and those more worried about failing to deliver. If the economy proves as fragile as some fear, Boris Johnson could find himself in a minority in his own cabinet as Mrs Thatcher did at the beginning.

A new-look Conservative Party

It's not just in terms of Europe and geography that the party has been transformed. So too has the make-up of the parliamentary party. The northern and midland working class towns which voted Conservative for the first time continued the move, albeit, slow until now, away from grammar and public school-educated Tory MPs towards those who went to comprehensives.

The change is not as great as Conservative Central Office might have you believe, but look at the Conservative Home website and you will see that instead of mentioning their public school education, or time as a special advisers, they are more likely to talk about their single parents or background in local government. The ultimate example of this culture change is 26-year-old Jacob Young, who went back to his job as a chemical process operator on Christmas Day because otherwise he would have let down his colleagues. Some of these MPs have themselves experienced the sharp end of globalisation. They will be far more worried about job losses in their own constituencies than preserving overseas aid or even perhaps global warming. These new members will have to co-exist with MPs from the shires, and Brexiteers who saw leaving Europe as a way of removing the British economy from its regulatory chains, and yearn for a smaller role for the state. Yet those very same left-behind towns, hit worst by globalisation, are the very ones that could suffer most from a hard Brexit. And how will the MPs representing these seats feel if they see money is being used to prop up wealthy farmers in the shires? Equally how will the Tories' traditional heartlands react if they believe the main beneficiaries of an end to austerity are in the north or the midlands, particularly if they think the Government is thrashing around to find projects they can put money into, and is ignoring deprived towns in the countryside. (Trowbridge in the otherwise affluent constituency of South Wilts has a ward which is in the decile of most deprived areas in England).

As it is many Tory MPs from rural constituencies felt aggrieved at the funding settlement for schools which favoured schools in areas of concentrated deprivation. And what about trade policy? Those first-time Conservative voters won't want to open up our market to cheaper imports from outside the EU if it means killing what's left of their traditional industries. And how will the various groupings react if the Conservative and Unionist Party ends up going back on its promise not to set up a border in the Irish Sea, or preside over the breakup of the union with Scotland?

Ted Heath's chief whip said managing a parliamentary party with a large majority was more difficult than managing one with a slim one. Theresa May might disagree, but these new MPs cannot afford to stay quiet if they want to be re-elected. Nor is Boris Johnson going to abandon them by sticking to the old gospel of financial rectitude and deregulation. He did not expand the Conservative territory into the working class rugger belt to impose old Tory agenda. If the going gets rough with the traditionalists he will look to the new generation to be his storm troopers. Activists speaking with the cut glass accents of the home counties may not feel at home in this new party but they will cheer Johnson to the rafters for having delivered such resounding victory, and continue to do as long as he delivers.

The risk to him is not defeat in Parliament, but disappointment which in turn fuels the very resentment that got him elected. All the more so if leaving the EU results in the recession which those he purged from the party warned would follow.

Note on the contributor
Elinor Goodman was political editor of Channel 4 News from 1988 to 2005, having joined the programme as political correspondent in 1982 from the Financial Times. In 2005 she was appointed chair of the Affordable Rural Housing Commission. In 2011 she was named as one of the six panel members assisting Lord Leveson's public inquiry into phone hacking.

The joyless election

Michael White analyses a contest between what many voters saw as two fundamentally disreputable candidates and worries about the public indifference to the parties' willingness to cut corners in the pursuit of power

Like everything else about the divided country which Brexit Britain had become, the 2019 General Election, held in mostly miserable weather on December 12, was the subject of wildly varying interpretations as to its desirability, its conduct and the meaning of the result. For the victors, those who had backed Boris Johnson's central campaign pledge to 'Get Brexit Done', it offered relief, resolution of the protracted political stalemate that emerged from the 52:48 per cent outcome of the 2016 EU Referendum. For others it was another downward step towards Donald Trump's dystopian brand of populist politics, a momentous step away, not just from membership of the European Union, but from responsible and relatively honest government.

For all that the re-elected Prime Minister asked both sides to 'let the healing begin', he emerged from the contest as he had entered it: the embodiment of the nation's conflicting, conflicted feelings. During a disciplined campaign which took few risks, Johnson made nugatory gestures towards his party's consensual 'One Nation' traditions. Despite efforts by more centrist parties, Liberal Democrats, Plaid Cymru and the Greens, to 'Unite to Remain' electoral pacts, the torn fabric of mainstream politics was not repaired. Fired up by its pro-Corbyn Momentum activists Labour purged dissident would-be candidates as enthusiastically as the Brexitised Tories. No MP who resigned from their party or crossed the floor to join another survived the cull. Tory grandee, Michael Heseltine, urged supporters to vote Lib Dem. More successfully, some disaffected Labour MPs endorsed the Conservatives. Win or lose, it was largely a joyless election in which turnout at 67 per cent was two per cent down and, by some estimates, one in three voted negatively – against something rather than for it. More people in lower social groups DE voted Tory than Labour, as did a plurality of voters over 39 – compared with 47 in 2017.

Biggest victory since Thatcher

In another bad year for experts the pollsters at least managed to end their losing streak. In 2015 few predicted either David Cameron's narrow Conservative majority or Theresa May's wanton squandering of it two years later – an incoherent attempt to fashion a parliamentary majority for any deal that both Brussels and Westminster could accept. Though the 2019 polls shortened odds on a hung parliament as the UK got closer to its fourth major vote in four-and-a-half years, none ever predicted a Labour win. To be on the safe side Tory Fleet Street still battered Jeremy Corbyn mercilessly. What turned out to be Johnson's 80 seat Commons majority – 43.6 per cent vote share against Labour's 32.2 per cent – was on the optimistic side of Tory expectations. Boris's appeal to Leave voters to abandon ancient tribal loyalties had breached Labour's northern 'red wall'. It was the largest vote share for any party since Margaret Thatcher's first triumph in 1979 and the largest Conservative majority since her last, hubristic hurrah in 1987. Down 60 seats to 202 MPs, Labour's result was its worst since 1935.

Unsinkable again at last, ministers sighed after three years when their ship had repeatedly come close to capsizing. May, who had campaigned, but not negotiated, on the slogan 'No deal is better than a bad deal' had failed three times to win MPs' approval for the lacklustre one she brought home – a withdrawal agreement with the EU27 and a non-binding political statement on future goals. That requirement had been imposed by a controversial Supreme Court ruling sought by pro-Remain campaigner, Gina Miller, a decision which had prompted the notorious Daily Mail headline denouncing the judges as 'Enemies of the People'. With passions high on both sides, ministers sounded less than eager to defend the courts.

Angry social media platforms erupted predictably. Growing public concern over the scale and scope of mass manipulation of millions of citizens online data – Cambridge Analytica-style – by shadowy commercial and government-sponsored forces made it less clear who was orchestrating much of the divisive uproar or exactly why. Except for zealots on both sides the worry did not improve morale.

With May constrained by the courts, harried by online activism and dependent on the votes of ten truculent DUP MPs, a Commons majority for her deal was duly denied by varying combinations of opposition parties and by both Leave and Remain wings of her own. Pro-Europeans feared that leaving the single market and customs union as well as the political union – once the primary goal of Brexit veterans – would be economically disastrous. Anti-Europeans convinced themselves Britain was being trapped as a 'vassal state' in perpetuity by way of the 'backstop' mechanism designed to prevent a hard border across the island of Ireland. Neither side wanted to jeopardise the Good Friday Agreement.

The impact of the European elections

For some, Jeremy Corbyn, Labour's most improbable leader since the much-loved pacifist, George Lansbury (1931-35), had misjudged a vote of No Confidence in Theresa May (defeated by 325 votes to 306) in January. The European Research Group (ERG) of hardline Brexiteers had already botched its own party leadership coup by 200 to 117 in December. After being forced to obtain a six-month extension to her Article 50 departure date of March 29, May's final attempt at compromise – a ten point 'New Deal' – included letting MPs vote on the principle of a second referendum. It enraged both sides. Though she announced her departure just ahead of the five-yearly European elections, the ones she had promised not to hold, May's sacrifice did not prevent the Tory vote share plunging to 9.1 per cent, just behind the pro-EU Greens (12.1 per cent). Nigel Farage's newly-formed pop-up Brexit Party, was the main beneficiary of Tory protest votes, on 31.6 per cent. In the subsequent leadership contest the then-Foreign Secretary Jeremy Hunt, put up a creditable show as the 'Not Boris' candidate. But there was little risk this time that Johnson would stumble as he did in 2016. The unruly boy, who once declared his ambition was to be 'World King' and grown into an unruly adult, entered his inheritance on July 23.

Yet by November his version of the 'strong and stable' government May had promised was looking even shakier than hers. Three times he failed to get two-thirds of MPs to back an election under the terms of the 2011 Fixed Term Parliaments Act, itself a constitutional sticking plaster adopted by the Cameron Coalition. In an unprecedented counter-move, a cross-party coalition of mainstream MPs, many of them exiles from their own front benches, took control of the parliamentary agenda to enact the 'Benn Act' in September. It prevented the No Deal Brexit they feared might take the economy over a cliff and 21 Tory MPs, including former chancellors, Kenneth Clarke and Philip Hammond, lost the party whip for backing the move.

People's Vote gains ground

To the indignation of government supporters, the UK Supreme Court then ruled unanimously that Johnson's attempt to prorogue parliament to avoid scrutiny of his Brexit plans was unlawful. In October MPs voted by 329 to 299 to give the revised Withdrawal Agreement Bill a second reading, but rejected Government plans to fast-track its passage. Johnson was forced to break his promise to 'die in the ditch' rather than seek a second extension until January 31. In retaliation he shelved progress on the legislation. The faltering campaign for a second referendum had once been a fringe campaign. Now grudgingly embraced by Jeremy Corbyn it began gaining ground as a means to resolve the deadlock. Brexit hardliners, long self-persuaded that 'the Establishment will never allow Britain to leave', were alarmed at the prospect.

But relief for embattled ministers was at hand. First the Scottish Nationalist Party (SNP) demanded an election, part of its strategy to justify its own second referendum on independence and thereby a return to the EU fold. Then the Lib Dems declared themselves prepared to share the gamble. Deeply divided Labour wobbled, then fell into what many warned Corbyn would be a trap if conceded without first achieving some form of Brexit. Torn between his Leave voters in Labour's traditional heartlands and Remain voters and activists in London and the south, Corbyn had finally come off the fence, but not before losing a trickle of MPs to defection over Europe and his mishandling of anti-Semitism. MPs passed the necessary legislation by 438 votes to 20. The election was on.

The party campaigns

The campaign that followed had a near-scripted inevitability about it to anyone who had witnessed the Bennite surge behind Michael Foot's doomed (1980-83) Labour leadership that ended in Margaret Thatcher's 143-seat election landslide. Labour's strategy was to shift the focus on to domestic issues, notably its plans to replace ten years of austerity with a package of current and investment spending on a scale unprecedented in peacetime. On Europe it offered a rapid and more closely aligned renegotiation of the withdrawal agreement, the outcome to be put to a referendum choice between the deal and Remain. Corbyn declared he would remain neutral on the issue.

The Conservative campaign was the opposite: to make 'Get Brexit Done' the necessary preliminary to every policy aspiration. During the autumn the party had already unveiled a more expansionary fiscal policy, promising more infrastructure spending and tax cuts, albeit on a more modest scale than Labour. Its manifesto added little new. But the Prime Minister took every opportunity to put the spotlight on Parliament's failure to deliver the 'will of the people', as expressed in the narrow referendum win. Under Jo Swinson's relatively untested leadership of the third UK-wide party, the Lib Dems adopted a provocative stance designed to attract Remain voters; that Swinson could become Prime Minister and that, if she did, her government would withdraw Britain's Article 50 application to leave the EU.

Both propositions rapidly showed themselves to be unpopular and were later ditched. Little else changed during the campaign, including the substantial Tory lead, though Labour surprised many of its own supporters by adding to its already considerable spending commitments. It made a previously undiscussed promise to provide a free and universal broadband connection, another to spend a further £58bn compensating so-called 'Waspi' women, those born in the 1950s whose official retirement age had been raised without sufficient notice. Sceptical voters told pollsters in increasing numbers they were not convinced such promises could be kept. Even Tory promises of 20,000 extra police officers, 40 new hospitals, more affordable homes and much else induced scepticism towards the historically 'fiscally responsible' party. In the age of fake news and emotionally-driven identity politics, many pledges were not made to be taken literally, others not even seriously.

The role of the Brexit Party

Such volatile times prompted attempts to exploit fractured party discipline and loyalties by making electoral pacts over specific seats – in Northern Ireland, Wales and England – and to maximise strength by way of tactical voting websites. Anti-Brexit sites unhelpfully offered conflicting advice, amid suspicions that some of it was being tailored to favour a particular party. At most such efforts swung four seats in Remain's direction. Far more significant was Nigel Farage's decision, made reluctantly under right-wing Tory pressure, to withdraw Brexit Party candidates from all 317-Tory held seats rather than split the Leave vote.

He resisted pressure to do the same in targeted Labour 'red wall' seats. It was a climbdown from his demand for a formal pact with the Conservatives. Acutely aware that Johnson's premiership had much reduced his leverage, Farage claimed both to have refused a peerage and to have extracted Hard Brexit concessions from No 10, endorsing a Canada-style trade deal and ruling out an extension beyond January 31. On polling day his candidates took just two per cent of votes cast. The Lib Dems also faded, its votes up, its MPs down from 12 to 11. The pro-Leave DUP lost two seats while the pro-Remain SNP went up from 35 to 48. Regional disparities as well as party fragmentation were part of the new landscape.

Learning from the Trump White House

Johnson had entered the campaign arena mired in personal controversy. Publication of a Commons intelligence committee report into Russian interference in British political processes was postponed amid suspicion it might embarrass his Brexit allies or donors. Allegations of impropriety in a £100,000 grant of public funds to Jennifer Arcuri, an American IT entrepreneur from whom the then-London Mayor had been receiving 'tech training' lessons, were kicked into the long grass. He dodged panel debates and one-on-one TV interviews which rival leaders reluctantly endured, most conspicuously with Andrew Neil, the BBC's interrogator-in-chief. Attacking the media messenger was historically Labour's 'bad loser' tactic. For a rampant Conservative party to do so suggested that Conservative campaign chiefs – led by Sir Lynton Crosby's media savvy young team of Australians and Kiwis – had been absorbing aggressive lessons from the Trump White House.

For all the Tories hardball day-to-day tactics and a 'Get Brexit Done' strategy that smacked of cynicism to those who knew the hardest phase of post-EU negotiation was yet to start, many voters seemed attracted by the Prime Minister's relentless optimism about the opportunities awaiting 'Global Britain' – opportunities to be shared more fairly by all regions and classes across the country, he stressed. Johnson was evasive, easily rattled by criticism and often close to incoherent. It was claimed that he ruffled rather than combed his hair before greeting the cameras. He would attempt a joke about anything as his default option and when a reporter tried to show him a photograph of a child lying on the floor of an NHS hospital, he actually took and pocketed the offending mobile phone.

Yet Johnson's well-documented shortcomings seem to have been priced in by voters weary of the exhausting EU stalemate. Many deplored being forced to choose between two fundamentally disreputable candidates for No 10. But, if pressed, they would go with the Etonian cavalier, not the bearded, dour and puritanical roundhead they saw in Jeremy Corbyn. Since Labour had little hope of winning an overall majority while the SNP dominated Scotland, the Tories were able to revive the claim that a Corbyn-led minority government would be in the Nationalists' pocket. When asked if they would concede a second Scotland referendum in return for 'confidence and supply' support, Corbyn and his shadow chancellor, John McDonnell, gave varying and unconvincing answers, as on much else.

On taxes the Conservatives had imposed a triple lock against raising income tax, VAT or national insurance, and rescinded a promised cut in corporation tax from 19 to 17 per cent, as well as one on higher rate tax thresholds. The then-Chancellor, Sajid Javid, had beaten back efforts by Downing Street's strategy chief Dominic Cummings, to further relax the purse strings, a victory which would not long survive in 2020. But Labour's plans to raise an extra £78bn in taxes, mostly on business and the better off, as well as borrow heavily to fund re-nationalisation and infrastructure projects, were described by the reputable Institute for Fiscal Studies (IfS) as representing 'enormous economic and social change'. Voters supported many such policies, Labour strategists pointed out, and were ready to abandon the unfair model of capitalism that had let down so many. Inasmuch as that was true the election result suggested they did not believe Labour could do all it promised, certainly not under Mr Corbyn, whose negative personal ratings were exceptionally poor. His Glastonbury moment had passed.

Only one other issue cut through…

As usual in such a campaign little serious attention was sought or given to detailed policy options or implementation. But commentators acknowledged one positive exception in 2019, a rare emphasis placed on climate change-related issues, perhaps because Australia's protracted bush fires were hard to ignore on TV. Even here the tendency to turn pledges into a bidding were was obvious. Rival camps vied to promise carbon-neutral policies and all-electric cars even sooner and the fashionable demand for more tree-planting culminated in Labour committing allotment-owner Corbyn's government to planting two billion, a costlier ambition than it appeared to realise. If 'Get Brexit Done' was Johnson's Ace of Hearts, Corbyn's character and record was his Ace of Spades.

An ever-larger number of TV debates where leaders surrogates could be deployed gave subordinates, even future Labour leadership candidates, potential breakthrough exposure. A surer performer than his boss, John McDonnell, bore the brunt of making Labour's economic case while Rishi Sunak, a rising Treasury star, was clearly deemed voter-friendly and trustworthy by Team Johnson. In the event TV delivered no game-changing moments. Newspapers and TV did better than previously at monitoring social media advertising and traffic and scored two notable hits: the revelation that Keir Starmer's image had been manipulated by the Conservatives to make him look indecisive and that Conservative HQ's website had briefly pretended to be an independent fact-checking site when adjudicated a debate.

Ugly tone of dispiriting election

Many voters shared the outrage expressed by rival parties at such questionable tactics and the apparent indifference of ministers to them. Labour produced 'leaked' documents to show greater access to the NHS might well be on the table for US trade negotiators and that Johnson had lied about EU checks on goods entering mainland Britain from Northern Ireland. None of it changed the dynamic. The imperative of delivering a clear Brexit mandate and of keeping out Jeremy Corbyn – anti-British, unpatriotic, underhand and incompetent, according to hostile newspaper profiles – overrode fastidious objections to some of the means deployed. This was not wholly new; all elections generate controversy and accusations of cheating. But the tone of the dis-spiriting 2019 election seemed uglier than before, the willingness of the parties to cut corners greater and the electorate's indifference to such behaviour more egregious. That did seem new.

Brexit supporters looking forward to restored national sovereignty and pride embraced the novelty of it all. They relished the Prime Minister's declared eagerness to slaughter sacred cows deemed to have held Britain back for so long. Others persuaded themselves the 'real Boris' could now reveal himself as a liberal internationalist at heart. Those who prayed that was emphatically not the case were joined by those who feared that Johnson's reliance on traditional 'red wall' ex-Labour seats and votes 'loaned' to him would prevent any such blossoming, as it would a deregulated lurch towards Singapore-on-Trent.

Looking at versions of authoritarian and populist nationalism emerging around the world, most conspicuously in the United States, progressives looked to the future with trepidation, Leavers, long versed in the rhetoric of 'betrayal', with suspicion. The new parliament met on December 17 and voted through the Withdrawal Bill four days later. On January 31 Britain became an EU 'third country' again and waited to see what would happen next.

Note on the contributor

Michael White is a former political editor of the Guardian (1990-2016) and currently a columnist for The New European.

The disconnect between the media and the people – come back Harry Hardnose, all is forgiven

"How did we all get it so wrong?" the BBC's Andrew Marr asked Huw Edwards on the morning of Friday December 13. As print journalist Allison Pearson wrote in response: "Hang on a minute, who did Marr mean by 'we'?" Vyv Simson wonders if journalism needs to look back in time

On the Monday before polling day I was in my village shop buying a copy of *The Daily Telegraph*. I said "Hi" to a neighbour and we chatted briefly about the extent of our local flooding. As I paid for my newspaper, he spotted it was *The Torygraph* and said: "I wouldn't wipe my arse on that."

I was momentarily taken aback. This wasn't a throwaway line or what Labour's Jon Ashworth would describe by the Tuesday as 'a bit of banter'. This neighbour is no supporter of the Tory Party in general, and in particular a man like Boris Johnson. His words were delivered to all within earshot with disdain if not downright vitriol. Now that day's *Telegraph* was carrying a large front page photo of Jeremy Corbyn. "Well," I reposted, "I think you *should* wipe your arse on it. Jeremy Corbyn needs as much ordure as we voters can dump on him."

In retrospect, this little exchange in my Nowheresville village shop says something fundamental about why so many of our political journalists in both the print and broadcast media failed in the very basics of their craft.

They failed to connect with or be curious about the blindingly obvious and, in so doing, became dismissive of the opinions of others. As a result they manifestly failed to spot perhaps the biggest domestic political story of their working lives: how a so-called old Etonian posh boy, narcissist, liar and glutton for power named Boris Johnson could possibly attract so many lifelong Labour supporters to his ranks that he delivered not only a 'stonking majority' but also an Exocet that has fatally torpedoed one of our two great political parties.

Extensive coverage

I followed the election coverage pretty extensively in print – *The Guardian* and *Telegraph* followed by *The Sun* and *Daily Mirror* – and on national broadcast media – BBC Radio 4 and 5 Live, BBC TV, ITV, Sky News and Channel 4. I didn't follow it through social media or local media. So my opinions and conclusions are drawn exclusively from the aforementioned facets of the media.

As far as I'm aware, no national broadcast journalist spotted the story or at least broke it publicly. The only national print journalist I'm aware of who did so was Sherelle Jacobs in *The Daily Telegraph*. In a November 14 piece – a full month before polling day – she wrote:

"Labour is on the brink of the most seismic wipeout in British election history. The polls and BBC have failed to pick up on the biggest shocker of this election. This could actually be it – the end of Labour. Some may scoff, pointing out that it has narrowed the gap with the Tories in some polls. But on the ground, in the heartlands, the party smells of death."

So how on earth can this be? Before I attempt to suggest some possible answers to this most damning of journalistic questions – a disclaimer. What follows is just the opinion of an old, retired, former hack and documentary programme maker. I have no inside information. I am not an expert on anything. I am not an academic. You will find no footnotes or references here. I now live under a bucket. It's simply my opinion based on what I have observed and what I have experienced over my working life.

My first point is that I was easily able to call the election result on the day the election was announced. I predicted a comfortable Tory majority. I don't say this with any pride or with any pleasure. Indeed it is a truly shocking state of affairs that should worry anyone who values the role of journalism in a free society.

How was I able to predict this? I believe that it's because even in my retirement I retain the hack's basic requirement of curiosity. Curiosity is the bedrock of journalism and it should have sent any half respectable UK political journalist's alarm bells ringing years ago.

What a journalist should do

My definition of what a journalist should do is pretty simple: get out of the office, find a story and report it. Everything else is just opinion or PR. Even if you're just motivated by self-promotion and advancement, any half way competent journalist should want to be finding and breaking the big new and preferably exclusive stories.

How do you find them? By being curious and spotting potential paradoxes. The particular paradox to be curious about, in this case, was what might happen as a result of Labour's moving position on Brexit.

As Labour moved away from its 2017 stance of respecting the referendum result towards becoming the 'party of Remain', the obvious journalistic question was how would those millions of the party's Leave-voting supporters react? In particular, come election time, what would those people say to their Labour candidates asking for their support, when most of those candidates and the bulk of the party membership had stopped supporting them?

If enough of those generational Labour voters felt betrayed, or let down, or unheard, then there was clearly the potential for a massive political shock.

To find the answer to this question the second basic tenet of journalism should have been applied. Go and talk to those people. Listen to what they have to say. I can only conclude that in much of the print and broadcast media this didn't happen. Or if it did, those voices went unheard or were dismissed.

So why the lack of both curiosity and basic journalistic trade craft? There are undoubtedly ingrained cultural and political reasons for this woeful state of affairs but put simply, many journalists – not just political journalists – simply failed to appreciate, let alone understand, that the referendum result was a truly revolutionary event.

It came from the bottom up and not from the top down. And whatever else it was or wasn't, the Leave result was a direct challenge to the status quo.

More failure

This fundamental lack of understanding led to a further failure. The referendum was the first opportunity that many people had to vote for themselves and not for their party. Come election 2019, those voters had already tasted the experience of being freed from the shackles of party loyalty – and many of them rather liked it.

So much so that many of them did it again following the farcical and surreal requirement for the UK to take part in the vote for a new European parliament. Having tasted the forbidden fruit, there was always the distinct possibility that they would want to eat more..

I don't call the national print journalists to task as much as the national broadcast journalists for this shocking failure of their trade. I think most national newspapers were in touch with large swathes of the electorate – albeit with their own particular readerships. Some titles even bothered to entertain opposing viewpoints without simply condemning them as the words of the devil.

But it's the national broadcast journalists who must face the truly damning indictment. They have the problem of attempting to maintain impartiality – particularly during an election. Not easy, I know. But they seem to me to have become blinded to the basics of their trade.

They have become overwhelmed by the need for TV in particular to entertain. They have allowed their bosses to marginalise true current affairs programming and seem to be more interested in empty chairing or highlighting blocks of melting ice than in actually finding and reporting a story.

Who's more important?

Big name national presenters and interviewers also now seem to think they are more important than their interviewees. Their questions, laced with interminable sub clauses, are often longer than their interviewees' answers. And, unlike Andrew Neil or Piers Morgan, I still believe that while it is undoubtedly any journalist's right to ask the questions, it's any individual's right to choose not to answer them.

It was a national print journalist who was the only one to spot and report what was really going on. I find it suitably ironic that it was *The Daily Telegraph*, seen by so many in the world of broadcast media as being old school, out of date and hopelessly out of touch that ran the real story. For all the undoubted goodness and morality of its many correspondents, it wasn't the BBC or *The Guardian*.

Steve Bell, *The Guardian's* long-time cartoonist, created the character of Harry Hardnose, journalist on *The Daily Mule*. Harry represented everything that was bad about old-school journalism: hopelessly right wing, crude, drunk, a womaniser, a man with a distant relationship with facts and totally unable to cope with the advance of the electronic media.

But I think many of today's scribblers and opiners might well take some time to dwell on one of old Harry's favourite dictums – and as it happens – one which takes me back to that exchange in election week in my little village shop: *'If you can't wipe your arse on it, it's not journalism.'*

Note on the contributor

Vyv Simson spent more than 40 years as a journalist, documentary programme maker, executive producer and commissioner. He has made factual programmes for BBC TV and BBC Radio, Granada TV, Channel 4, Discovery Networks, National Geographic, The Smithsonian Channel and many other broadcasters. He is also the co-author of two books dealing with institutionalised corruption: *Scotland Yard's Cocaine Connection* and *The Lords of the Rings*, an expose of the Olympic movement. He has been lucky enough to win many awards and nominations from many organisations, including the RTS, Bafta and Grierson. He was often called an 'investigative journalist' but, in his view, all journalism should be investigative. He is now retired and lives under a bucket in a small village in Somerset.

The election in the media: against evasion and lies, good journalism is all we have

Political manipulators in the UK proved they have learnt from the US how to blur truth, but one local paper points to the antidote, says former Guardian editor Alan Rusbridger

In his first thousand days in office Donald Trump made 13,435 false or misleading claims, according to the good folk at the Washington Post who painstakingly monitor the president's habit of bending the truth. How we Brits have smiled at this con man's Teflon gift. Could never happen here.

But consider the lessons political managers around the world might have learned about our election and how we struggled to negotiate the increasingly blurred lines between truth and falsehood; facts and propaganda; openness and stealth; accountability and impunity; clarity and confusion; news and opinion.

It rather looks as if one or two skilled backroom manipulators (we can guess) studied Trump's ability to persuade enough people that black is white and, rather than recoil in disgust, came to the opposite conclusion: it works.

Promises, evasions and outright lies

One far off day we will discover whether 40 new hospitals will be built, and whether 20,000 new police officers will materialise along with 50,000 'new' nurses. It won't be long before we learn whether we've now finally got Brexit 'done' or whether this is just the start of a long and painful process of negotiating our future trading relationships with a greatly weakened hand.

We'll learn the reality of whether there is to be frictionless trade between the mainland of Britain and the island of Ireland. We will read the truth about alleged Russian interference in the 2016 Brexit Referendum … and much more. But by then life will have moved on, and maybe many of us will have forgotten the promises, evasions and outright lies of late 2019.

Lessons learned? That, in an age of information chaos, you can get away with almost any amount of misleading. You can doctor videos, suppress information, avoid challenging interviews – but only after your opponents have been thoroughly grilled. You can expel dissenting journalists from the press pack or hide in a fridge. You can rebrand a fake 'fact-checking' website. In the end, none of it matters.

Coin one unforgettable message and stick to it. 'Get Brexit done' was brilliant, never mind that the meaning of 'Brexit' and 'done' was far from clear: this is an age of simplicity, not complexity. Even the so-called mainstream media will do far more to amplify that slogan rather than question it. Try this stunt: slap the words on a JCB digger and drive it through a pile of polystyrene bricks ... and watch as news editors obligingly clear their front pages for the image. They are making posters, not doing journalism.

Threats to broadcasters

And remember that in most countries, governments have unusual power over public service broadcasters. So, in the event that television journalists seem to be getting too big for their boots, it is often useful to drop a heavy hint there will be a price to pay. Maybe Channel 4 has outlived its usefulness? Possibly it's time to privatise the BBC? That should do the trick.

Old-fashioned press conferences should be kept to the minimum. A manifesto should say almost nothing. Gaffe-prone colleagues should be 'disappeared'. If in real trouble, make things up. You'll be amazed how readily even the best journalists will repeat unattributable fictions (see the 'row' over the four-year-old boy in Leeds General Infirmary and what 'happened' during the subsequent visit of health secretary Matt Hancock). By the time the journalists have corrected themselves and Twitter has spent 24 hours arguing about the truth, the world will have moved on.

So, as Trump has discovered, the liars, myth-makers and manipulators are in the ascendancy – and however valiantly individual journalists attempt to hold them to account (and many, especially at a local level, have tried magnificently) the dice are loaded against them.

The one over-riding thought is that for many years I looked at US newspapers and pitied colleagues there who 'just' ran the newsroom, leaving comment pages to others. Pity has turned to envy. I now think it would be cleansing for all British national newspapers to split the responsibility for news and comment. It's simply too hard for the average reader – especially, but not only online – to tell the difference.

Local hero

And a hero? After the Yorkshire Evening Post's reporting of the Leeds story was questioned, its editor-in-chief, James Mitchinson, wrote a long and considered reply to a reader who, on the basis of something she read on social media, thought the story was fake. Mitchinson's reply courteously asks the reader why she would believe the word of a total stranger (who might not even exist) over a newspaper she had read for many years in good faith.

The fact the paper knew the story to be true was, said Mitchinson, down to 'bog-standard journalism'. It was a powerful statement of why good journalism – independent and decently crafted – should matter. So let's hear it for bog-standard journalism. There's too little of it. It may not be enough, but it's all we have.

This article first appeared in The Observer on December 15, 2020.

Note on the contributor
Alan Rusbridger is chair of the Reuters Institute for the Study of Journalism and Principal of Lady Margaret Hall, Oxford. He was editor of The Guardian from 1995 until 2015.

Section two

Broadcasters and the Brexit election

***

Decline and fall?

Richard Tait

For the last half century every UK general election has been described as a 'television election'. And with good reason – television's mass audiences and British broadcasting's unique reputation for accuracy and impartiality have made it the key battleground. Today, for the first time, that dominance looks less assured. For the broadcasters, the 2019 election was an awful experience – unprecedented levels of complaint and dissatisfaction from the public and vicious rows with the politicians, not helped by some embarrassing missteps of their own – but followed by the nightmare of a government with a huge majority talking about unpicking the whole structure of public service broadcasting which has always sustained high quality broadcast journalism in this country.

At Channel 4 News, Gary Gibbon stood out as a political editor who preferred analysis to haring around the country in search of the latest leader photo opportunity. One memorable report showed a group of Labour Leave voters in the midlands repeating the Vote Leave slogans of 2016 – they wanted the Brexit they had been promised and they didn't trust Jeremy Corbyn. What was to become the story of election night was there in one piece of hard-headed, analytical journalism.

He believes the politicians think they no longer have to engage with the broadcasters in the old way – with a growing focus on social media. The television interview is there to be mined (by both sides) for 'gotcha' clips that can then go viral. Reporters' Twitter feeds leave a 'paint trail' which the parties then use to categorise journalists for bias. Boris Johnson refused the Andrew Neil interview, seen even by a rival broadcaster as 'one of the last gateposts of scrutiny'. Not that Gary Gibbon had any better luck – he did not get the chance to ask Johnson a single question during the campaign and his one interview with Corbyn was only his third with the Labour leader in four and half years. So much for Channel 4's alleged 'left-wing bias'!

Cardiff Professors Stephen Cushion and Justin Lewis have been producing definitive analysis of the impartiality of broadcast news for many years – working for the BBC Trust and now Ofcom. They offer a bleak verdict on the overall performance of the broadcasters in the 2019 campaign. They echo Gary Gibbon's worry that the politicians are now in control. 'Broadcasters' they write, 'referee a contest in which politicians argue between themselves with only limited external scrutiny'. In a situation where the levels of public knowledge are often alarmingly low, the broadcasters need to raise their game with analysis and challenge. "The issue of public knowledge about politics and public affairs raises an inconvenient truth about British democracy."

Their conclusion is alarming: "The ideal of a healthy democracy in which people have high quality information on which to make independent decisions is floundering and we will not progress unless we take serious action to address it."

Roger Mosey, a former head of BBC Television News and now Master of Selwyn College Cambridge, is almost equally unimpressed. For him, it was a wretched and dispiriting election campaign, 'a grim cycle of aggressive politics and battered journalism'. The main channels missed the story of the collapse of the Labour vote.

There was too little analysis. The parties had abandoned the morning press conferences which had allowed scrutiny of individual policies; but equally the broadcasters seemed to have abandoned the editorial grids and commitments which used to mean that whatever the parties were doing, there was also space through the campaign for analysis of the key issues. He takes the current level of threats seriously: "Public service broadcasting is under threat as never before. Its imperfections were sometimes glaringly apparent, but nobody should be in any doubt that we'd be worse off without it."

Phil Harding, another distinguished BBC executive – former editor of the *Today* programme and BBC chief political adviser – has some sympathy for his colleagues in the trenches – elections are, as one of them said, 'hell on wheels'. But he too thinks the BBC needs to raise its game despite unprecedented pressures. He is critical of the way the BBC used one its greatest assets, its excellent political editor, Laura Kuenssberg, who tweeted a false story about a protestor punching Matt Hancock's adviser:

"Those at the top of the BBC need to think harder about what they really want their political editor to be. Is it reasonable to expect one person to be reporting on the ground; to appear on multiple outlets, live from the back of a travelling car sometimes; to be across social media; to tweet breaking news; and, at the same time, to make the necessary calls to contacts and still have the time to stop and reflect and come up with authoritative summaries and judgments for the main outlets?"

Perhaps the one positive to be taken from the 2019 campaign is the broadcasters succeeded for the first time in staging head-to-head prime ministerial debates between the two main contenders, Johnson and Corbyn. Sue Inglish, as head of BBC political programmes, had chaired the negotiations which brought about the first televised leaders' debates between David Cameron, Gordon Brown and Nick Clegg in 2010. She chronicles the grim battle to keep debates alive in the face of political opposition, particularly from the Conservative Party.

Theresa May's refusal to take part in any debates in the 2017 election now seems something of a turning point – playing its part in further damaging her image in her already catastrophic campaign. The fact that Johnson and Corbyn agreed to two debates on the two main channels – BBC1 and ITV – was 'a historic prize which had eluded the best efforts of TV broadcasters in all previous elections'. She thinks they are now here to stay – despite the complaints of those parties (and those broadcasters) who felt excluded.

One of those broadcasters was Channel 4, who tried and failed to persuade all seven party leaders to debate climate change. The refusal of Boris Johnson and Nigel Farage to take part led to the now notorious ice sculptures being placed symbolically on their empty chairs in the set and the farcical scenes as Michael Gove turned up at the studio with Boris Johnson's father and a film crew and asked to take part. Dorothy Byrne, Channel 4's head of news and current affairs, argues that the ice blocks were making an important point. Writing from Australia at the time of the bush fires, she argues:

"Our planet isn't just warming; all around me it is in flames."

She has no time for those who think television's role in elections is fading. "if you want to reach voters en masse, go on the telly" – three quarters of the public trust television news compared with 10 per cent who trust social media. Despite the rows and controversies, the various debate and interview programmes achieved healthy audiences. She believes the public want to see more robust engagement and she was disturbed by the derision some of the ITV audience showed in the first prime ministerial debate – 'I had never seen mockery like that before'.

However, the bitter arguments about debates and interviews did much to poison the atmosphere between the parties and the broadcasters. Trevor Barnes, a programme maker-turned-lawyer, was Ofcom's Director of Broadcasting Law and then Senior Standards Manager. He is worried about leaving these issues unresolved: "What was arguably damaged was the unwritten understanding that during a general election campaign the party leaders of all the main parties, without exception, would submit to a long-form interview by the BBC's Rottweiler interviewer of choice."

He does not think there is at present any chance, as some have suggested, to take the negotiations over debates away from the parties and broadcasters and set up an independent debates commission as in the US. However, he does have a practical suggestion to make the current situation less fraught. Ofcom is now the referee for all broadcast journalism, whether commercial broadcasters or the BBC. Its word on what is or is not impartial is final. His proposal is that Ofcom should make clear in its election code that if a leader does not want to take part in a scheduled debate the broadcaster can 'empty chair' that individual without running the risk of being found in breach of impartiality rules.

If, as David Cameron's former spin doctor, Sir Craig Oliver, says, 'the parties now have the cheat codes for dealing with broadcasters', the BBC, ITN and Sky had better just get used to the fact that future elections will continue to be 'hell on wheels'. The broadcasters still have public trust – perhaps diminishing but still in a different league from trust in newspapers or social media – or politicians, for that matter. They still have large and engaged audiences. Recent Ofcom research pointed to audiences wanting braver, more challenging journalism. There is no public enthusiasm for smashing up public service broadcasting, despite the self-interested campaigns of some newspapers. In a situation where the Government is threatening Channel 4's remit and the BBC's licence fee, being brave is not going to be easy – but there really is no alternative if the broadcasters are to keep the public support which is ultimately their best defence against those who want to destroy them. They have to remember that if they are not independent, they are no use to the rest of us.

'Permission not to engage' – Broadcasters and politicians before, during and after the 2019 election

The 2019 General Election campaign was markedly different from its predecessors and may well have heralded a change in the relationships between politicians and journalists to come in the near future, warns Channel 4 News political editor Gary Gibbon

Just when we thought covering politics couldn't get more challenging to cover, along came the 2019 General Election. Insults flew between broadcasters and politicians. There were stand-offs, boycotts and threats. It was a high octane, high risk roll of the dice by Boris Johnson that might just change our media landscape forever.

Broadcasters were accused of arrogantly assuming it was some kind of 'travesty of democracy'. One senior figure who helped to run the Tories' 2019 General Election campaign told me: "Both sides are eroding the conventions… you've given us permission not to engage." If broadcasters want to preserve their central role in our national life they need to work out if they have indeed given politicians room to take this kind of action with impunity. Have mistakes been made on both sides of the microphone?

Partisans backing both the two main parties piled in behind their leaderships with complaints of bias in both directions. Some called in evidence the online activities of reporters. Broadcasters were accused of ludicrous self-regard portraying a skipped interview as a travesty of democracy. Threats were made against the continuation of public service broadcasting. Are those threats in deadly earnest? Is the death of public service broadcasting a done deal?

Parliament in paralysis

You can't divorce this election from the unique tensions and pent up frustrations of the preceding year or so in Parliament which had raised tempers and temperatures. The UK political system was in paralysis. The hung parliament produced by the 2017 General Election could not agree how to implement the 2016 EU Referendum decision. Hardliners on both sides of the argument were emboldened to think they might get their own dream outcomes (either a harder Brexit than Theresa May was ready to settle for or a second referendum that might overturn the first). Parliament was incapable of deciding anything and tolerance was frayed. We saw this in microcosm every day as pro-Leave and pro-Remain demonstrators shouted at each other and sometimes at the media just outside Parliament. One demonstrator played a repetitive refrain on a glockenspiel, a fittingly eerie soundtrack to our national nightmare.

The Conservative Party decided the way out of this was to get a leader with strong Leave credentials to deliver Brexit. What followed in the autumn of 2019 with the Government's attacks on convention, courts and customs, left even some Boris Johnson early adopters feeling very queasy. But those rather unconservative moves laid the foundations for the December 2019 General Election Tory victory.

Boris Johnson needed to convince Leave voters he was deadly serious about delivering Brexit and that required the normal bounds of behaviour to be broken. He needed to show exasperated Leave voters he was truly more 'one of them' than he was 'one of the establishment' or 'just another Theresa May'. "We did some petty extreme things," one senior Tory acknowledged to me.

Was that outburst of unTory behaviour a tactical ploy necessary to the moment and to be jettisoned and forgotten about in the aftermath of the election, or was it part of a new pattern of behaviour which means there is nothing to stop the 80-strong majority Government taking on parts of the national furniture, such as public service broadcasting?

The BBC under threat?

Some Tories are nervous about a continuing revolutionary approach to institutions like the BBC. Journalists at the *Daily Mail* talk about how their longstanding editor Paul Dacre would happily urge on BBC-bashing by his editorial team but drew the line at bringing down the corporation altogether because many *Mail* readers struggled to find the multitude of other available channels on their TV sets.

The avowed and longstanding intent of the Prime Minister's top aide, Dominic Cummings, is to change the media landscape starting with the de-criminalising of non-payment of the BBC licence fee. Some have suggested that would slice close to £200m off the BBC's funds. I suspect it would do much more than that and be the end of the corporation as we know it. It would, as one close ally of Dominic Cummings told me, be accompanied by viral campaigns by hostile media rivals encouraging citizens to opt out of payment. This is not intended to be a minor moment in the history of the BBC but the final chapter. Changing the basis on which Channel 4 was set up gets talked about in the same breath by some around the Prime Minister but as a second order priority to re-thinking the BBC. Have public service broadcasters got what's coming to them? We have certainly made mistakes. Need it all end this way? Maybe not.

The allure of Twitter

In the December 2019 General Election we again saw some of our collective failings on display. Many of them are rooted in the arrival of social media and alternative news platforms. Broadcasters want to reach the fragmented audience in all its new hide-outs. But we risk damaging our core work and raison d'etre in the rush to build 'follower' markets and get 'hits'.

Twitter is deployed as a way of building up reach either for the broadcast outlet, the individual journalist or both. Some journalists use their Twitter handles as an alternative news agency service, pumping out news lines that are available in many other places either simultaneously or a moment earlier or later. They hope to become the 'go to' Twitter feed but run the risk they're publishing material that is not checked with the same rigour as the reports they'd put on air in a bulletin.

Some combine this with showing a little more ankle or personality which, judging by the number of followers some attract, has a strong appeal for many on Twitter. All this need for presence and activity and personality then kicks off other activity. Some broadcast journalists join in online debates, they 'like' or re-tweet material which may itself express an opinion.

The individual journalist may not have written an op-ed piece declaring their views but this sort of online activity can leave paint trails that build up a picture of a clear set of opinions. Tory HQ believes the paint trails are usually red, pink or green and it along with some of its allies in the print media rinse the web to put together political profiles of broadcast journalists which they claim is evidence of deep bias against the Right in the broadcast media.

Another great challenge facing the broadcast media is the form that interviews take. Social media, yet again, has had quite an impact. It encourages political parties to think they can avoid the risks of an encounter with a TV reporter or presenter and send their message direct through ads or messaging and go over the heads of the regular bulletins. But political leaders' teams on both sides of the divide argue that social media has bred a desire among some interviewers to secure a 'gotcha moment' that can then go viral on the internet. The rest of the interview merely serves as a vehicle for getting that click-bait clip which boosts the online statistics of the programme and/or the interviewer. Political parties realise there has always been a search for a news line in an interview and something that will get 'pick-up' in the newspapers to reflect glory on the outlet and keep its name in people's minds. But, the argument runs, the desperation to be trending on Twitter has magnified this and altered their calculations about whether to take part in conventional broadcast interviews.

Members of Boris Johnson's team say the main reason he swerved the encounter which the BBC expected him to have with Andrew Neil was not because of the immediate TV viewing audience but the potential impact of re-tweeted clips of a mis-judged answer or an on-air howler. Andrew Neil is a legendary forensic interviewer but I would argue his election programmes are particularly ferocious pressure points because politicians are not exposing themselves to more interviews throughout the year. Andrew Neil has 30 minutes to try to tackle the wildest claims a politician has been making unchecked for months or years as he or she deftly dodges and swerves what used to be the standard routine of high profile broadcast interviews. There is a sense these Andrew Neil encounters are the last gateposts of scrutiny and the politicians have sneaked past all the previous pat downs and bag checks. Some of the intensity of these interrogations would reduce if political leaders subjected themselves to long-form interviews earlier in the political cycle, outside elections, in political peacetime.

Breakdown of traditional relationships

In this same spirit of self-criticism, the broadcast media probably has to admit its combined approach to TV election debates produced a mess that served no one in the last election. Frenzied competition between broadcasters resulted in new, untested and flawed formats that didn't produce much enlightenment. None of which is to excuse the political leaderships who know full well that they have been playing a game ducking scrutiny because they can. I never got the opportunity to ask Boris Johnson one single question in the 2019 General Election campaign. Even the microphone-shy Theresa May did better than that in 2017 (though I remember her then press aide stretching over camera equipment boxes on the floor to tug at my trouser leg to finish an interview he felt had outlived its usefulness). When I got an allotted slot with Jeremy Corbyn for an interview in Nottingham in November 2019, it was only the third interview I had been granted with him in his four and a half years of leadership.

Boris Johnson wanted the election to be about three words: Get Brexit Done. Anything else beyond campaign pictures showing him at ease with real people was getting in the way. The Leave/Remain split energised divisions and tensions in the broadcaster/politician relationship. One senior Tory told me: "The way (the Tory leadership team) see it: they won the argument and you people (the broadcasters) represent the part of the country that lost and you're not doing enough to represent the majority of the people."

In truth, the tensions were added to by Brexiteers sometimes playing fast and loose with basic facts about the future relationship that would be possible with the

EU after the UK leaves. Broadcasters felt under an obligation to challenge wildly optimistic promises of the 'cake and eat it' type. Some Remainers, for their part, were merely pretending to have accepted the 2016 referendum result when deep down their avowed intent was to overturn it not to moderate it. The special tensions of this bizarre and painful period in British political history have contributed to the bust-up we are witnessing between senior politicians and the broadcast media.

The hostility from the Right was mirrored on the Left in the Labour leadership team around Jeremy Corbyn. Their long-held feeling that the mainstream media was drenched in the establishment outlook and institutionally incapable of engaging with the re-think or insurgency represented by Jeremy Corbyn's world view intensified in the 2019 General Election. The Labour leader, like the Tory leader, has been increasingly drawn to friendly media or to in-house, unmediated direct online messaging. That direct messaging is, of course, much harder to challenge.

As I write, speculation swirls on what policies the Government will actually craft from the slogans of the 2019 General Election. There is much revolutionary language in the court of Boris Johnson but he himself is a politician marinated in the establishment. Is this government seriously interested in a reset of relations with the broadcasters or is it determined to transform the broadcasting landscape? Can public service broadcasting win back lost support in an age of angry debate and polarised, fearful tribes? Can broadcasters reverse 'permission to disengage'? We probably don't have long to find out.

Note on the contributor
Gary Gibbon is political editor of Channel 4 News.

Were broadcasters biased? Interpreting impartiality during the 2019 General Election campaign

The impartiality of broadcasters during election campaigns always attracts critical attention but throughout the 2019 UK General Election campaign allegations of media bias became more prominent, most notably with BBC news under fire for its editorial decisions. Stephen Cushion and Justin Lewis assess accusations of bias levelled at broadcasters during the campaign and suggest ways the impartiality of news could be enhanced by the adoption of more robust journalistic conventions and diverse newsgathering practices

In an increasingly fragmented digital media environment, the origin and destination of complaints about bias is beginning to develop distinctive patterns. Broadly speaking, younger people, and those holding left-wing political beliefs, tend to use social media to vent their frustrations with media bias rather than complain through official channels. Conversely, older people, and those with more right-wing political beliefs, are more likely to address complaints to Ofcom – the UK regulator who investigates infringements of impartiality – or the BBC itself.

So, for example, social media – in particular Twitter – was widely used as a platform to express disaffection with BBC coverage towards the Labour Party, including sloppy editorial mistakes that undermined the credibility of Jeremy Corbyn and appeared to favour Conservative leader Boris Johnson. Given the rising social media backlash against the BBC, this motivated its director of news – Fran Unsworth (2019) – to write a response to critics in *The Guardian* a week before the election, where she vehemently defended the BBC's impartiality.

By contrast, post-election analysis by *The Guardian* showed there were more public complaints to Ofcom alleging bias against the Conservative Party rather than Labour (Waterson and Brennan 2019). In particular, there were thousands of objections about the treatment of Johnson by Andrew Marr during a live television interview. This had more than a hint of irony since Marr was under pressure to be tough, following Johnson's refusal to be interviewed by the BBC's Andrew Neil, which in itself led to accusations from Labour and other parties about unfair treatment – see below. But these grievances tended not to trend on social media because complaints to Ofcom were largely made by older, Conservative supporters who tend to be less active on Twitter.

While it is useful to understand the demographic and political inflections of where and how people complain about media bias, the volume of complaints is *not* a measure of their veracity. Complaints about the Marr interview are a case in point: Conservatives are more likely to watch their leader under scrutiny and, taken on its own, Johnson faced a tough interview with challenging questions. But to make a serious assessment about interviewer bias, we would need to systematically compare this with Corbyn's journalistic treatment.

Intentional bias or sloppy journalism?

Much of the furore during the election campaign centred on editing mistakes – whether intentional or not – in BBC news that favoured Conservatives and undermined Labour. So, for example, in one news report BBC Breakfast used out of date footage – from 2016 – of a younger and smarter looking Johnson laying a wreath at the Remembrance Day services, while the BBC's Saturday lunchtime television news bulletin the day after the *Question Time: Leaders Debate* featured a clip that edited out audience laugher after a response by Johnson about trustworthiness. In both instances, the BBC apologised for editorial mistakes, but it reinforced the perception among sceptics that there was a systematic bias in news output that favoured the Conservative Party.

Prominent accusations of bias also centred on the construction of live television debates and extended one-on-one interviews with party leaders. There were, for instance, complaints from Liberal Democrats, the SNP and other parties about their exclusion from debates between the leaders of Labour and Conservatives. Channel 4 was criticised for not allowing Michael Gove to take the place of Johnson in a TV leaders' debate about the environment – and for replacing the Conservative leader with an ice sculpture. This decision was subsequently judged to be consistent with 'due impartiality' guidelines by Ofcom after a Conservative Party complaint.

Another television election BBC format – extended prime time interviews with Andrew Neil – attracted attention because all the leaders signed up to it apart from Johnson. Corbyn, who was grilled intensely, was led to believe the Prime Minster would also agree to an interview with the same journalist. Johnson's decision to then decline to submit himself to a Neil interview led the Labour Party to cry foul.

From specific instances of poor editing, to the style and format of programming and the inclusion and exclusion of certain political parties and their leaders, allegations of broadcasting bias were a recurrent theme throughout the election campaign. But taken individually or collectively, in our view they represent either the difficulties of balancing political perspectives in a multi-party system or, in many cases, sloppy journalism rather than any intentional bias towards one party or another.

There are, however, undoubtedly lessons broadcasters can learn. Extended prime time interview dates with party leaders, for example, should be pre-determined and announced in advance – as they were in a previous election campaigns – making it more difficult for parties to drop out. Similarly, the form and structure of leaders' TV debates could be a matter for an independent body to establish over an election cycle – as it is in the US – rather than for something for parties and broadcasters to squabble over. But we would like to make a broader point here. In our view, the focus on individual editorial decisions or the composition of particular programmes detracts attention away from more deep-rooted and systemic questions of editorial bias that limit public understanding of election issues and political debates.

Bias against understanding?

In a systematic analysis of broadcast and press coverage, Loughborough University's (2019) research established that television news on the UK's main broadcaster featured a broadly similar proportion of appearances by Conservative and Labour politicians over the campaign. Indeed, as research about election reporting has long established, political parties make up the vast majority of all sources during campaigns, followed by citizens in vox pops (Cushion 2018). According to Loughborough University's (2019) study, this was the case during the 2019 election campaign. This leaves little space for experts from a range of professions, such as independent think tanks, economists and academics, to comment upon the credibility of the parties' claims. In other words, broadcasters referee a contest in which politicians argue between themselves, with only limited external scrutiny. This is exacerbated by the time-honoured journalistic narrative of following party leaders around the country on the campaign trail. This may be enlivened by chance encounters or gaffes, but it rarely offers insight into substantive policy areas or manifesto promises. While correspondents are often given time to take a more forensic and independent look at the differences between parties in their approach to issues, these pieces generally fall outside the main news narrative.

When independent analysts were consulted on the BBC nightly bulletins when Conservative and Labour manifestos were launched, Berry's (2019) research found that it was only the Institute for Fiscal Studies that was used as an external source. The IFS was strongly critical of Labour's tax and spend policies, which was at odds – he argues – with other economists who were *not* given any airtime (notably, for example, a letter to the Financial Times supporting Labour's programme from 163 prominent UK economists, a view that was given far less coverage). This point was reinforced by Loughborough University's study, which found in week three of the campaign "The most high-profile of these authorities has been the Institute for Fiscal Studies. IFS Director Paul Johnson has been more prominent than every campaigner in the Top 20 apart from Jeremy Corbyn and Boris Johnson".

The problem here is partly one of economic literacy and partly one of limiting debate. The IFS's reputation for impartiality is well earned, but their focus is not macro-economic. A key argument made by many macro-economists was that increasing public spending and public investment (as Labour planned to do) would stimulate the economy, spurring economic growth. For macro-economists, this is seen as particularly important when interest rates are at rock bottom, which removes the other main option (in this case, the Bank of England lowering interest rates) for economic stimulus. This argument is outside the IFS's main area of focus, which is to use models based on existing assumptions about the money available to governments, rather than model how this might be changed by macro-economic policy. In other words, there is an economic debate here that was ignored, with broadcasters favouring one branch of economics (practiced by the IFS) and ignoring a key debate about macro-economic policy (articulated by the 163 economists).

Oxford economist Simon Wren-Lewis (2018) argues that, over the last decade, this bias, while not *overtly* party political, has tended to favour pro-austerity economics, with its fixed assumptions about the money available to governments for tax cuts or public spending. In short, the voice of many mainstream macro-economists who argued that austerity policies slowed UK economic growth – reducing government revenues as a result – was rarely heard, allowing the Conservative Party to make (some might say questionable) claims about their economic record.

As the BBC Trust report into the coverage of statistics suggested (Cushion et al 2018), journalists could be bolder in challenging claims made by politicians, and, more importantly, more focused on developing an independent knowledge base by which claims can be measured and assessed. Conservative Party claims about the 'strong economy', for example, were rarely challenged, despite plenty of available evidence to do so (so, for example, the economic recovery since 2010 has been one of the weakest on record, a point rarely made on broadcast news). The media bias against understanding, in this sense, is about the narrow sourcing practices which often privilege the same institutional views and which favour a particular understanding of the world. This is particularly important in an era of populist politics and easy slogans, with strong 'common sense' emotional appeals that bypass evidential scrutiny. In this election 'Get Brexit Done' is the most obvious example – an idea that depends on low levels of public knowledge about the realities of trade negotiations or the economics of Brexit. Broadcasters recognised the need to rigorously assess some of the parties' dubious claims. As Unsworth (2019) acknowledged in her *Guardian* article, the BBC 'ramped up' its Reality Check service during the campaign in order to fact check the parties' statements and manifesto pledges. But most people do not consult such services, and as we argued during the campaign, broadcasters could have taken more radical steps to challenge the parties' campaign spin and enhance public understanding (Cushion 2019).

The issue of public knowledge about politics and public affairs raises an inconvenient truth about British democracy – one that it is difficult for politicians or journalists to raise (it is much easier for both to flatter their audiences, than ask awkward questions about how well informed they are). Surveys show that levels of public knowledge about a whole range of prominent public issues – from the EU to immigration – are often alarmingly low. More worrying is that many people are not just uninformed but misinformed. This was illustrated during the campaign when Channel 4 News showed excerpts from a focus group with Leave voters in traditional Labour areas (although the report was used to highlight why Labour was in trouble, not to explore the quality of information used to form judgments).

The ways in which journalists engage with members of the public – mainly through vox pops (or variations thereof) – do little to address this. Indeed, as we have argued elsewhere (Cushion 2018; Lewis et al 2005) vox pops are a poor, unscientific measure of public opinion, which often recycle conventional wisdom rather than challenge it. While they superficially tick a box marked 'public engagement' for journalists, they provide little informative content for audiences. If they occasionally signify a democratic deficit, they do little to address it.

Beyond the rushed immediacy of the newsroom, we would argue that the starting point for broadcasters (especially PSBs) should be to understand, respond to and address levels of public knowledge. This is, in some ways, quite a radical departure from a newsroom culture dictated by instinctive judgements about what news is and how to communicate it. But the ideal of a healthy democracy in which people have high quality information on which to make independent decisions is floundering, and we will not progress unless we take serious action to address it.

References

Berry, Mike (2019) UK election 2019: why the BBC's approach to the IFS is a threat to its impartiality in *The Conversation*, 3 December 2020: https://theconversation.com/uk-election-2019-why-the-bbcs-approach-to-the-ifs-is-a-threat-to-its-impartiality-128032

Cushion, Stephen (2018) 'Using public opinion to serve journalistic narratives: rethinking vox pops and live two-way reporting in five UK election campaigns (2009-2017)', *European Journal of Communication*, Vol. 33(6), pp. 639-656.

Cushion, Stephen (2019) Broadcasters must take radical steps to challenge campaign spin and enhance understanding, *New Statesman*, 15 November, https://www.newstatesman.com/politics/media/2019/11/broadcasters-must-take-radical-steps-challenge-campaign-spin-and-enhance

Cushion, Stephen and Thomas, Richard (2018) *Reporting Elections: Rethinking the logic of Campaign Coverage*. London: Polity.

Cushion, S., Lewis, Justin and Callaghan, Rob (2017) 'Data journalism, impartiality and statistical claims: towards more independent scrutiny in news reporting', *Journalism Practice* Vol.11 (10): 1198-1215

Lewis, Justin, Wahl Jorgensen, Karin and Inthorn, Sanna (2005) *Citizens or Consumers? What the Media Tell Us about Political Participation*. Maidenhead: Open University Press.

Loughborough University (2019) General Election 2019 Media Research: https://www.lboro.ac.uk/news-events/general-election/

Unsworth, Fran (2019) 'At the BBC, impartiality is precious. We will protect it', *The Guardian*, 4 December 2020: https://www.theguardian.com/commentisfree/2019/dec/04/bbc-impartiality-precious-protect-election-coverage

Waterson, Jim and Brennan, Martha (2019) BBC election coverage draws more complaints from Tory than Labour supporters, *The Guardian*, 31 December 2020: https://www.theguardian.com/media/2019/dec/31/bbc-election-coverage-draws-more-complaints-from-tory-than-labour-supporters

Wren-Lewis, Simon (2018) *The Lies We Were Told: Politics, Economics, Austerity and Brexit*. Bristol: Bristol University Press.

Note on the contributors

Stephen Cushion is a Professor at the Cardiff School of Journalism, Media and Culture at Cardiff University. Stephen is currently a PI four on research projects that total more than £1.2m. This includes a three year £517,731 research grant awarded by the ESRC entitled 'Beyond the MSM: Understanding the rise of alternative online political media' (2019-2022); a two year £9,839.80 research grant awarded by BA/Leverhulme entitled 'Accurate or misleading? The portrayal of MSM in alt-left media' (2019-2021); A two year £579,183 research grant awarded by AHRC entitled 'Countering disinformation: enhancing journalistic legitimacy in public service media' (2020-2022); and an Ofcom review of BBC News and Current Affairs (2019-2020).

Justin Lewis is Professor of Communication at the Cardiff School of Journalism, Media and Culture at Cardiff University. He is Director of Clwstwr, a £10m R&D inovation centre for the Screen and news sectors. He has conducted research with the BBC, the BBC Trust, Channel 4, and a number of EU and UK research councils. He has written widely about media, culture and politics. He is Chair of the UK Government's Research Excellence Framework panel on Media and Communication.

Could the broadcast media have done better?

The 2019 General Election was a difficult one for the broadcasters, says Roger Mosey, former head of BBC TV News, and while there were some major successes, most of them missed the big story happening in front of their cameras

Whatever your view of the result, it was a wretched and dispiriting election campaign. Politicians seldom broke away from churning out the same soundbites and on social media there was a level of viciousness that was unbearable. It's therefore not exactly a surprise the mainstream media, pressured by parties and harried by online trolls, had a rough ride in Election 2019 too. It is difficult, as the proverb goes, to make a silk purse out of a sow's ear. But the question is whether the broadcast media could have done better, or whether we're doomed to be in a grim cycle of aggressive politics and battered journalism.

Without any doubt, the best bit of this campaign for television was when it ended. From the striking graphics of Sky's realisation of the exit poll onwards, all three of the main channels had an excellent results night. Huw Edwards took to the BBC anchor's chair with charm and authority, and the strength in depth of the BBC's talent line-up was evident. A special round of applause to the designers and directors who, working within the confines of Broadcasting House for the first time, made the operation feel big and spacious even if it wasn't Elstree or TC1.

Praise for political pundits

Often, though, the most watchable moments were on ITV. Their panels were the sparkiest. Ed Balls and George Osborne, first paired in 2017, remain a wonderful combination. And then the interaction of Labour centrist Alan Johnson with Momentum's Jon Lansman produced some of the most telling exchanges in the early coverage. Widiane Moussa, who led the guest booking team, should take a bow. On Sky, John Bercow looked like a good hire before the event, but his value crumbled as the scale of his opponents' triumph became clear.

The coverage of the election campaign itself was less sure-footed. It has to be said political journalism these days is much more difficult than it used to be. That's because the parties are trying to control much more – the open daily news conferences disappeared long ago – and also because the scrutiny from social media is so intense. An error, or worse still an imagined error, is immediately pounced upon and cited as an example of bias or conspiracy. The BBC was absurdly criticised for two cock-ups, one when the wrong footage of Boris Johnson at the Cenotaph was used on Breakfast, and the other when laughter directed at Johnson during a peak-time live programme was edited out of a subsequent news clip. Within the vast amount of BBC output, and with journalists working under intense pressure, it's understandable that mistakes happen, and it's daft to ascribe them to partisanship.

The big Johnson no-show

But there were much more serious challenges to impartiality. The Prime Minister sent his apologies for Channel 4's debate on climate change, and was irreverently replaced by a melting block of ice instead. The Conservatives' bullying response to this, and its threats to the BBC licence fee, were disturbing. It was, however, the saga of Boris Johnson's invitation to be interviewed by Andrew Neil that dominated the middle part of the campaign. The media love to talk about the media. Neil's interrogations of the party leaders on BBC One were one of the television highlights – first unsettling Nicola Sturgeon and then eviscerating Jeremy Corbyn. But Johnson's refusal to commit to the same treatment gave the BBC a headache.

It reacted by first talking tough and saying it would not let him take part in the Andrew Marr programme if he didn't also appear with Andrew Neil. Then, citing the London Bridge terrorist incident, it gave in and let the Marr interview go ahead anyway. With Marr obviously under orders to be super-tough, and Johnson determined to bash ahead with a political agenda, it was the most unwatchable prime ministerial interview in television history. A few days later, when it was clear Johnson was a no-show for the peak time programme, Neil delivered a withering put down of the PM – which was not to the taste of many former senior broadcast executives, who saw it as too much of a political intervention into a campaign.

There was a happier experience with the party leader debates – unless you were Jo Swinson, of course. It was good for viewers that the two men contending to be prime minister agreed to take part in head-to-head encounters and there was a coup for ITV in having Johnson and Corbyn standing alongside their presenter Julie Etchingham as a piece of political history was made. Etchingham was, as ever, terrific, and Nick Robinson also did a fine job in refereeing the BBC equivalent. The virtues of the two-way debate were reinforced by the unsatisfactory seven-way alternatives. It is right that all the parties should be featured, of course, but the more politicians who are involved the messier and more difficult to control it becomes.

Similarly, studio audiences can be a nightmare to balance. I was struck by the relatively subdued role of the public in the prime ministerial debates by contrast with the vociferous BBC Question Time broadcast with four party leaders from Sheffield. The latter seemed to have an over-supply of Corbynites, some of whom got to put soft questions to their leader – whereas Jo Swinson was battered by opponents with no contingent of Liberal Democrats to cheer her on.

Did broadcasters miss the big story?

But the biggest questions for the broadcasters are whether they missed the actual story of the election. There was an enormous effort to get out and about around the country. It didn't, however, prove to be particularly illuminating. Too often a constituency piece majored on voters doing everyday tasks such as buying Christmas trees or visiting livestock markets, while grumbling about politicians in general. One person would be quoted giving one view, while another would then immediately reply with the opposite. It was impartial, in the sense that both sides of an argument were represented, but it lacked insight into which view would prevail. The most common line from correspondents was that both party leaders were equally unpopular and many voters had not decided which way to vote. With hindsight, we know that is untrue. Jeremy Corbyn was markedly more disliked by traditional Labour voters than Boris Johnson was by potential Conservative supporters, and the Remain versus Leave fault line was the determining factor of this election.

More editorial decisions made in the north of England and fewer in metropolitan London would have helped. Some reporters did identify and dwell on the collapse of the Labour vote – Lewis Goodall on Sky was one – but it was never as clearly defined in this campaign as it was in 1983 when Michael Foot actually won more seats.

Trivial pursuits

Accompanying this was a tendency to spend too much time on the parties' agendas rather than the public interest. Or, worse still, the preoccupation with trivia when the future of the country was at stake. At its most extreme, this was manifested during the mid-campaign NATO summit when any questions about Russia or China or the future of the alliance were subverted by an obsession with the disrespectful joke that Justin Trudeau may have told about President Trump. It was also manifested in the late flurries about Boris Johnson confiscating a reporter's phone and then a couple of days later allegedly hiding in a fridge to avoid an interview with Good Morning Britain. These dominated the news agenda in a way that the substance of our negotiating mandate for Brexit never did, and the electorate didn't seem to be swayed by them, anyway.

I have some nostalgia for the days of the former BBC director-general John Birt's journalism empire, and subsequently the election grids produced by Mark Byford as deputy DG. They ensured proper attention was given to all the big issues: defence, housing, social care and all the rest. It is difficult, though possible, to divert the politicians from their preferred topics. It is well within the broadcasters' control to focus more on policy than on process. This campaign showed the terrain for television journalists is tougher than ever. Public service broadcasting is under threat as never before. Its imperfections were sometimes glaringly apparent, but nobody should be in any doubt that we'd be worse off without it.

This article first appeared in Television magazine.

Note on the contributor

Roger Mosey is Master of Selwyn College, Cambridge. Previously he was Head of BBC Television News and Editor of the *Today* programme.

The BBC under fire as usual, but this time it's different

The BBC was attacked from all sides in the 2019 election. Phil Harding argues that in changing media times the BBC must decide on its real priorities – but that the need for a bold, confident and independent public-service broadcaster is greater than ever

If you followed this sour and dispiriting election campaign for any length of time, it soon became clear who the real enemy was: the BBC.

It received some 60,000 complaints from the public during this election. It copped it from all the parties. A Labour front-bencher claimed the vilification of Jeremy Corbyn had fuelled its election defeat. The Conservatives accused the BBC of being completely out of touch with the public, part of a pro-Remain metropolitan Islington bubble. The *Today* programme came in for particular criticism: "Radio Misery... full of interviews with left-wing, entitled, virtue-signaling students."

The Lib Dems were extremely unhappy about being squeezed out of the leaders' debates and felt excluded from much of the rest of the coverage. The SNP felt it was ignored by the London media. Comments about the BBC and its correspondents (#bbcbias) on social media were far worse. It seemed as though all the political neuroses of this campaign were directed at one organisation. Laura Kuennsberg came in for particular attention, much of it personal and vitriolic.

Election campaigns are always a testing time for the BBC. A former colleague of mine once described them as "hell on wheels". It's a time when politics is at its most febrile, the parties at their most partisan and bellicose.

From Bernard Ingham bristling during Margaret Thatcher's time to Alistair Campbell's shouting and bullying on behalf of Tony Blair, the pressure on the BBC has always been intense. It can take even the most seasoned of observers by surprise. James Harding, who had previously been through some rough times as editor of *The Times*, said that when he took over as BBC news boss he was "quite astonished by the ferocity and frequency of complaints from all parties" and that was during the 2015 election with only 5,000 complaints.

That the BBC should find itself the main target of such attacks is perhaps not surprising. For all the talk of the demise of the mainstream media – and audience behaviour is changing – the BBC remains the dominant source of news in this country. Some 78 per cent of the population use it as a news source whether on television, radio or online. It is this dominance of the market that has caused many of its media enemies to question its role.

Andrew Neil's monologue with the empty chair was always going to kick over a Conservative hornets' nest. It was when Boris Johnson mused aloud during the middle of the campaign about whether the BBC licence fee was sustainable that you realised that this might be an election with consequences. This was the most explicit juxtaposing of editorial pressure on the BBC and its funding during an election that I can remember.

The BBC didn't help its cause with the left either by some stupid errors – using the wrong library footage of Boris Johnson laying a wreath, editing out the laughter from an audience question, using an unfortunate phrase in a live report.

In thousands of hours of coverage produced by human beings it would be extraordinary if there were not mistakes. In previous campaigns most would have gone unremarked. No chance of that now when the denizens of social media can pick out the slightest imperfection, retweet it constantly and incite thousands who never saw the original report to complain about it.

Given how much in this campaign the BBC became part of the debate, it found it harder and harder not to be seen as an active political participant. And many at the BBC felt there was little they could do that was right. This level of intense scrutiny is new and something the BBC is not designed to deal with..

Impartiality: it's getting harder.

Impartiality has been a core value of BBC political output almost from day one. Part of its remit as a national public broadcaster is to cover fairly all significant shades of opinion on controversial issues. In a nutshell, the BBC must not 'take sides'. Like all broadcast media in this country – but unlike the press – the BBC is statutorily regulated to be impartial.

That has got harder and harder. Politics has become more complicated. What was once a neat two-sided debate between Labour and Conservative with fairness consisting of giving equal time to both sides has morphed into a multi-party debate with the Liberal Democrats occasionally surging into significant contention.

UK politics has changed. In Scotland we now have an SNP First Minister; in Wales Plaid Cymru has moved from the fringe. We have had surges of support for Ukip and the Brexit party. A lot of politics has moved beyond Westminster to the pressure groups and protest movements.

We have had the deeply disruptive issue of Brexit, which has divided parties and pitted MPs of the same party in violent debate with each other. The 2016 referendum also sharpened the debate about the role of reporting, with the BBC being accused of deploying false equivalence and not 'calling out lies' such as the NHS slogan on the Leave campaign bus.

In addition, the last decade has seen the rise of identity politics which has become intense and highly personal.

As a result the parameters of impartiality – never precise in the first place – have become vastly more complicated and blurred. The old bipolar model of impartiality has been overtaken by a multilayered multi-polar paradigm of Einsteinian complexity. The BBC's claim to be impartial is increasingly disputed.

As if that hasn't made life complicated enough there has been the advent of social media.

The rise and rise of social media

Two thirds of the UK population now use Facebook, a site that only started in 2004. Twitter, founded two years later, today has more than 13m users in this country. While social media does not change the fundamental principles of impartiality, it certainly changes the practice and leaves some of the tensions and contradictions much more exposed.

Social media has made the successful operation of a mutually agreed democratic space much more difficult. There are fewer agreed benchmarks; there are 'alternative facts'. Each partisan side only trusts its own highly selective sources of information.

The rise of websites like Breitbart and the Canary has accelerated this process. Increasingly some people only want to see material which re-confirms their own views and prejudices. This leaves little middle ground for sources of news which seek to offer a rounded impartial view. (Some news outfits such as LBC have tried to get round this, while staying within the rules of impartiality, by scheduling a range of opinionated presenters at different times of day with Nick Ferrari and James O'Brien offering milder versions of Fox News and MSNBC.)

The path of impartiality was always narrow and hard. It has got a whole lot tougher.

All of this is happening against a background of declining trust in institutions in general and the media in particular. According to the Reuters Institute, trust in the news in the UK has fallen by more than 11 percentage points since 2015. Although broadcasters have higher levels of trust than tabloids or digital only sources, even the most trusted brands like the BBC are seen by many as pushing or suppressing agendas – especially over divisive issues like Brexit and climate change. If this trend continues, it could become a massive problem for the BBC.

One of the reasons people trust the BBC more than other outlets is that the BBC takes a lot of trouble to get it right. When it comes to trust, accuracy matters a lot.

The decision-making process over what and when to publish or not publish has changed a lot over the years. Once it was standard practice in BBC newsrooms that nothing went out on air unless it had been confirmed by at least two news agencies (the 'two-source rule').

'Better second and right rather than first and wrong' was the motto. That started to change with changes in media consumption and increasing competition in the news market. A turning point came with the London bombings of 2005 when the BBC was noticeably behind the curve on reporting that the explosions were bombs (the authorities at first blamed power surges). From that point on it became accepted practice for the BBC to publish unconfirmed reports provided that that the source of such reports was made clear and properly attributed.

Social media has made the whole issue of editorial thought and oversight much harder. The BBC Editorial Guidelines on the use of social media are fine in principle, but much harder to put into practice:

'*All BBC activity on social media…is subject to…editorial oversight in the same way that our on-platform content is*'.

With Twitter that is just about impossible. Most tweets are not seen by a second pair of editorial eyes before they are published.

Twitter during the campaign

Social media is a valuable source of news, quick for tip offs and offering a broad agenda. It has also radically changed the pace of news; every correspondent can be in direct touch with the audience at the touch of a screen. Social media has become a branch of publishing in its own right. The BBC quite rightly has decided it needs to be where the audience is.

For the BBC, social media has grown from just publicising programmes and republishing programme content to becoming a separate branch of BBC content in its own right. Correspondents and producers now have their own Twitter feeds. They often break stories first on Twitter. They have thousands of followers. Laura Kuennsberg alone has a 1.1m (though whether she welcomes all of them is another matter!). The dividing line between personal and BBC use and endorsement is often far from clear. This has brought problems for the BBC both over editorial accuracy and the fine line between judgment and opinion.

During the election, the BBC received a lot of stick for one incident when Laura Kuennsberg – along with other broadcast journalists not from the BBC – tweeted that an assistant to the Conservative health secretary Matt Hancock had been hit by a Labour protester outside a hospital.

"*So Matt Hancock was dispatched to Leeds General to sort out mess. Hearing Labour activists scrambled to go + protest, and it turned nasty when they arrived – one of them punched Hancock's adviser.*" @bbclaurak

ITV's Paul Brand also tweeted that the Conservatives were saying that Labour had paid for taxis for 100 activists to turn up. In fact as the later video showed there was no punch, just four or five protesters turned up, shouting at Hancock's departure.

Somebody, presumably on the Conservative campaign had, knowingly or unknowingly, been briefing false information. Kuennsberg took her source at face value and got it wrong, albeit briefly. In the demanding and competitive world of Twitter journalism she didn't want to be beaten to the punch by her rivals.

In past elections this would have been a 10-second row. But now, thanks to the instant amplification of social media, it became a much retweeted talking point alleging BBC bias. But only the BBC got it in the neck. For some time before the election, Kuennsberg had been the subject of much abuse – some of it vile – from left-wing activists alleging she was a Tory stooge and worse. She quickly deleted her original tweet and posted footage of a harmless encounter. But that was not enough for the furious Twitterati who wanted an apology broadcast on every BBC outlet.

It's not an incident that is going to feature hugely when the political histories of this campaign come to be written, but it is one that made a further dent in the BBC's reputation for fair journalism. Those dents start to accumulate.

The debate also takes us into the murky world of non-attributable political sources – a world in which increasingly aides and ministers think misleading is all part of the game. In this case, a more explicit explanation of where the story had originally come from would have helped. But Twitter is a medium that compresses, there isn't much room for attribution or nuance.

The election also raised a further issue for the BBC in how it deploys its political resources. Laura Kuennsberg is a highly skilled and energetic political editor. A first-class broadcaster with good political judgment, she is in much demand by the many BBC outlets. Every editor wants her on their show.

As with her predecessors, appearances have to be rationed. She also has experienced colleagues who are very good at their jobs. Those at the top of the BBC need to think harder about what they really want their political editor to be. Is it reasonable to expect one person to be reporting on the ground; to appear on multiple outlets, live from the back of a travelling car sometimes; to be across social media; to tweet breaking news; and, at the same time, to make the necessary calls to contacts and still have the time to stop and reflect and come up with authoritative summaries and judgments for the main outlets?

Beyond the sound and fury, there are some important issues for the BBC here. What does it want to use social media for? Does it matter if in the rush and bustle of reporting there is the odd high-profile mistake? And, over and beyond that, what are the BBC's real priorities in news? Does it want to be known for getting it first or getting it right? The BBC's political editor is an important and influential figure. If he or she reports or says something, people sit up and take notice. It's a balance of course but in terms of its reputation and trust in it, the BBC can't afford to get it wrong very often.

The aftermath of the election

Many of the political rows whipped up during elections are usually forgotten fairly quickly. Governments have too many other things to worry about. This time though it looks as though some of this is not going to disappear quickly.

Government ministers are currently refusing to appear on the *Today* programme; a similar ban is reported to be in operation for *Newsnight*. At the same time there are proposals to decriminalise the licence fee, the row over over-75 licence fees rumbles on; large cuts loom; ministers have started talking about a 2022 review of the licence fee already.

The political and editorial pressure on the BBC is going to be enormous. Its enemies want it to buckle. It has to withstand the pressure with among other things bold and confident journalism – but bold and confident journalism needs clear direction and a clear sense of priorities. Some rebalancing is needed.

In the wake of a polarising election, one of the things Britain needs now more than ever is a reliable and trusted BBC with journalism which can speak truth to power. The example of the United States, which abandoned the fairness doctrine in favour of partisan news channels and shock jocks, acts as a dire warning to us all about what can happen to the polity of a country when it thinks impartial news no longer matters.

Note on the contributor

Phil Harding is a journalist and broadcaster. He is a former editor of the *Today* programme and chief political adviser to the BBC.

The debate on the debates:
After the 2019 election, are leaders' head-to-heads here to stay?

The 2019 General Election campaign marked a historic moment – the first head-to-head live TV debate between the two main contenders for the key to Downing Street. After years of controversy, Sue Inglish asks, are prime ministerial debates now an accepted part of general election campaigns?

For the first time in any UK election the leaders of the two main political parties vying to become the next prime minister agreed to take part in head-to-head TV debates. In such turbulent political times with two such unpredictable party leaders, these debates could have produced moments of high jeopardy for both men. One ill-advised comment and the campaign could be in trouble. Yet somewhat to the relief of campaign aides, the two hours of prime-time television debate failed to provide many highlights.

Ironically, the more memorable TV moments were the programmes for which the Prime Minister failed to show up and was replaced by a melting ice sculpture on Channel 4 and an empty chair next to Andrew Neil. But the very fact that two head-to-head debates took place at all was a historic prize which had eluded the best efforts of TV broadcasters in all previous elections. So are leaders debates now established as regular fixture or are they always going to be dependent on the whim of politicians?

How did we get here?

In 2010 despite several unsuccessful attempts at past elections and after months of discussion, three prime ministerial debates finally made it to the screen. Eight months earlier the BBC, ITV and Sky had come together determined to have one more push to get the parties to agree to debates. Ric Bailey, the BBC's chief adviser politics and I represented the BBC and at the outset neither of us were particularly optimistic about the likely outcome.

We had watched colleagues embark on the same task at several previous elections only to end in bitter disappointment. 1997 was the closest anyone came to success. The Prime Minister John Major, facing dire opinion polls, agreed to debate but Tony Blair, riding a wave of popular support, saw little advantage. Richard Tait, who led the 1997 ITV/ITN bid for debates, described it as 'a missed opportunity of epic proportions' (Tait 1998).

As Ric Bailey concluded in his study of the history of debates, the parties' decisions on participating are based 'squarely on political self-interest. Either incumbency or a substantial opinion poll lead – or both – always meant agreeing to debates presented too high a risk for one or other of the parties' Bailey (2012). But in 2010 the circumstances were different. David Cameron had been a vocal advocate of debates since 2007 missing no opportunity to taunt Gordon Brown. He even offered to drive the Prime Minister to the studio to take part.

Initially the PM was reluctant but by the summer of 2009, Labour had privately decided Gordon Brown had nothing to lose and the party, short of cash to fight the campaign, could see the attraction of debates paid for by the broadcasters.

Learning the lessons of past failures, the broadcasters agreed working together would be essential to avoid the political parties playing them off against each other. Negotiations with the Conservatives, Labour and the Liberal Democrats started in the autumn of 2009 and by Christmas an agreement on the key principles was reached. The three leaders agreed to take part in three debates, one per week during the campaign. The first produced by ITV, the second by Sky and the final debate on the BBC a week before the vote.

In spite of hostile press coverage the debates were the highlight of the 2010 campaign. Four and a half hours of prime-time television with the three leaders of the largest political parties in the UK debating audience questions ranging across the economy, foreign and home affairs. 22 million people saw the debates and two thirds of people surveyed said they learned something new. One of the most striking features was the response of young people, traditionally hard to reach with political programmes. 18-24 year olds seemed to have been particularly energised by the debates with more than half saying they had become 'more interested' in the campaign and 75 per cent said they had learnt something about the parties' policies (Coleman, 2011).

In some ways 2010 was the high water mark for election debates. By 2015, the Conservatives had come to the view that the 2010 debates were a mistake with David Cameron claiming the debates had sucked the life out of the rest of the campaign. Lynton Crosby, responsible for the Conservatives' election strategy, made it clear privately he disliked being dictated to by a 'cartel' of broadcasters. He advocated the Australian model in which he decided whether the PM took part in a debate and with which broadcaster.

The political landscape was more complex too in 2015 with the rise of Ukip and the success of the SNP requiring a format which reflected the increasingly multi-party state of UK politics. After months of fractious discussion David Cameron agreed to take part in a single, seven party debate on ITV. There was one other debate involving five opposition parties on the BBC. In addition to debate programmes, a Question Time Leaders Special featuring Cameron, Miliband and Clegg took place, and Sky and Channel 4 co-produced a programme just before the start of the campaign where David Cameron and Ed Miliband appeared separately being interviewed and taking questions from live studio audience. 21m people saw some of the four programmes, slightly fewer than the 2010 debates. The principle of election leaders' debates survived but only just and the previously unified approach of the broadcasters had comprehensively broken down.

The 2017 General Election

Calling a snap election in April 2017, Mrs May immediately ruled out taking part in a prime ministerial debate – the first of several errors of judgment which turned an apparently commanding poll lead into an electoral debacle. It was a mistake she subsequently admitted in an interview at the time of her resignation: "I should have done the TV debates. I didn't because I had seen them suck the life blood out of David Cameron's campaign [in 2010]." (Mail 2019)

ITV bravely went ahead with a leaders debate minus the two main players. The viewing figures were disappointing but ITV stuck to its principles. Labour aides realised they had missed an opportunity by ducking the first debate and at the last minute agreed to take part in the BBC debate. Research after the election confirmed refusing to debate had greatly damaged Theresa May in the eyes of the electorate. One leading pollster declared: "There is now a clear expectation that party leaders are accessible, open and willing to debate... After this election, only a fool would make the mistake of refusing to take part." (Hawkins, 2017).

The Brexit election

With politics in turmoil in the run-up to a crunch parliamentary vote on the EU Withdrawal Bill in late 2018, Downing Street advisers persuaded Theresa May to take part in a head-to- head debate with Jeremy Corbyn. Discussions were held with the BBC but amid dark mutterings of a BBC 'stitch-up' and disagreements over format, the talks failed to reach agreement. Following Mrs May's resignation, ITV hosted the only leadership debate between Boris Johnson and Jeremy Hunt, notable for Julie Etchingham's increasingly robust attempts to control Mr Johnson, including her use of a quizzically raised eyebrow. Julie's eyebrow trended on Twitter.

In September, as the likelihood of an early election grew, the broadcasters individually approached the parties to discuss debates and other election programmes. It was clear Boris Johnson would not take part in a multi-party debate and the BBC and ITV agreed to accept substitutes for the leaders. For all the broadcasters the main objective was to achieve the prize of a head-to-head contest between Boris Johnson and Jeremy Corbyn. Conservative campaign strategists believed the studio audience in a head-to-head debate would be more balanced than previous multi-party debate audiences which they claimed were biased against the Tories, a claim the broadcasters refute.

The BBC's head of newgathering, Jonathan Munro, detailed the audience selection criteria in a blog announcing the BBC's programme line-up: "When it comes to selecting audience members for our UK debates… supporters of the Conservatives and Labour will be roughly equal in most audiences, followed by a smaller number for the SNP and the Liberal Democrats, and a handful for the smaller parties. But with this election there is one extra issue to grapple with. Namely, the majority of people who voted in 2016 backed a departure from the EU. With that in mind, the complexion of our audiences for network news debates in the venues are, for this election at least, also being weighted to have a slim majority of people who voted Leave over Remain." (BBC News online, November 8, 2019).

The announcement of two head-to-head debates on BBC and ITV and the exclusion of the Liberal Democrats provoked an immediate outcry from Jo Swinson in the House of Commons: "At this general election, voters deserve better than a choice between the two tired old parties, and in the TV debates people deserve to hear from a leader who wants to stop Brexit and build a better future. So will the Prime Minister commit today to take part in those three-way debates, or is he going to run scared of debating with 'a girly swot'?" (PMQs, October 30, 2019).

The Lib Dems and the SNP went to court to demand a judicial review of ITV's decision but it was to prove a futile and costly challenge. On the eve of the ITV debate on November 18 the requests were turned down by the High Court which ruled that: "The decision to schedule tomorrow's debate in this format was a matter for the editorial judgment of ITV, which cannot be said to have displayed a want of due impartiality for the purposes of the Broadcasting Code: especially in the light of subsequent planned interviews, further debate and other programmes, which are properly to be regarded as a series of 'linked' programmes." (*Guardian* November 2019).

It was not just other political parties who were unhappy with the head-to-head debates. Sky and Channel 4 were excluded from the process, leaving the debates to the mass audience channels. Sky's 'Make Debates Happen' campaign in 2018 aimed to take politics out of the discussions and called for an Independent Commission on the lines of the US model to regulate election debates. More than 140,000 people signed a petition in support and a debate was held in Westminster Hall.

One prominent backer at the time was Boris Johnson. He told Sky News: "My feeling is that they are essential… and I think the way for politicians to allay their worries about leadership debates is to have as many of them as possible. So, you can make a cock-up in one and say something sensible in the next." (Sky News online, September 29, 2018). In the intervening 12 months, the Lynton Crosby playbook appears to have won and chances of 'a cock-up' minimised.

Channel 4's relationship with Downing Street, not easy at the best of times, was further complicated by a speech given by Dorothy Byrne the channel's head of news and current affairs (see chapter 14 below) in which she described the PM as 'a known liar'. The channel's invitation to the party leaders to take part in a Climate Change Debate during the campaign was turned down by Downing Street. Michael Gove arrived uninvited to take part but was turned away and an ice sculpture was put in the studio in place of the Prime Minister. The Conservatives complaint to Ofcom that this contravened impartiality rules was turned down on the grounds that: "Broadcasters have editorial freedom in determining the format of any election debate… providing they take steps to ensure the programme complies with our due impartiality and elections rules." (Ofcom November 2019).

The 2019 election debates
The first debate on ITV between Boris Johnson and Jeremy Corbyn covered a range of subjects including Brexit, the NHS, the future of the Royal Family and trust in politics. Both men were laughed at by the studio audience for some of their claims. It attracted an average audience of 6.7m viewers, with about a million younger viewers in the 16 to 34 age bracket. A snap Yougov poll suggested the public thought there was no clear winner, with Boris Johnson polling 51 per cent and Jeremy Corbyn 49 per cent.

The BBC held a special Question Time a few days later with four party leaders which was notable for the unfavourable audience reception given to the leader of the Liberal Democrats, Jo Swinson. Both ITV and BBC held multi-party debates. The BBC's head to head debate six days before the election reached an audience of 7.2m across BBC1 and the BBC News channel. Once again there were no shocks and BBC political editor Laura Kuenssberg concluded: "Boris Johnson and Jeremy Corbyn were both markedly on their best behaviour tonight. They didn't harangue each other, there was no heckling from the audience. There was a wide range of subjects certainly and profound disagreements naturally. But there was no… massive gaffe on either side, or political car crash in the most public of forums." (BBC News Online, December 6, 2019).

Where next?
There seems to be a general consensus that leaders debates in some form are now part of the electoral ecology, an important element in a range of TV output which includes long-form interviews and Question Time-style audience programmes rather than a special category of their own. In past campaigns concerns were raised that participating in debates makes it easier for the leaders to duck the rigour of a

forensic one-to-one long-form interview. The refusal of Boris Johnson to submit to an interview with Andrew Neil underlined that fear. But as Ric Bailey points out: "Neil's caustic three-minute monologue, setting out the questions he wanted to ask, was viewed on social media around ten million times before polling day – significantly more than watched debates or Neil's interviews with other party leaders." (Bailey 2020).

Arguments around the regulation of debates including the establishment of an Independent Commission will no doubt continue to be made but it's hard to see a case for contesting the conclusion of the House of Lords Select Committee inquiry into TV debates, in 2014: "We have found no good arguments for the introduction of such a body." (House of Lords, 2014).

In the ten years since the first prime ministerial debates took place, the political and media landscape has changed radically. By the time the electorate are once again asked to cast their votes, the UK will be out of the EU and the digital transformation of media and information will have thrown up new challenges. One certainty remains – politicians will always need to sell themselves and their policies. Debates have proved to be an effective way of communicating with voters and it looks like they are here to stay.

References

Bailey, R. (2012) Squeezing out the Oxygen – or Reviving Democracy? The History and Future of TV Election Debates in the UK. Oxford: Reuters Institute for the Study of Journalism

Bailey, R. Juárez-Gámiz, J., Holtz-Bacha, C. & Schroeder, A. (publication due mid-2020) Routledge International Handbook on Electoral Debates. Routledge. London.

Coleman, S. (2011) Leaders in the Living Room. Oxford: Reuters Institute for the Study of Journalism.

The Guardian, Lib Dems and SNP lose high court bid over TV election debate. November 18, 2019

Hawkins, A. (2017, June 16) Election Unpredictability, Retrieved from https://www.comresglobal.com/electoral-unpredictability/

House of Lords Communications Committee. (2014). Second report: Broadcast general election debates.

Jonathan Munro, BBC News online, November ,8 2019.

Jo Swinson MP, Hansard PMQs, October 30, 2019.

Laura Kuenssberg, BBC News online, December 6, 2019. https://www.bbc.co.uk/news/election-2019-50695598

Daily Mail, July 12, 2019.

Ofcom, November 28, 2019, https://www.ofcom.org.uk/about-ofcom/latest/media/media-releases/2019/election-committee-decision-channel-4-news-climate-debate

Tait, R (1998) 'The Debate that Never Happened', in I. Crewe et al, Why Labour Won the 1997 General Election (Cass 1998)

Note on the contributor

Sue Inglish is chair of the Disasters Emergency Committee and a member of Sky News Board. She was head of political programmes at the BBC from 2005 to 2015 and chaired the working party which delivered the prime ministerial debates of 2010.

A big debate about the big debates

The television debates on BBC, ITV, Channel 4 and Sky were vital elements in the election campaign, attracting millions of viewers. The six primetime UK-wide debates, including head-to-head meetings between the nation's potential prime ministers, covered a huge range of policies. However, leading politicians limited their appearances and the formats were tightly controlled. Going forward, Dorothy Byrne asks, how can we ensure these debates happen at every election, are less rigid in form, and encourage all our leading politicians to take part?

I write this from Australia. I'm 500km from the nearest bush fire, which is so huge that our air is filled with its smoke and breathing is uncomfortable. I came to this burning continent as our election campaign ended and from here, even Brexit, the towering issue of the election, pales into insignificance beside the red glow in the sky we have just been told can be seen from New Zealand.

The melting ice blocks, which took the place of prime minister Boris Johnson and the Brexit Party's Nigel Farage when they declined to take part in our *Channel 4 News Climate Change Debate*, were dismissed by Conservative spokesman Lee Cain as a stunt. But, from here, it feels like they were making a very important point.

Our planet isn't just warming; all around me it is in flames. So, looking back on the debates, my first thought as Head of News and Current Affairs at Channel 4 is that I am very glad that our team conducted the first ever election debate on climate change.

However, across all broadcasters we didn't have enough coverage of climate change and, going forward, we all need to up our game.

If some politicians have their way Channel 4 and the BBC, as we know them now, will be doomed for allegedly failing to be duly impartial during the election campaign. But, if we don't sort out the planet, the whole lot of us – politicians, television journalists and voters – could all be equally doomed.

Impressive figures

Judged by the viewing figures, the TV debates and special coverage were a great success with voters.

The BBC's statistics were impressive. Its BBC1 and News Channel head-to-head prime ministerial debate had an average audience of 4.6m. The seven-way debate had viewing of 2.26m. *The Question Time Leaders' Special* gained nearly 4.71m viewers and the four Andrew Neil interviews with Nicola Sturgeon, Jeremy Corbyn, Jo Swinson and Nigel Farage had averages of 2.49m viewers.

All these figures refer to at least three minutes viewing. Combined BBC programmes reached a total of 19.7m individuals on television and 2.9m requests on BBC iPlayer. ITV's Corbyn vs Johnson won 7.1m viewers and its seven-way debate 1.8m. The *Channel 4 News Climate Change Debate* had 900,000 viewers. Its *Everything But Brexit* debate gained 600,000 viewers.

It was widely claimed there was too much coverage of Brexit so it interests me that a programme, which made a feature of trying to avoid the subject, was the lowest rating debate.

One of the other debates avoided having a question on Brexit for the first 30 minutes, but the topic kept coming up. It's hard, arguably impossible, to separate issues of the economy or the health service from the effects of leaving the EU.

Remember all those figures when you hear some politicians say television is now irrelevant.

If you want to reach voters en masse, go on the telly. Newspapers can't rack up numbers like that and are massively distrusted even by their own readers. And social media posts will tend to appeal to people who already support you.

A question of trust

To win the trust of the electorate, you need to reach beyond social media. It is important to remember that latest research from regulator Ofcom shows three quarters of the public trust television news but, according to a Reuters survey across Europe, only 10 per cent of people trust social media news.

By chance, 10 per cent is also the proportion of the public surveyed by Savanta ComRes for Channel 4 who thought that politicians and candidates had been generally honest and trustworthy during the campaign. So if you want to reach a lot of people on a massively trusted platform, television is still overwhelmingly the best way to do it.

Of course, for a politician, television represents a risk for those very reasons. If you make a mistake, millions see it and, because they trust TV, the large majority of the population will believe it's your mistake and not some set-up by TV journalists.

That's why, sadly, some of our leading political figures now do only the minimum of in-depth interviews they can get away with during election campaigns.

In this election, the most notable example was Boris Johnson's refusal to be interviewed by Andrew Neil. In a fascinating article by Ian Griggs in *PR Week* headlined, 'Facing a 'new normal' for political media relations', Laura Sainsbury, chair of Women in Public Affairs and board member of Labour in the City said: "What might be a dodgy political practice – appearing to avoid scrutiny – is at the same time good comms management. Would you put your CEO in front of Andrew Neil? Unlikely."

And Sir Craig Oliver, David Cameron's PR supremo, said in the same article: "The truth is the parties now have the cheat codes for dealing with broadcasters. For years, they have understood that in many circumstances they have the power to say no – and there isn't a thing the broadcasters can do about it."

The risk of being empty-chaired

The damage of being empty-chaired is judged lower than the risk of saying the wrong thing. Nor do our party leaders any longer conduct major morning press conferences in election campaigns during which, in the past, they would have been grilled daily by leading journalists. So the TV debates are even more essential during elections.

It's been claimed by some politicians that the debates were not duly impartial. In fact, they were at times excruciatingly impartial.

Four of the debates had rigid rules. I felt I could hear the stopwatches ticking at times. It is likely that most viewers don't quite get the significance of the severe restrictions which politicians insist on for TV debates:

- The audience member who asks a question is not permitted any come-back. So no danger of great embarrassment of the type suffered when Margaret Thatcher was questioned by an irate and informed woman about the sinking of the Belgrano.

- No other audience members are allowed to speak.

- The presenters are not allowed to ask any questions of their own but only follow-ups.

- You also can't get through many questions or get into issues in real depth with two people in an hour or with seven speakers in 90 minutes.

Arguably, the debates were too short. And, as I noted above, not nearly enough attention was given to climate change. On the ITV debate, the climate change question was in the quickfire question section.

Across all debates, it was inevitable that politicians were sometimes able to make statements which were demonstrably untrue in a way which would have been impossible during an in-depth interviews.

In the head-to-head debates, the BBC's Nick Robinson made more use of the follow-up to challenge statements than did ITV's Julie Etchingham. In all debates candidates successfully challenged each other several times.

After the referendum debate, it was claimed that people didn't have sufficient correct information on which to make a judgement. I believe that if you watched the TV debates in this election campaign, you would have had a good understanding both of the policies of different parties and criticisms of those policies.

The audience's understanding would have been greater had there been more in-depth interviews and daily press conferences with party leaders. The debates couldn't make up for those deficiencies, but they did a good job for democracy and were informative and fair.

The two Channel 4 debates were not bound by a stopwatch or the rule that each person's initial answer had to be of a set length. Instead, speakers received broadly the same amount of time in a more free-flowing format. None of those who took part objected afterwards of any unfairness.

The climate change debate had no audience and all the questions came from the presenter. The Conservative Party complained to Ofcom that it was not duly impartial because Channel 4 declined to accept the Chancellor of the Duchy of Lancaster, Michael Gove, as a stand-in for Boris Johnson who had declined to take part.

Michael Gove turned up literally at the door and asked to be let in. Other leaders were asked if they were prepared to let him join what was always a party leaders' debate. They declined. The Conservative standpoint was outlined during the debate by presenter Krishnan Guru-Murthy. Ofcom rejected the complaint and said the debate was duly impartial.

Who's in charge?

The rigid rules, which some politicians insist on, are thus proved not to be necessary for due impartiality. They give politicians control, but I believe viewers would appreciate a more natural form of debate. To borrow a political term, in the next election, broadcasters should aim to take back control of the formats.

It was also good to talk about one subject in-depth. There was an uncanny similarity to the questions in some of the other debates. Going forward, the audience would benefit from more of the debates specialising in subject areas.

That *PR Week* article is interesting both in itself and because it's important for us as journalists to understand how PR people see the political state of play. Griggs concluded that the No 10 comms team can be confident it has 'effectively neutered' media scrutiny. *The Guardian* also wrote: "Political parties are increasingly confident in their ability to ignore certain channels and dictate the terms of engagement for debate appearances amid falling broadcast news figures."

On the face of it, that might seem obviously true and very depressing.

Boris Johnson declined to take parts in debates on Channel 4 and Sky. His press team made clear he wouldn't do a three-way debate with Jo Swinson, so none took place. He declined to take part in the larger seven-way ITV and BBC debates and sent a replacement. He wouldn't be interviewed by Andrew Neil and many others. When he did appear, he repeated the same message over and over again – I counted eight repetitions of 'Get Brexit Done' in the ITV debate and 11 in the BBC debate.

And he won. So avoiding tricky interviews and limiting television appearances succeeded for him. Some of his advisors might therefore imagine he should continue with that policy over the next five years. The boycott of the *Today* programme signals that attitude.

The need to explain

However, our new government has major policies it needs to explain and justify to the public, especially as its stated aim is to unify the country. It doesn't want to appear to be riding roughshod over voters and indeed, I am sure it wants to win over as many voters as possible to its strategy.

Leaving the EU will be complex and many voters, whatever their views on Brexit, will be anxious about how they will be affected. The best way to talk to voters about these issues is by appearing on television. The way to win voters over is to explain policies properly and be seen to answer difficult questions.

The opposition is also likely to have a much higher television profile. Jeremy Corbyn hated what he dubbed 'the mainstream media' and avoided challenging interviews. But a new Labour leader is going to want to get out onto the front foot and establish themselves by giving major television interviews.

That will make it difficult for Boris Johnson to decline to do the same. Will that *Today* boycott continue when an invigorated new Labour leader dominates the airwaves on Budget Day?

There is an even more important reason why leaders of both parties should go onto the telly.

The most disturbing aspect of the debates was the derision shown by the audience in the first ITV debate. They laughed out loud at some of the responses, notably when Johnson spoke about truth and trust and Corbyn said his policy on Brexit was clear.

I had never seen mockery like that before. It's a symptom of the low trust revealed in that Channel 4 survey, which showed only 10 per cent of voters thought candidates were generally truthful. That figure is around the same as a poll carried out before the election campaign for Channel 5.

All politicians have to be concerned at this loss of trust in them as this undermines democracy. And sitting on a breakfast sofa making announcements doesn't do it.

Esme Wren, editor of *Newsnight* puts the case well: "Clips to camera and Facebook messages don't earn respect. Over time, avoiding challenging interviews is not sustainable. The public wants to see robust engagement.

"If a politician comes on television and fights his corner, people think, 'Good for him. He really believes what he's saying. He's not dodging the question; in fact he's answered the difficult questions'."

Of course, we journalists need politicians to appear on our programmes. But that's not why they should do it. It's because the public needs to hear from its representatives.

Note on the contributor

Dorothy Byrne is the Head of News and Current Affairs at Channel 4 and the author of *Trust Me, I'm Not a Politician'* She is a visiting professor at Leicester De Montfort University.

Leaders' television debates – why Ofcom must step into the breach

With Boris Johnson's towering Commons majority there is no prospect of new laws to force the leaders of all the main parties to participate in future television election debates. Former Ofcom standards executive Trevor Barnes proposes a practical way forward

To hate is natural. As the great essayist Hazlitt declared at the start of the 19th century: 'Without something to hate, we should lose the very spring of thought and action.' This is especially true of the politically committed on the left and right.

After the Conservatives trounced Labour in the 2019 election, supporters of Jeremy Corbyn pointed the finger of blame at a biased media, while right-wing commentators castigated liberal bias in the BBC and Channel 4 and called on the new government to 'liberate ' them 'from the grip of the Left.'[1]

The newspapers of course were their usual partisan selves. Nothing new there. High levels of engagement on social media gave Labour false hope as activist spoke to activist. Both platforms – subject only to the general law of defamation and hate speech – were largely a free for all. Only the broadcast media were under a duty of due impartiality, imposed under statute and enforced by the regulator, Ofcom.

During the campaign there were the usual complaints of alleged bias in general coverage. Twenty-four thousand winged their way to the BBC in the fortnight to December 7 alone, and 1,781 to Ofcom against all broadcasters.[2]

During the two UK general elections when I was Senior Standards Manager at Ofcom overseeing election complaints (2010 and 2015), this was normal. We knew all the major parties had activists monitoring coverage and firing off complaints.

In 2019 those activists hyper-ventilated over the predictable alarums and excursions of the daily campaign coverage: for example, Boris Johnson refusing to look at the photo on a reporter's mobile of a child lying on the floor of an accident & emergency department, and the political editors of the BBC and ITV News mistakenly tweeting that a Labour activist had punched a Tory staffer. But during the campaign much of the focus was on a relatively new phenomenon for British general elections: leaders' debates.

The debates from 2010

The first head-to-head leaders' debates only took place in the 2010 general election. There were three broadcast, featuring the heads of the three main parties. The first demonstrated their potency, temporarily catapulting to political stardom the leader of the Liberal Democrats, Nick Clegg. In 2015, with the splintering of political allegiances, there was only one head-to-head debate with the leaders of the seven main political parties. Prime Minister Theresa May, refused to appear in any leaders' debates in 2017.

During discussions after the 2015 election, Labour and the Democratic Unionist Party (DUP) proposed an independent commission should be created to put the debates on a statutory footing. The Government rejected the idea, saying broadcasters and the parties should make arrangements for any debates. Two years later the Liberal Democrats became the first political party to include in their manifesto a commitment to compel leaders' debates on TV during general elections, based on rules produced by Ofcom.

2019: just two head-to-head debates involving two main party leaders

And so we arrived at the rancorous 2019 election, dominated by Brexit. Once again there were tortuous negotiations between the broadcasters and the parties, culminating in just two head-to-head debates involving the main party leaders (Johnson v. Corbyn) on ITV; and a BBC *Question Time* special with four leaders (Johnson, Corbyn, Swinson and Sturgeon).

The first of these debates was challenged by the Scottish National Party (SNP) and the Liberal Democrats by means of judicial review – the legal process to check the rationality and reasonableness of decisions of public bodies. It failed dismally. The judges ruled on November 18 that the case was not even 'realistically arguable' because ITV was not exercising 'a public function'.[3]

Channel 4 staged a leaders' debate focused on the climate change 'crisis'. Two of the main parties, the Conservatives and the Brexit Party, decided their leaders would not attend. The Tories offered Michael Gove instead of Boris Johnson as their spokesman but the broadcaster spurned the offer. The channel replaced Johnson and Nigel Farage (leader of the Brexit Party) with two blocks of ice.

Crying foul, the Conservatives lodged a formal complaint of bias with Ofcom. Meeting with great haste during the campaign, the regulator's Election Committee dismissed the complaint unceremoniously. This was because a broadcaster has editorial freedom to determine the format of the election debate, and they may choose to proceed without having agreed the participation of a particular political party or politician, providing they take steps to ensure the programme complies with Ofcom's due impartiality and elections rules (as happened here through Channel 4's broadcast of linked and timely programming).[4]

The BBC held a debate with representatives of the seven main parties, but Labour, the Conservatives and the Brexit Party did not send their leaders.

There were also separate interviews with the party leaders. Those that perhaps attracted the most attention were conducted by the BBC's grizzled griller, Andrew Neil. His interviews with Corbyn and Swinson drew some blood but Johnson refused to submit to Neil's forensic interrogation, leading the journalist to taunt the Prime Minister by posting a video monologue challenging him to be interviewed.

Johnson's decision – as no doubt anticipated by his advisers – did not damage his electoral prospects. He ended after all with a stonking parliamentary majority of 80, the largest since 1987.

What was arguably damaged however was the unwritten understanding that during a general election campaign the party leaders of all the main parties, without exception, would submit to a long-form questioning by the BBC's Rottweiler interviewer of choice. This is particularly important because head-to-head debates tend to be rather stolid, staged affairs with few opportunities for either the presenter or audience to follow up on the inevitable half-truths and evasions.

All of this matters because leaders TV debates *do* influence voters. This is not a matter of opinion but objective polling.

In 2017 for example 56 per cent of voters said the TV debates helped them decide how to cast their votes.[5] And despite the explosive growth in social media, especially among the young, the power of the broadcast media remained dominant in the 2019 election. Ofcom's research that year underscored that broadcast content still made up the majority (69 per cent) of daily video viewing for UK consumers.[6]

So what should happen about leaders' debates before the next UK general election, which is not likely until 2024 at the earliest?

An independent commission to run leaders' debates?

One proposal that has gained traction is legislation to mandate TV debates and the establishment of an independent commission to oversee them. After the 2017 election Sky News inspired an online petition calling for these changes. It attracted 130,000 signatures and triggered a debate on the issue in Parliament in Westminster Hall in January 2019.

The general consensus was that the commission should be paid for by the broadcasters and not the taxpayer, and the number and timing of the debates needed to be carefully considered to avoid 'sucking the life' out of the campaign on the ground (as David Cameron phrased it in 2010).

Whatever the merits of this proposal, there is no prospect at all of a Conservative government with a majority of 80 agreeing to it. There is however another way forward – a way to encourage broadcasters to organise debates and party leaders, and it requires no new legislation and no new commission.

Ofcom should act before the 2024 general election

Ofcom already regulates all UK broadcasters for due impartiality, including the BBC. It has been operating since 2003 and on the whole has an enviable reputation for the way it polices standards on TV and radio. Sections Five and Six of the Ofcom Broadcasting Code set out the somewhat complex web of rules governing impartiality, including the special ones applicable during elections and referendums.

Ofcom has the power to change the code at any time, provided it holds a public consultation first. The code in fact is ripe for a wholesale review under Ofcom's latest chief executive, who will take over in 2020. Whether Ofcom will have the vision and courage to undertake this work remains to be seen.

Since the code was first introduced in 2005 the media landscape has been transformed, but Ofcom's response has been piecemeal (if usually helpful) reform. The code has simply become longer and longer, with some of its new rules (for example on product placement) arguably too restrictive.

With Britain leaving the EU in 2020, and Ofcom being given dramatic new powers to regulate social media companies for harm against users,[7] the moment has come to consider a root and branch review to ensure the code is fit for purpose for the challenges ahead.

One of those challenges is leaders' debates. Ofcom should – whether as part of a wide-ranging overhaul of the code or separately – introduce a new rule in Section Six of the code. It could read along the following lines:

"A public service broadcaster may organise televised party leaders' debates during the election or referendum period. If a leader chooses not to participate in one of these debates and the broadcaster decides to 'empty chair' that individual, that decision in itself will not mean the broadcaster has failed to maintain due impartiality."

An evolutionary and symbolic step

This would not be a radical change. From one point of view it would merely turn the principles behind Ofcom's 2019 decision on the Channel 4 'climate change' leaders' debate into a code rule. But it would be evolutionary and symbolic. For the first time the concept of leaders' debates would be referred to and so enshrined in regulation. It would send a signal to public service broadcasters (meaning the BBC, ITV, and Channels 4 and 5) to be more confident in organising leaders' debates and help them resist pressure from the main parties to send an alternative spokesperson to the debate.

Equally, no leader would be under any statutory or regulatory compulsion to appear. He or she would keep their freedom to decide whether to participate or not, but secure in the knowledge that the broadcaster who 'empty-chaired' them was still under an obligation to remain duly impartial in their election coverage overall.

The proposed new rule could of course be broadened to include Sky News as well as the existing public service broadcasters. But it should not have a wider compass. Other broadcasters might be tempted to exploit it for a stunt by inviting the party leaders in the expectation they would refuse with the deliberate intention of 'empty-chairing' them.

A small step by Ofcom perhaps. But a big and symbolic step towards making the heads of UK political parties slightly more accountable and transparent to the voters when it counts most – during a general election or national referendum campaign.

Notes

[1] See e.g. Andrew Roberts, p.3, *The Daily Telegraph* , 14 December 2019

[2] *The Times*, 7 December 2019

[3] https://www.judiciary.uk/wp-content/uploads/2019/11/Lib-Dems-v-ITV-decision.pdf (accessed 10 January 2010)

[4] https://www.ofcom.org.uk/__data/assets/pdf_file/0035/182969/decision-election-climate-debate.pdf (accessed 10 January 2010)

[5] *The Times*, p.35, 18 November 2019

[6] https://www.ofcom.org.uk/research-and-data/tv-radio-and-on-demand/media-nations-2019, page 5

[7] *The Times*, p.1, 31 December 2019

Note on the contributor

Trevor Barnes runs barnestvcompliance, offering media and compliance advice to broadcasters, and is a consultant solicitor with leading London media law firm, Simons Muirhead. He was Ofcom's Director of Broadcasting Law and then Senior Standards Manager until early 2017. Previously he had been a BBC news trainee and later senior producer in BBC News and Current Affairs. Barnes regularly blogs on Ofcom standards issues, and in 2020 publishes the first history of the Portland Spy Ring, *Dead Doubles*, based on hitherto secret MI5 files (Weidenfeld).

Changing media, different influencers

***

Was it the papers wot won it?
Or did social media take the prize?

Neil Fowler

After the 1992 General Election, when the Labour Party under Neil Kinnock crashed to an unexpected defeat to John Major's Tories, it was *The Sun* under Kelvin Mackenzie which famously claimed to have won it.

But do newspapers have the same influence now? Does the general public care what they say? Have falling print circulations and diminished business models led by declining advertising sales meant they are now just bit players? Have their digital footprints saved them? Or have the various newish branches of social media taken over ownership of who makes and who crowns the Victor Ludorum?

We start this section by looking back at the 2016 EU Referendum. Michael O'Sullivan and John Mills, who ran the Labour Leave campaign then, in *How digital tools can help win a big political victory* believe newly developed digital and social media operations have not only changed the direction the country heads in but also evolved the way campaigns will be run forever.

"Politics is no longer divided into one third left, another third right, with those who persuade the remaining third in the middle or centre, victorious. The typical swing voter is today both more left and more right wing than ever before. Political sentiment is now far more complex, as are voters," they write.

Alex Connock, of Oxford University's Said Business School, is in no doubt about what has changed, though he takes a slightly different angle. In *Dark Patterns in the online 2019 General Election* he believes the digital battle wasn't principally about bots and Russian money. This time, he says, it was won and lost by actual human beings, millennial professionals, being extraordinarily clever, using the most modern of techniques.

"Dark patterns drive the consumer to make choices they otherwise wouldn't make – leaving their user journeys misleading and manipulated. They are a form of information warfare, but in the retail space. They are legal but often unethical," he says.

Hugo Dixon, deputy chair of the People's Vote, in *Ten Top questionable Tory Brexit claims*, believed a successful election slogan-based fight by the Tories, based on 'Get Brexit Done' helped the party to avoid getting into detail on the EU. But when Europe was raised as an issue, the level of accuracy left much to be desired, he says.

"It was supposed to be the Brexit election. In fact, there was hardly any proper scrutiny of Boris Johnson's Brexit deal in the media, in part because he avoided tough interviews. The Prime Minister wanted to talk about almost anything but Brexit. And when he and his colleagues did use the 'B' word, it was mostly to spray around misleading statements and sometimes outright lies," Dixon writes.

Steven McCabe, of Birmingham University's Centre for Brexit Studies, believes there is still plenty of life left in the old dog of newspapers. In *Did the media crucify 'Marxist enemy' JC in the 2019 General Election?* he says it was inevitable the right-wing media would go all out to keep Jeremy Corbyn out of Downing Street.

"Many news organisations attack any politician daring to challenge orthodoxy that UK politics is located in the centre to centre-right. Corbyn, however, was subject to opprobrium verging on frenzy," he writes.

However, Paul Connew, long-time Fleet Street editor and now sagacious observer, in *A toxic leader and a manifesto like Father Christmas on acid* believes there were more fundamental issues that caused Labour's loss. Although a staunch Remainer, he was a rare pundit to predict Leave would win based on research in Labour heartlands. He revisited his original research sample in the wake of the general election.

And one quote was apposite: "It was the first time in my life I hadn't voted Labour," said one voter to Connew. "Brexit wasn't the deciding factor. I'm yet to be convinced Boris Johnson can even deliver on his Brexit promises. But I just couldn't envisage Corbyn as prime minister and that decided where I put my X when I reached the ballot box." And his voice was far from alone, as the result showed.

Nigel Willmott was that rare beast – a Leaver who worked for *The Guardian*. In his chapter – *How 'them' showed how out of touch 'us' were* – he argues that politicians and journalists who believe the long-held attitudes of the so-called forgotten voters will change, do so at their peril.

"As many found on the doorstep in the election, the issues that concern and motivate the people 'out there' are often very different from those defined by the politicians, activists, lobbyists and commentators," Willmott says. "But how did two whole sections of society become so detached from each other that in the 2016

EU Referendum the country was split down the middle in an uncomprehending face-off? Why did no one see it coming?"

How digital tools can help win a big political victory

The digital and social media operation at Labour Leave in the 2016 EU Referendum may have persuaded the crucial winning margin of 1.2m voters, argue Michael O'Sullivan and John Mills, who ran that campaign. This not only changed the direction the country was headed but also evolved the way campaigns would be run forever.

The work carried out by the various Leave campaigns has introduced a new doctrine and methodology on how best to categorise, segment, target and persuade voters. This may not have been possible without a cross-party national referendum to demonstrate its core principle which has been ignored by Westminster politicians for far too long. Politics is no longer divided into one third left, another third right, with those who persuade the remaining third in the middle or centre, victorious. The typical swing voter is today both more left and more right wing than ever before. Political sentiment is now far more complex, as are voters.

Political divides for the typical swing voter are now issue-focused, with many on the right passionate supporters of the NHS, social housing and many on the left wanting tougher polices on crime, security and military intervention. The old-fashioned campaigns of centrism are long dead. Those who recognise this are victorious and those who do not, are often doomed to failure. At Labour Leave we identified this early on and were therefore able to help convince around 930,000 Labour voters to switch from voting Remain to Leave. Ten per cent of the 9.3m people who voted Labour in the 2015 General Election changed their voting intentions. This cumulative swing was 1.8m voters for Leave. The Leave campaign won the EU referendum by a majority of 1,269,501 votes or 3.78 per cent. When an unnamed strategist for the Remain/Stronger In campaign during the referendum campaign said: "The Labour vote is critically important. I'm tempted to go further and say the Labour vote will decide the outcome,"[1] they were correct, yet they still managed to fail to understand who these voters are and what motivates them. The

Westminster/London bubble was safely insulating the David Cameron and Will Straw machine from any fears of reality, David Dimbleby's tones still can be heard echoing through the empty offices of Stronger In: "The British people have spoken, and WE'RE OUT!"

The journey for Labour Leave to get to the position where we were able to operate freely, build up our data/digital tools and use these to persuade voters was laborious, challenging and at times looked uncertain. Labour Leave in January 2016 was fully integrated into what would become the official designated Leave campaign, Vote Leave. Headed by Matthew Elliot and Dominic Cummings, Vote Leave was chaired at this time by John Mills, Gisela Stuart had yet to be recruited and Kate Hoey was suspicious and mistrusting of the Vote Leave hierarchy.

Three Leave groups the key to victory

To some onlookers the organisations were in disarray and to a certain extent this was true, but this early chaos and lack of bipartisan cooperation primed the landscape for genuine innovation. Had all the Leave campaigns come together working in unison, then targeting specialisation could not occur, messaging would have been compromised by majority rule, too broad to be effective and the result would have been a comfortable Remain victory. Instead three key individual organisations formed with a unique ability to target their own base of voters, with greater trust than any unified movement.

Leave.EU was able to target the most anti-immigrant and anti-EU demographic, the Ukip vote. This was always going to be the campaign they would advocate. The campaign was a simple turnout or get out the vote operation, no persuasion was necessary. This demographic wanted out and was not shy. Vote Leave was able to run a campaign which could convince the undecided Tory and Labour voters it was safe for them to vote to Leave the EU while simultaneously trying to demotivate the Remain supporters, suggesting through fear tactics to just stay at home, do not vote to Remain. Then last but not least, Labour Leave was able to target the traditional working class Labour voter; anti-EU but likely to be too afraid to vote for change, feeling some security in the status quo but influenced by the London Labour Party so cautious about speaking freely about their views of the EU, likely not to be living in any major city and certainly north of the M25.

These three campaign groups were essential and trusted by their respective bases, with the additional benefits of Vote Leave and Labour Leave being able to actually persuade voters. Given Remain was miles ahead in the polls, the Leave campaign had to demotivate Remain voters, persuade undecideds and turn out their respective bases. This was the only path to victory. The ability to work without constraints and independent of each other was critical, but without each of these organisations, the Leave vote could not possibly have won.

Disruption in the end did indeed lead to innovation, the underdogs prevailed through dogged determination, coupled with a more motivated and committed voter base (polling demonstrated Leave voters were more committed to turning out to vote, Remain ignored this X factor[2]) and more intelligent campaigning and targeting techniques. Leave knew it had to work harder, we had less money, resources and no Government machinery at our disposal. Leave was able to define the campaign as stagnation vs ambitious change, coupled with loss aversion techniques invoked by the campaign slogans. The Leave campaign finally had all the right ingredients to take back control of the narrative.

With a unified message, synergy between the media, digital and politicians, the polls demonstrated the electorate were indeed shifting their opinions towards Leave. An alternative government-in-waiting was formed and treated as such by the press lobby. The multiple fronts set up by the Leave campaigns were disrupting the best laid plans of the Remain methodology, who in the face of sudden and looming failure quickly reverted to declaring Remain the good guys and Leave the bad guys. This of course furthered and hastened the Remain decline.

Understanding the background to these three organisations is important because by the time Labour Leave had left the confines of Vote Leave, our digital infrastructure had been taken over by Vote Leave. This included the Facebook page, website domain and @voteleave.uk email accounts. By the time Michael O'Sullivan left Vote Leave to work as head of digital at Labour Leave it was the end of April. Labour Leave had no digital infrastructure whatsoever, nothing other than a Twitter account which the team had managed to keep out of the Vote Leave clutches. This was a major problem, although we had learned much from working at Vote Leave with Dominic Cummings and AIG with regards to digital campaigns techniques, without any of the tools we needed, how could we possibly campaign effectively? This was going to be our first major challenge and with very little time to effect substantive change, we got to work in earnest.

We needed tools that could help us store voter contact and voting intention profile information, we needed channels to reach these voters, we needed ways to be able to understand and rank our voters and we needed to be able to reach potential undecided voters with accurate and targeted messaging. These were our basic strategic requirements. The suite of digital tools we then went on to build was in response to these requirements.

Nationbuilder

We immediately identified the software provider Nationbuilder as a viable tool to manage our core campaign requirements. The platform would not only allow us to build a complex advocacy content management web portal but would also provide us with the technology to manage our voter database, store voter information and contact these voters via mass email and SMS campaigns. This was the critical first step in building our digital infrastructure.

After a 56-hour coding sprint with no sleep, we deployed our brand-new Labour Leave web platform on our new domain: LabourLeave.org.uk. For the first time in the campaign we could now begin to build and manage our own email lists, deploy unlimited numbers of varying landing pages which were designed to encourage voters to give us their contact information and take a positive campaign or advocacy action. We could finally collect small donations via our staged donation page connected to PayPal and Stripe payment processors. We were able to deploy surveys, petitions, pledges and numerous additional advocacy tools to help supporters find ways to get involved.

When a new voter/supporter signed up on our website we were able to store their information in our voter database and then contact these voters via both email and SMS (assuming the correct permissions were granted by each specific person). This is the foundation all political campaigns and most digital businesses are built upon. Email marketing is to this day still one of the most effective tools for selling products or generating greater political advocacy.

But more than just storing voter contact details, using Nationbuilder's tools we were able to build accurate voting intention profiles of each of our voters/supporters. Each time someone completed our surveys we could tag them with the answers they provided and use these tags for voter segmentation, helping us to build detailed targeting lists. For example we may ask you who you voted for at the last general election and then create a list of people to target who voted Labour, or a different list of people who voted Tory, offering both different messaging that was more likely to result in a positive advocacy action. If you told us you were particularly hopefully of a more global trading outlook for the UK post Brexit for example, you would likely see messaging both on Facebook, Twitter and via Email describing how new trade deals outside of the EU would be beneficial and achievable. Whereas your siblings or parents for example for may receive something completely different, perhaps on immigration or the NHS. This is how effective the targeting available to us was, just based on the information given to us directly from voters/supporters. The website was also used as a digital brochure detailing the campaign team, objectives, campaign information, events and guidance on how voters could find opportunities to get involved.

Surveys and Polls

Hosting multiple surveys and polls, petitions and pledges gave our campaign a much more detailed and effective window into the minds of the average swing Labour, Conservative and Liberal voter than traditional polling ever could. Polling processes haven't changed much over the past 50 years. Standard polling is not the optimum solution. Although a random sample of say a thousand people from a representative pool does provide some detailed and interesting insights, it is not the best way to truly understand a mass of people or in this case the plebiscite. Asking hundreds of thousands if not millions of people and utilising machine learning and languages like R and python to process this information will provide much more accurate and detailed outcomes. You also have the opportunity to define smaller subsets of demographics during the survey analysis. This can help understand the specific motivations of and parallels between different subsets of voters. You can then use this data to better target individuals. A representative sample of a thousand people will only return 510 women for example, whereas the types of surveys we ran helped us understand the motivations behind 51,000 women or more, and this provided a great deal more information than standardised polling and some unpredictable and unexpected patterns/outcomes, all which we could use for targeting.

It is also possible to upload customer or voter contact information directly into Facebook ad accounts and use this data to target individuals with even more sub-categories, as Facebook matches your customer or voter data file with that of its own. Even if we didn't know a voter was motivated or supported Y, but Facebook did, it would allow us to target individuals with the Y variable directly on Facebook. However, this was done without us specially knowing who these voters that were motivated, or supported Y, were as individuals. This process itself was vital in targeting undecided voters with the correct messaging that was most likely to persuade them to make a positive advocacy action and helped us synergise our email, Facebook and Twitter followers.

Facebook and campaign messaging

It may not have been possible for us to be so effective, both in terms of output and return on investments if it was not for Facebook as a marketing and advertising tool. In this context Facebook was essentially a public database which contained the personal information and key special category information of at least 60 per cent of the UK population, allowing campaigns such as ours to target these Facebook users, directly for a very small fee. We would in fact target and retarget voters multiple times during our persuasion campaigns.

We decided to build our own Facebook page to retain full control. Quickly building up around 30/40k likes and followers, we used this data to connect Facebook to our Nationbuilder database API and then pull in all the users from Facebook who were engaging with our digital campaigns, adverts and posts, comments, likes, emotive responses and video views (we did the same via the Twitter API to a lesser extent). Using Nationbuilder's profile matching technology, we could then link/match social media users to supporters/voters in our own database.

Our voter/supporter data was collected only by each specific person providing this information directly to us, usually in response to a positive advocacy action such as providing an email and first name in order to sign up for email updates, complete surveys, sign petitions, make a donation or pledge. This helped us further expand our voter profiling, iterating and improving our understanding of individuals, then by uploading these customer/voter lists into Facebook we could re-target voters based on our ever increasing understanding of them, but more critically, we could now target them with information that Facebook held on them, not just what they had provided to us.

Voters/supporters would see the same messaging in their email inboxes, Google search results and Facebook feeds. Politicians would be using the same slogans and messaging on TV and in the press and then all of a sudden you had specific demographics being targeted with the same messaging on multiple platforms, resulting in effective persuasion. The microtargeting made available by Facebook was unbelievably effective and accurate. And given Facebook's tendency to favour older voters, Facebook ended up becoming the perfect platform for us to reach our most valued and supportive demographic.

But it wasn't just the ability to micro target that gave us the edge, after all the Remain campaign had access to all the same tools. It was how we used our messaging, how we built on simple slogans/messaging created by Vote Leave, this is what made the difference. While the Remainers warned of the dangerous and terrifying life outside of the EU, burdening their political advocates/spokespersons with cumbersome and convoluted details which resulted in dull discussions centred around the Single Market and Customs Union or the soon to be crashing economy, the Leave campaign demonstrated the opposite, simple to understand and relative slogans would work much better. Protein politics. Take each Remain argument, rebut with a simple solution in varied ways depending on your target demographic.

Ambitious and patriotic voters also just didn't buy the Remain fear campaign that the British state could not function and thrive outside the EU. This talking down and fear tactic was a big mistake, it asked the question of who wanted to vote for the status quo when the said status wasn't working for them. Turns out, not many.

Like every other major country outside the EU, Labour Leave argued the UK could just agree a Free Trade Agreement (FTA) with the EU. It will be one of the 'easiest international treaties we have ever negotiated'. We will have the best of both worlds, the benefits of European trade arrangement, but the restrictions on freedom of labour movement, which could damage workers' rights and incomes. The state aid rules could now be lifted, freeing Jeremy Corbyn to renationalise at will, 'Jez we can'. Couple this with the opportunity provided by Vote Leave for voters to vote FOR the NHS while voting to Leave, we had enough ammunition to target and persuade the demographics closest to our movement that voting to Leave the EU was safe, ambitious, worker protectionist and would benefit the NHS and future generations. It could even lead to more manufacturing jobs and the return of more investment into forgotten towns and cities.

Having collected a large amount of data from voters and supporters interacting with our campaign, we could run policy and messaging experiments on Facebook. Seeing what worked and what didn't work. How best to target individuals and how we could synergise the whole process, and if we did, what type of changes we might see in our engagements and support. This process gave us the crucial information we needed regarding where to best place, target and deploy our campaigns online to ensure the maximum engagement and persuading opportunities for the least amount of cost. Seven days away from polling day, we began to deploy much of our budget, gradually increasing until polling day itself, where we spent the rest on our 'get out the vote' budget, again a data directed process guided by our previous experiments and learning outcomes.

YouTube, Twitter and Google Ads

We did make use of platforms such as YouTube for hosting our videos and Twitter to reach fellow politicians or journalists, but neither of these platforms are widely used to micro target or persuade voters. Twitter tends to be preaching to the converted or arguing with your political opposites. However, Twitter was quite effective at helping us generate additional donations and support for our two GoFundMe campaigns, which were both very successful. Twitter and its retweet function opened up our messaging to a much broader Leave political audience, many of these new supporters were not typical Labour supporters but were pragmatists who understood the need for Labour voters to hear a strong Labour voice advocating for Leaving the EU.

We did use Google Ads via the search platform to dramatically increase our audience reach during our get out the vote campaign and for some general campaigning. This helped us reach any potential Labour Leave voters who were not on Facebook and who may not have known how and where to vote on polling day. This was a very important aspect of our work but was focused largely on turnout rather than persuasion.

Tracking

Monitoring and tracking our progress through our surveys and with third-party polling companies we soon realised we were moving the needle in the right direction. Between May 1 and polling day, when we ran our campaigns at full throttle, we recorded the polls moving from 26.4 per cent to 39.1 per cent (ICM, five days prior to polling day) in Labour leaning voting intentions towards the Leave vote.

The polling of most interest was:

- June 10: OBR puts Labour support for Brexit at 44 per cent
- June 10-13: ICM puts Labour support for Brexit at 39 per cent
- April 15-17: ICM put Labour support for Brexit at 26 per cent

By the end of the campaign, we had reached more than six million Labour learning voters. two million saw our get out the vote adverts on referendum day, June 23. 116,028 people had joined our movement, we convinced 930,000 Labour leaning voters to not vote Remain, but to now vote to Leave. The vast majority of our persuasion work took place online, via our website and via Facebook. The public rallies and canvassing did play a key part, in particular by generating interesting and engaging content, but these tend to help get out the vote and keep the base enthused. Synergy between TV debate and online campaigns were also highly important at reinforcing campaign messaging and further engaging active and emotional supporters.

Targeting the right people with the right message across multiple relevant platforms at the right time is effective at persuading people to vote in the way you want them to, and the best way to do this is through the strategic and innovative use of digital and social campaign techniques.

Notes

[1] https://www.theguardian.com/commentisfree/2016/feb/14/eu-referendum-labour-tories

[2] https://www.icmunlimited.com/historical-polls/page/12/

Note on the contributors

Michael O'Sullivan is a digital campaign organiser and fundraiser, data scientist and web developer. He has provided these services for Vote Leave, Labour Leave, The Labour Party and Labour Future within the political sector. He worked on the EU Referendum and the general elections of 2015, 2017 and 2019. Michael has recently developed a decentralised, blockchain verified news network named Bywire News and is soon launching the new political news channel, Labour Buzz.

John Mills was chair and then vice-chair of Vote Leave until he left Vote Leave at the end of April 2016 to concentrate on Labour Leave during the last two months of the EU Referendum campaign. During the two months between April and June 2016, Labour Leave provided a home for Leave leaning Labour voters which had not been there before. Polling evidence suggests this resulted in something like a million additional tradition Labour voters opting for Leave, providing a winning overall margin for Leave which might not otherwise have been there.

Dark Patterns in the online 2019 General Election

Whatever the debate about 2017, the election online in 2019 wasn't principally about bots and Russian money. This time, says Alex Connock, the digital battle was won and lost by actual human beings, millennial professionals. They used disciplined, iterative digital marketing straight out of a particular playbook: online retail. The techniques are effective but sometimes highly manipulative, which means this was the election which brought the 'dark patterns' of global ecommerce into UK politics

2019 was the pre-Christmas election. The nights were drawing in. Black Friday – the ritual millennial online retail blowout, a critical pivot in the ecommerce year from athleisurewear to fridge-freezers – dropped in the middle of the campaign. It was not the only darkness in the online political landscape.

From paid search to programmatic ads on social media, this was an election campaign won online in the same way companies win the hour-by-hour, programmatically automated war to sell cheap hotel rooms, makeup or protein shakes online. Through micro-segmentation of the audience, iterative A/B testing of ad copy, and the most devious of digital marketing tools and tricks, a brand's awareness is translated into activation, in the form of sales, or votes.

Andrew Neil may have complained that the PM didn't go on his BBCOne TV programme, but the Tories saw the real wins were in the programmatic advertising platforms, in Google adwords and Facebook ad manager. And they reaped the dividend.

The month before, November 2019, a Princeton University team[1] published an academic article in a journal which no one – except perhaps Dominic Cummings – reads in British politics. In Proceedings of the Association for Computing Machinery on Human-Computer Interaction, they presented a study of 11,000 shopping websites worldwide, categorising and quantifying the manipulative techniques behind commonly used strategies in online retail. The term for these techniques: 'dark patterns'.

Dark patterns drive the consumer to make choices they otherwise wouldn't make – leaving their user journeys misleading and manipulated. They are a form of information warfare, but in the retail space. They are legal but often unethical. Modern digital marketing's most Machiavellian tools have multiple characteristics in common with modern politics (or indeed intelligence war): asymmetry, covert design and deception. In the Princeton analysis, dark patterns fall into 15 recognisable categories. These include forced action, forced enrolment, obstruction, high-demand (as in 'these rooms are going fast'), hard to cancel ('please call our customer retention team during office hours'), low-stock message ('only two remaining'), testimonials of uncertain origin ('I loved this product'), deceptive activity notifications, pressured sell and trick questions.

Almost all of these tools were visible in the 2019 election campaign. In fact, there was one retail trick which underpinned the whole project: Countdown Timer, indicating to users that a deal will expire. All the parties in effect agreed to this last chance proposition. The election was marketed by Tories as a last chance to get Brexit done, on a hard deadline of January 31. The Brexit Party said it was the last chance, full stop. The SNP and the Lib Dems proposed this as the last chance to stop Brexit. The Greens said it was a last chance to save the planet. And Labour retailed it as the last chance to stop a Tory Brexit.

Of course, 'nudging' is not new in politics – in fact it was thought to be a positive asset when it hit marketing around 2008 through Richard Thaler's book Nudge[2] (although the term originated in the mid 1990s). It was hailed as a solution to public health challenges like smoking or bad diet. Don't force people to do things that are good for them, the argument went. Just point and tempt them the right way subconsciously, perhaps with arrows on the floor that they don't even notice, as they are guided unwittingly towards that vegetable aisle. Now for vegetables, read 'Get Brexit Done'. By 2019, the human frailties targeted by nudging – like framing effect, anchoring effect and scarcity bias – are to be readily found in the darker heart of manipulative online retail, including retail politics.

In 2019 we saw the real-time, technically adept, A/B-iterated (that means testing multiple versions of an advert at the same time) sometimes deliberately amateurish, dark art of digital marketing. To borrow Boris Johnson's phrase, the Princeton dark patterns piece is an 'oven-ready' taxonomy to take us through what the political parties did online. It said: "Bösch et al. used Kahneman's dual process theory which describes how humans have two modes of thinking – 'System 1' (unconscious, automatic, possibly less rational) and 'System 2' (conscious, rational) – and noted how 'Dark Strategies' exploit users' System 1 thinking to get them to make a decision desired by the designer." The 2019 election, with its relentless focus on key, emotive labels ('Get Brexit Done') and proliferating non-fact-based facts, was all about System 1 thinking.

Let's get started with two dark patterns to be alert for: (1) Visual Interference (misdirection): Using style and visual presentation to steer users to or away from certain choices and (2) Testimonial of uncertain origin. And a quintessential example of both? To change a Twitter handle in real time, aiming apparently to misdirect users as to the credibility of a source of information.

"Misdirection uses visuals, language, or emotion to steer users toward or away from making a particular choice," said the Princeton team. This is what Conservative Central Office did in the BBC TV debate on November 19, 2019, by putting out 'factcheckUK' tweets. The Economist explained the Twitter landscape that night: "There was Full Fact, an established charity, FactCheck, run by Channel 4 – and then there was factcheckuk, a new Twitter-based outfit which seemed particularly keen to pick holes in Mr Corbyn's arguments. Closer inspection revealed the account was in fact run by @CCHQPress, the Conservative Party press office." Conservative Party chairman James Cleverly was game for a sequence of interviews the next morning to robustly defend the strategy, but not everyone was convinced the project did not involve an intended trick.

Of course, politics has always been about the familiar retail dark pattern of 'sneak into basket' – adding additional products to users' shopping carts without their consent – via un-manifestoed ideas ranging from the Poll Tax to PFI. Indeed, the Labour voter's shopping cart was so full by the end of the campaign (free stuff for everyone, from pensions catch-ups to university tuition fees) that the manifesto itself was potentially discounted on grounds of economic credulity.

One dark pattern is Forced Enrolment, or coercing users to share their information to complete their tasks. Anyone who thinks they don't share information on a coerced basis is either delusional, has never browsed online, or has not read the superb New York Times primer – These Ads Think They Know You[3]. The Times took the simple step of buying programmatic online display adverts, where the copy shown told the viewer what it was about their browsing history (or cookies, put simply) that made them get served programmatically in the first place (by a rather complex process of automated auctions between advertisers and platforms, lasting around a fifth of a second). This targeting and segmentation, at multiple levels both demographic and psychographic, forces enrolled users of social media (or simply viewers of any programmatic advertising like banner ads or paid search results) into a tunnel of content designed to appeal specifically to that micro segment of the audience. And so it is with modern politics too.

This time round, even the wholesome Lib Dems were toying with A/B tested, programmatically distributed multi-version adverts at scale, on Facebook AdManager. WhoTargetsMe showed how different versions of a Stop Brexit advert with Jo Swinson in various outfits and visages were tested online. £2985 was spent sending 15 different looks[4] of the leader to a combined 128,000 people – from smiley and determined, through severe, to thoughtful and humorous.

From those 15 ads, they decided to drop ten on October 31 and stick with five. As WhoTargetsMe said on Medium: "Today party campaigning is Janus-faced, a fantastic example of this phenomenon is via the many faces of Jo Swinson the Liberal Democrats were recently pushing.[5] We the Facebook audience are in fact lab rats in a giant experiment."

Another dark pattern: confirm shaming. It's the use of language and emotion (shame) to steer users away from making a certain choice (like spending less money). It's used by some charities ('would you want to see these animals starve?'.) More or less legitimately, depending on which social feed you believe, Labour used the picture[6] of the boy on the floor of A&E at Leeds Royal Infirmary in an ad that ran on Facebook and Instagram, linked to the Yorkshire Evening Post article that first highlighted the story on December 8. One effect of the proposition was to shame potential Tory converts into sticking with Labour. The text which accompanied the picture on the ad read: "You can't trust the Tories with the NHS. If the Tories win on Thursday, patients will suffer five more years of this. Vote Labour to save our NHS." By the next afternoon, the advert had been seen by around 850,000 users costing the party around £5400.

There are other dark patterns at play in any election of course. Hard to Cancel makes it easy to sign up for a service and hard to get out of it, a *sine qua non* of the Fixed Term Parliament Act. Or there is Low Stock Message: indicating to users that limited quantities of a product are available. This messaging is universal in the online adverts of the political parties. We could continue with the analogies between retail and politics but the point is made.

The dark pattern we all see almost every time we go online shopping is Activity Message: informing the user about the activity on a website, with the implication something good is about to become scarce. This is the 'Six users are looking at this hotel right now' message. Political retailers have been doing that too, by a process of driving momentum on social posts. This is sometimes done through natural momentum on high-follower sites (like those of Momentum, with a useful and proactive, if not stellar, 41,000 followers on Instagram, and 156,000 on Twitter) and/or through the use of paid placement to seed it – a standard practice in digital marketing. If enough people like an ad, that gives it traction. An Instagram picture[7] of Jeremy Corbyn holding a plate got 46,029 likes.[8] *The Guardian* pointed out that a clip of Corbyn rattling through Labour's manifesto was the most seen of all Instagram posts by the main parties and outriders one week, watched almost 123,000 times. In fact, the Labour leader was the top performer on Instagram, taking all five places in the most viewed/liked posts in another week in late December.

But if Labour won Instagram, in contrast to the immediate previous election, the Tories did much better on Facebook. Their campaign was driven by Sean Topham and Ben Guerin, social media experts from somewhere Down Under, hired by the Conservatives' director of politics and campaigning via their agency TG in London, having formerly worked for the Liberal Party's Scott Morrison in Australia. They were reputedly known for making 'boomer memes' – content deliberately crafted to look simple and basic, targeting demographics like older people, or using content from Game of Thrones to gain attention. Their *bona fides* are not in doubt, but that doesn't mean their team was always seen as having the facts right. First draft said the Tories had created 6000 ads in a four day period December 1-4 alone.[9] They found[10] on December 6 that nearly 90 per cent of the Facebook ads posted by the UK's Conservative Party in the first days of December were pushing figures about the NHS, income tax cuts, and more that had already challenged by Full Fact, one of election's higher profile fact-checkers.[11] A total of 5,132 Conservative adverts, such as the one footnoted here,[12] pushed the idea that the Conservatives would build 40 new hospitals. Full Fact claimed, even before the start of the election, that the actual figure was six. (The Tories consistently disagreed with that figure.)

So do we need more and better regulation of this fast-moving, digital retail politics? Yes. The LSE Truth, Trust and Technology Commission report in late 2018 concluded: "The UK should not find itself having to go to the polls again before the legislative framework is modernised." (We did, a year later.) Highly specific targeting, psychographic, behavioural and demographic (the three pillars of segmentation), questionable transparency and non-party groups all complicate the mix. Non-party groups[13] were targeting voters on issues including Brexit. Since the last election in 2017 the number of non-party campaign groups registered with the UK watchdog the Electoral Commission rose from 43 to 67. The Electoral Commission's framework on Transparent Digital Campaigning[14] needs updating.

As Lisa-Maria Neudert and Phil Howard of the Oxford Technology and Elections Commission said on November 11, 2019, there need to be changes to the way political advertising online is regulated, in the name of transparency[15]: "Social media companies should be archiving all ads all the time. If political parties are spending money on different platforms, in a variety of formats, they should also archive the ads they buy." Not all archiving worked this time round, including at Facebook. The more archiving there is, the less darkness exists for dark patterns to hide in.

So digital marketing now drives elections. If you want to understand the dynamics of future election campaigns, rather than listening to Andrew Neil complaining about non-appearance by the Prime Minister on election specials, you might be better off looking at how BooHoo.com are marketing fast fashion. BooHoo is, after all, substantially closer to how the next demographic is interacting with media. Even the 'BBC *Question Time Election Special*, Under 30s,' actually scored its biggest audience with over-65s, 31.4% on December 8.

Dark Patterns are as much an intellectual construct as a forensic description of retail online politics in the 2020s. But as Martin Luther King said: "Darkness cannot drive out darkness: only light can do that." Shining an analytical light on political digital marketing is as vital public service as putting the PM on the spot.

Notes

[1] Dark Patterns at Scale: Findings from a Crawl of 11K Shopping Websites. Proc. ACM Hum.-Comput. Interact., Vol. 3, No. CSCW, Article 81. Publication date: November 2019.

[2] https://www.amazon.co.uk/Nudge-Improving-Decisions-Health-Happiness/dp/0141040017

[3] https://www.nytimes.com/interactive/2019/04/30/opinion/privacy-targeted-advertising.html

[4] https://www.facebook.com/ads/library/?active_status=all&ad_type=all&country=GB&impression_search_field=has_impressions_lifetime&view_all_page_id=5883973269

[5] https://medium.com/@WhoTargetsMe/the-many-faces-of-jo-swinson-55a7f766c324

[6] https://www.ft.com/content/121eca30-1a97-11ea-9186-7348c2f183af

[7] https://www.instagram.com/p/B5K4-_NJ42l/

[8] https://www.theguardian.com/politics/2019/nov/29/which-parties-are-using-instagram-most-successfully

[9] https://firstdraftnews.org/latest/thousands-of-misleading-conservative-ads-side-step-scrutiny-thanks-to-facebook-policy/

[10] https://firstdraftnews.org/latest/thousands-of-misleading-conservative-ads-side-step-scrutiny-thanks-to-facebook-policy/

[11] https://blogs.lse.ac.uk/medialse/2019/12/12/online-political-advertising-in-the-uk-2019-general-election-campaign/

[12] https://www.facebook.com/ads/archive/render_ad/?id=498520917416279

[13] https://www.ft.com/content/f42f9aa2-16ba-11ea-8d73-6303645ac406

[14] https://www.electoralcommission.org.uk/who-we-are-and-what-we-do/changing-electoral-law/transparent-digital-campaigning

[15] https://www.theguardian.com/commentisfree/2019/nov/11/online-politics-facebook-twitter-social-media-political-parties

Note on the contributor

Alex Connock is a Fellow in marketing at Said Business School, Oxford University.

Ten top questionable Tory Brexit claims

The Conservative Party's 'Get Brexit Done' slogan dominated its message in the 2019 General Election, and the party avoided getting into detail on the EU, but when it did raise Europe as an issue, the level of accuracy left much to be desired, says Hugo Dixon

It was supposed to be the Brexit election. In fact, there was hardly any proper scrutiny of Boris Johnson's Brexit deal in the media, in part because he avoided tough interviews. The Prime Minister wanted to talk about almost anything but Brexit. And when he and his colleagues did use the 'B' word, it was mostly to spray around misleading statements and sometimes outright lies. Here are ten of the top ones.

The EU doesn't stop us planting trees

This was one of Michael Gove's whoppers. He told the BBC on November 16, 2019 that leaving the EU 'will allow us to meet... tree-planting targets which will ensure that we deal with the climate crisis that we face'. What he didn't mention was the EU actually provides cash to encourage tree-planting – and our Government doesn't use it.

EU migrants aren't scrounging on the NHS

This was another Gove slur. He wrote in the *Mail on Sunday* on November 17: "It's unfair that people coming from European countries can access free NHS care without paying in while others make significant contributions."

EU citizens living in the UK contribute more to the public finances than Brits. Their net contribution a year is £2,300 more than the average UK resident, according to analysis done for the Government's own Migration Advisory Committee. This is because they pay more taxes and use the NHS and other public services less.

What's more, Brits have the right to use other EU countries' health systems: 145,000 of our pensioners get free healthcare in other EU countries, while 27 million Brits have EHIC cards giving them free healthcare when they travel to other EU countries. What's unfair about that?

We didn't need to leave the EU to scrap the tampon tax

Johnson again and again cited the tampon tax as a reason for Brexit. For example, he told the BBC on November 15: "We'll be able to cut VAT on things that we currently can't under EU rules – sanitary products, you name it."

What he didn't mention was that the EU plans to change the VAT regime to allow a zero rate for sanitary products, after David Cameron pushed for it when he was Prime Minister. Nor did he say the Conservative government stopped campaigning for a change to the tampon tax after the referendum. If it had kept up the pressure, the tax might already have been scrapped.

No fish quotas? Pull the other one.

Johnson said again and again things like 'we will take back 100 per cent control of the spectacular marine wealth of this country' after Brexit. This flies in the face of the 'Political Declaration' sketching out our future relationship he agreed with the EU. This says the UK and EU should try to 'establish a new fisheries agreement on, inter alia, access to waters and quota shares' by July 1.

EU migration isn't nearly as big as non-EU migration

The Prime Minister got his facts on migration spectacularly wrong in mid-November 2019. Asked by a BBC listener what proportion of UK immigrants come from the EU, he said: "From memory the total net migration proportions are about 50-50," before adding, "but I may be wrong about that."

At the time he made this statement, migration from the EU was barely a quarter as big as the non-EU flow. A couple of weeks later new data came out showing it was only a fifth of the size. Given Johnson was at that stage of the election weaponising migration, it's odd he didn't know the basic facts.

Live animal pledge wasn't what it seemed

In the Conservative manifesto the Prime Minister gave 'abolishing the cruel live shipment of animals' as an example of how 'where we choose, we will be able to do things differently' if we leave the EU. Listening to the rhetoric, you might have thought he was promising to abolish the live transport of animals. But examine his weasel words and he wasn't actually making such a hard and fast commitment. All he was doing was saying he would tighten up the rules, but that's something we could have done without quitting the EU.

Nope, our rights aren't guaranteed

Johnson claimed again and again his Withdrawal Agreement would protect workers' and consumers' rights, and environmental standards. Just before the election was called, for example, he told the House of Commons workers' rights will 'never be inferior' to those in the EU. The deal never promised such a thing. In fact, the Prime Minister removed a legally-binding commitment to precisely that from Theresa May's Withdrawal Agreement. What's more, after the election, he watered down the already weak protections in the original legislation needed to enact the deal.

Freeports aren't a reason for Brexit

When Johnson was casting around for reasons to leave the EU, he kept coming up with 'freeports'. For example, in the manifesto, he said: "From freeports to free trade deals… we will be able to do things differently and better." What he didn't say is we could have created freeports without quitting the EU. The EU currently has more than 80 of them. Whether creating freeports is wise is another matter. Margaret Thatcher tried and they weren't a great success, so they were scrapped.

Tidal wave of investment? Another pipedream

As part of his optimistic spiel, the Prime Minister promised in his manifesto a 'pent-up tidal wave of investment into our country'. Nowhere did he justify this implausible claim. Foreign firms, such as Nissan and Honda, have already cut investment fearing we'll lose access to the EU market. The London School of Economics' Centre for Economic Performance (CEP) makes what it calls a 'very conservative' prediction Brexit will cause foreign investment to fall by 22 per cent over the next decade.

No checks in the Irish Sea? Who are you kidding?

The only way Johnson managed to clinch a Withdrawal Agreement with the EU so quickly was by agreeing to what the EU wanted on Northern Ireland. But again and again he denied he had given ground. He told businesses in Northern Ireland on November 7, 2019 there would not be checks on 'goods coming from GB to NI that are not going on to Ireland' or 'goods going from Northern Ireland to Great Britain'. In fact, the Prime Minister had agreed Northern Ireland would follow hundreds of EU rules to do with customs and so forth. As a result, there will be checks in the Irish Sea – in both directions. This was made abundantly clear in a Treasury analysis. When this was leaked during the election, Johnson dismissed it saying voters should ignore the civil servants and 'believe what I say'.

Get Brexit done

But the biggest misleading statement of all was that slogan: *Get Brexit done*. It was on the side of Johnson's bus and the front of his manifesto. The truth is all he had agreed was a sell-out divorce deal. The proper negotiations about a future deal with the EU hadn't started. The voters were bored of Brexit and wanted to believe they could forget about the whole goddamn business if they kept Johnson in Downing Street. But that is not the case. Day in day out we will continue to wake up to news about Brexit.

Note on the contributor
Hugo Dixon campaigned to stop Brexit as chair and editor-in-chief of InFacts and deputy chair of People's Vote. Previously he was editor-in-chief of Breakingviews, which he founded in 1999 and chaired until it was sold to Thomson Reuters. Before that he worked at the Financial Times in various jobs including head of Lex.

Did the media crucify 'Marxist enemy' JC in the 2019 General Election?

Labour leader Jeremy Corbyn's political back story did him no favours, but it was inevitable the right-wing media would go all out to keep him out of Downing Street in the 2019 election, says Steven McCabe

Every Leader of the Labour Party expects to be scrutinised by the mainstream media. Many news organisations attack any politician daring to challenge orthodoxy that UK politics is located in the centre to centre-right. Corbyn, however, was subject to opprobrium verging on frenzy. His lifelong commitment to extreme left-wing politics, support for groups engaged in 'liberation struggles', perceived lack of patriotism, ambivalence on Brexit and equivocation on anti-Semitism were used against him. Encouraged by those resenting his ideology, Corbyn, was reported as being an unapologetic Marxist who posed a significant threat to national security and the economy.

Corbyn the anti-imperialist rebel

Corbyn has always been an outsider to what some contemptuously call the 'establishment'. He never attempted to endear himself to either the Labour Party hierarchy, the majority of fellow MPs or the system of rule or privilege. As successive Labour leaders and MPs found, Corbyn's antipathy was as great for them as the Conservative Party. Possessing the zeal that had motivated him in his youth and had led to him becoming Labour councillor in Haringey in 1974, when Harold Wilson was Prime Minister (PM), Corbyn believed that radical social change was essential.

Until he was included as a 'makeweight' candidate for the left to become the leader of the Labour Party in 2015, Corbyn was almost unknown to the general public apart from some brief notoriety in the 1980s. He's been a lifelong supporter of groups engaged in 'anti-imperialism' across the world. One such group was especially infamous in carrying out terrorist atrocities in the UK; the IRA.

Two weeks after bombing Brighton's Grand Hotel in 1984, in which the IRA had attempted to murder Mrs Thatcher and her cabinet, killing five and injuring 31, Corbyn invited convicted IRA volunteers to the House of Commons and was ferociously condemned by the press and denounced by MPs. Though he felt entitled to hold whatever views he wished, and though an MP with no hope of progression, he would, nevertheless, have been aware that anyone, especially with his access to Westminster, having close links to Irish republicans would be monitored by the police and security services.

Labour under Corbyn, 2015-2017

Corbyn's election by the vastly increased membership would have seemed inconceivable in the 1980s when he was being excoriated for his links to Irish republicans. His surprise victory in the leadership contest had been made possible by Ed Miliband who had beaten his brother David, the favourite to become Labour's leader in 2010. This was due to anger by Labour members exasperated by what they saw their party having become too right-wing under Tony Blair and Gordon Brown (Bower, 2019, Kogan, 2019).

The reaction of the public to Corbyn's victory as leader, led by the media, was puzzlement. Though Blair's victory in 1997 had been feted by, in particular, the so called 'Murdoch press' (*Sun, Times, Sky* Television), his involvement in Iraq had led them to question his judgement. His successors were subject to criticism as being incompetent and too closely associated with Blair's 'New Labour' project (Brown) and, in the case of Miliband, too left-wing and, curiously, being the son of a refugee who'd been an intellectual.

Corbyn's past was a gift to those in the press wishing to find fault. His defenders pointed out that he'd previously been proved correct on many issues. These included opposition to war in Iraq, advocating the need to engage with terrorist groups in Northern Ireland as part of a process of achieving peace, and arguing the innocence of the Birmingham Six and Guildford Four (Bennett, 2016). However, Corbyn's continued commitment to the creation of a Palestinian state and regular criticism of American international interventionism and interference, meant no shortage of material to be used against him

Many commentators in the media appeared to believe, undoubtedly gleaned from MPs critical of him, that Corbyn's election as leader was an aberration. He was too left-wing to be popular in an election and should be deposed. Accordingly, political reporting of Labour was of internal struggles between supporters of Corbyn – frequently members of his support group Momentum – and those MPs considered not sufficiently dedicated to returning the party back to its founding socialist ideology.

For the general public, such matters were seen through a lens of reporting all-too-often anti-pathetic to Corbyn. Labour under Corbyn was increasingly disunited and fractious. Resignations amongst the shadow cabinet were presented with accompanying narratives of incompetence and varying degrees of mendacity. The issue of anti-Semitism within Labour started to emerge. Labour under Corbyn, it was reported, was unelectable.

Brexit altered everything. David Cameron, who'd won a slim majority in the 2015 election, implemented a manifesto promise to hold a referendum on EU membership in June 2016 that, as well as ending his premiership, proved toxic for his successor Theresa May and became destructive to Corbyn at the 2019 election. Corbyn's support for the UK remaining in the EU during the referendum campaign was criticised by MPs and media as 'lukewarm'. Hardly a surprise. *The New Hope for Britain,* the 1983 manifesto Corbyn had wholeheartedly supported when he'd been elected as MP for Islington North, committed to leave the European Economic Community.

Following Corbyn's sacking of shadow minister Hilary Benn, for organising resignations against him, a vote of confidence he lost, a second vote on his leadership was held. Corbyn won this vote as decisively as the first the year before cementing his position as well as supporters, some of whom were rewarded by shadow ministerships. Confidence that Corbynism would eventually be rejected by voters was tempered by the fact that May was not required to call an election until 2020.

Hoping to increase the slim majority inherited from Cameron and ensure she could implement Brexit in the face of hostility within her party, May called a surprise election for June 2017. Media reporting was that Labour under Corbyn was expected to perform badly, extremely badly. Nonetheless, some outlets carried stories of how dangerous Corbyn would be if he became PM. One story, 'MI5 opened file on Jeremy Corbyn amid concerns over his IRA links', carried in *The Telegraph* a little under three weeks before the election. The Conservatives spent £1.2m on social media adverts portraying Corbyn of being a terrorist sympathiser (White, 2017).

Defying predictions, Labour under Corbyn achieved a net gain of 30 seats and increased vote share to 40 per cent; a swing of 9.6 per cent, the largest since 1945 when Labour under Clement Attlee had proposed a radical socialist manifesto. As many in the media suggested, discontent among those suffering from austerity policies and especially the young, contributed. Corbyn's detractors had been proved wrong. Perhaps, after all, his commitment to socialism could enable Labour to regain power and make him PM. Many, including a good number in the media, saw such a vista as appalling. It would damage the UK's economic interests. They would do all they could to stop it by reporting Corbyn's deficiencies and the dangers he posed, most especially during any future election.

The 2019 Election – completing Corbyn's socialist dream

It may be argued Corbyn's misfortune in December 2019 was his main opponent was Boris Johnson who ruthlessly wielded Brexit as a weapon. The public were treated to daily election reporting when they heard Johnson repeating, *ad nauseam,* that he'd get Brexit 'done' provided they gave him a mandate to unblock

Parliament that was 'against the people'. Whilst Labour's position had shifted to being committed to negotiating a new deal to leave the EU followed by another referendum, Corbyn's stance was agnostic. The media lapped up the confusion.

Though Johnson had many critics, they compared him to Corbyn considered more of a liability. Johnson's boss, at *The Telegraph,* right-winger and seminal historian, Max Hastings, wrote in *The Guardian* that though Corbyn was more honest, "[he] harbours his own extravagant delusions [and]… may yet prove to be the only possible Labour leader whom Johnson can defeat in a general election." More generally, Johnson was presented as an optimist who could move the country on against Corbyn, the Marxist, whose party had blocked Brexit.

With the exception of *The Mirror* and, to a lesser extent, *The Guardian*, reporting of Corbyn's campaign was rarely less than hostile. Corbyn was portrayed as less a 'man of the people' than his Old Etonian opponent. Corbyn's past and present links to Irish republicanism and terror groups supporting a Palestinian state were regularly raised portraying him as dangerous. The implication was, *qui cum canibus concumbunt cum pulicibus surgent*, "He that lieth down with dogs shall rise up with fleas."

Disgruntlement amongst party workers, particularly by those thwarted by Corbyn's supporters in attempting to root out anti-Semitism, was given exposure in the media. Besides his lack of patriotism and relationships with unsavoury groups, he was held to have been intimately involved in the 99 page manifesto, *It's Time for Real Change;* resonant with Labour's 39 page 1983 offer, described by leading Labour MP of the time Gerald Kaufman as 'the longest suicide note in history'. *It's Time for Real Change* commentators maintained, represented Corbyn's dogmatic and unaltered certainty in state intervention, socialism and, significantly, a profligacy that was economic recklessness.

Headlines of December 12, the day of the election, are instructive. *The Sun* led 'Save Brexit' and juxtaposed pictures of lightbulbs with Johnson and Corbyn's faces on them indicating, respectively for each leader, a 'bright future' and 'the lights will go out for good'.

The *Daily Mail* wrote "Your vote has never been more vital. Today YOU must brave the deluge to go to your local polling station and back…BORIS" beside a picture of 'national treasure' and (Jewish) former Labour supporter, Maureen Lipman. 'Brexit and Britain in your hands' said the *Daily Express*. Contrast these with, 'For them … vote Labour', in which *The Mirror* used pictures of social issues raised during the campaign, and *The Guardian* 'Corbyn urges voters to deliver shock to the establishment'.

Conclusion

Corbyn surely knew his relationships with individuals and groups engaged in liberation struggles would be used against him? Harold Wilson's experience as PM demonstrated that once the security services consider you to be a threat, information collected has an uncanny habit of ending up in the hands of sympathetic journalists. Corbyn's sympathies and his unwillingness to use nuclear weapons proved he wasn't a true patriot who'd act to in the national interest. Corbyn's unwillingness to be decisive on Brexit demonstrated he vacillated and against Johnson's simple 'Get Brexit Done' message proved damning.

If Corbyn feels he was 'crucified' by the media, they fashioned 'nails' provided by him to achieve maximum damage. After his 'glorious defeat' in 2017, the potential for an avowed socialist such as Corbyn to become PM needed to be dealt with more forcefully. The 'establishment' using their extensive contacts in the media were happy to see stories denigrating him. Analysis of policy and any merits were inevitably drowned out in the cacophony of criticism contained in papers read by the very voters Corbyn hoped to appeal to; *The Sun* and *Daily Express* with lower sales, arguably being the worst offenders.

Even the BBC, the supposed stalwart of objectivity was accused of failure to maintain objectivity in its reporting of Corbyn and Labour during the election. Labour's manifesto contained too much of his imprimatur to attract approval from all but the *Mirror* and, grudgingly, *The Guardian*. For the remainder, it represented a return to 1970s socialism. Britain under Corbyn as PM would be an economic catastrophe.

Corbyn always faced an uphill battle to become PM. The majority of the media, aided by enemies within and outside of Labour, including the establishment he'd spent his whole life condemning, did everything they could to make this objective impossible.

References

Bennett, Ronan (2016), Jeremy Corbyn has been on the right side of history for 30 years. That's real leadership, *The Guardian*, 16th September, https://www.theguardian.com/commentisfree/2016/sep/16/jeremy-corbyn-leadership-david-cameron-libya-labour

Bower, Tom (2019), Dangerous Hero, Corbyn's Ruthless Plot for Power, London: Williams Collins

Hastings, Max (2019), I was Boris Johnson's boss: he is utterly unfit to be prime minister, *The Guardian*, 24th June, https://www.theguardian.com/commentisfree/2019/jun/24/boris-johnson-prime-minister-tory-party-britain

Kogan, David (2019), Protest and Power: The Battle for the Labour Party, London: Bloomsbury Reader

Newell, Claire, Dixon, Hayley, Heighton, Luke and Yorke, Harry (2017), Exclusive: MI5 opened file on Jeremy Corbyn amid concerns over his IRA links, *The Telegraph*, 19th May, https://www.telegraph.co.uk/news/2017/05/19/exclusive-mi5-opened-file-jeremy-corbyn-amid-concerns-ira-links/

White, Charles (2017), Tories spent £1,200,000 on negative anti-Jeremy Corbyn social media adverts, *The Metro,* 10th June https://metro.co.uk/2017/06/10/tories-spent-1200000-on-negative-anti-jeremy-corbyn-social-media-adverts-6699774/

Note on the contributor

Dr Steven McCabe is Associate Professor and Senior Fellow, Centre for Brexit Studies and Institute of Design and Economic Acceleration (IDEA), Birmingham City University, and writes/comments regularly in the national and international press on politics and the economy. He is joint editor with John Mair, Neil Fowler and Leslie Budd of Brexit and Northern Ireland, Bordering on Confusion (published by Bite-Sized Books, 2019)

A toxic leader and a manifesto like Father Christmas on acid

Although a staunch Remainer, Paul Connew was a rare pundit to predict Leave would win the 2016 referendum, based on research in the north and midlands Labour heartlands he was convinced would decide the result. He's revisited his original research sample in the wake of Labour's 2019 general election debacle

It may be 2020 but the vision for the UK's future remains far from perfect and decidedly blurry. OK, the general election of December 12, 2019 radically reshaped the electoral landscape but it revealed that millions of voters behind Labour's fabled, traditional Red Wall preferred a charismatic charlatan Tory with a deceptively simplistic but highly effective bumper sticker slogan *Get Brexit Done* to a Labour leader they deemed light on leadership, lacking in patriotism and hooked on an economic fantasy manifesto.

'I held my nose and voted for Boris'

As one defecting Labour supporter (in Tony Blair's old Sedgefield stronghold) confessed to me in the cold light of dawn on December 13: "I held my nose and voted for Boris Johnson, a man I despise, because I despised Jeremy Corbyn even more. I didn't trust Corbyn on patriotism and, while it was a December election, I couldn't believe in a manifesto that was the equivalent of a Christmas present wish list for Santa compiled by someone on an acid trip.

"It was the first time in my life I hadn't voted Labour. Brexit wasn't the deciding factor. I'm yet to be convinced Boris Johnson can even deliver on his Brexit promises. But I just couldn't envisage Corbyn as prime minister and that decided where I put my X when I reached the ballot box."

His voice and verdict was far from alone.

The reason I was talking to him, and others, was that he was among the sample of Labour heartland voters I'd consulted just before the 2016 referendum when, despite being a staunch Remainer, I was a rare pundit predicting on air and in print that Leave would win.

It was a rough-and-ready research project focused on those Labour midlands and northern areas where I was convinced the referendum result would be decided. But rough and ready or not, it proved (to my personal chagrin) rather more accurate than the big, sophisticated pollsters, with a 53-47 per cent margin in favour of Leave.

Since then I've periodically returned to my original data base (primarily for *The New European*) and there were at times a marked shift in sentiment with up to 50 per cent of my Leave sample changing their minds, or at least subscribing to the notion of a second referendum/people's vote.

When a blue tsunami hit a creaking red wall

Significantly the shift from Leave to Remain (or second referendum) was more pronounced among the Under 40s and those with children at school or university. Among the over 60s, however, the commitment to leave remained rock solid and the hostility to any thought of a second referendum unshakeable.

So how did this all play into a general election tsunami that swept so many solid Labour MPs out of parliament in a blue tidal wave breach of that creaking red wall, a wall that had admittedly been creaking slowly since Tony Blair was in his election-winning New Labour pomp? (Cue a startling stat: of the 28 general elections since the First World War Labour has won just eight.)

Well, around half of those in my Leave sample who'd changed their minds about Brexit revealed they'd either voted Tory, not voted at all or, in a handful of cases, voted Lib Dem. So why not Labour, a party which, for all Jeremy Corbyn's fudge-coated fence-squatting, was offering the democratic opportunity to the people to reaffirm or reverse the 2016 referendum via an up-to-date, specific people's vote?

Encore for 'the longest suicide note in history'?

Again and again, the answers came back. Corbyn can't be trusted on defence or the economy or believed on Brexit, too close to terrorists and extremists, an apologist for Russia, an anti-Semite or at least a weak, prevaricating leader incapable or unwilling to crack down on anti-Semitism in the Labour Party.

'He's out of touch with people like us' was a recurring quote, defying the question of how in touch could Boris Johnson, Old Etonian, Oxbridge and well-endowed with a toff's sense of entitlement truly be either after a decade of austerity. The list ran on and on and, illogically or not, added up to an electorally toxic mix.

Their views echoed the big post-election polls by YouGov and others that showed how Corbyn's Brexit non-committal stance led to a slump from 66 per cent in 2017 to 56 per cent amongst young voters in 2019.

Significantly, too, these polls revealed strong sympathy across the broader electorate for the principle of Labour's manifesto plans for nationalising the rail and utility sectors individually but a fatal scepticism around delivering such a blanket pledge and, equally crucial, in the competence of Labour leadership to deliver on such huge ambitions.

This helps explain why, for the first time since Harold Macmillan in 1959, a government that had been in power for a decade has been re-elected with an increased majority. And why Labour had suffered a defeat arguably even more catastrophic than that in 1983 of Michael Foot, another non-telegenic left winger seen as vacillating, unpatriotic and unrealistic.

Foot's manifesto was famously dubbed at the time 'the longest suicide note in history' by the former *Mirror* leader writer turned senior Labour politician, the late Gerald Kaufman. His words could almost be resurrected as Jeremy Corbyn's political epitaph in 2020.

On the eve of the election, I was again asked on air for a forecast. My pundit credentials took a bit of a knock when I predicted an overall Tory majority of 'around 25'. My only consolation? On polling day Boris Johnson and his inner circle were apparently only counting on 'around 10', as several polls (wrong again) suggested the Tory lead was evaporating and a hung parliament might even be on the horizon.

Chuckling at *Private Eye* through gritted teeth

In many respects, *Private Eye's* Christmas edition cover captured the mood music. Beneath the headline: '*Bearded old man hands Boris Christmas present*', a mocked up image of the Labour leader as Father Christmas shakes Boris Johnson by the hand, declaring 'Happy Christmas, here's a landslide', to which a beaming prime minister responds: 'Thanks, Jeremy!'

Several ousted Labour MP friends told me that, although they had to chuckle through gritted teeth, they saw that *Private Eye* cover as stark reality, not satirical send-up.

Inevitably the scale of Labour's defeat has triggered an internal investigation, vicious in-fighting and of course the electoral battle to be Corbyn's successor. Inevitably, too, there are those questioning the party's very survival, just as happened after Michael Foot's 1983 defeat debacle. Yet 2020 is an historic year when an effective, credible opposition (beyond the SNP with its own particular battleground) remains vital to hold the Johnson government to account.

So who succeeds Corbyn and the direction in which the new leader takes the party is more than a democratic sideshow. A personal confession here: after decades as a Labour loyalist and editor of pro-Labour titles, I voted Lib Dem in both the last European election and the December general election.

In the latter case, it was a tactical decision because my St Albans constituency is strongly pro-Remain and I was happy to actively support an excellent young Lib Dem candidate in Daisy Cooper to oust a pro-Brexit hardline Tory MP with a hefty 11 per cent swing in what was a rare bright spot for the Remain and Lib Dem causes on the night.

On reflection, the pro second referendum campaign's influence on the election was also badly holed by a combination of tactical disagreements, personality clashes and rival power struggles. Sadly, that was something of a betrayal of the hundreds of thousands of ordinary anti-Brexit marchers. That said, both Boris Johnson and the post-Brexit Labour leadership face a pivotal problem posed by a deep generational gulf the election outcome will do little, or nothing, to bridge.

Anyone but Long-Bailey

But, rather like my old friend and colleague Alastair Campbell, I always hoped my 'defection' would be temporary. It was one driven by my hostility to Jeremy Corbyn's leadership shortcomings, most notably over Brexit, the anti-Semitism crisis, and a growing conviction he was electorally toxic in places where Labour had to win to even replicate the 2017 election result.

For what it's worth, any one of early front runner Sir Keir Starmer, Emily Thornberry or the analytically astute Lisa Nandy would swing me back into the Labour fold. Thornberry's late failure to make the cut disappointed admirers of the shadow foreign secretary. If nothing else, her sharp barrister's wit and flair for a killer phrase would have made PMQs' jousts with Boris grand theatre. Jess Phillips' belated withdrawal from the race and acceptance that she couldn't be a unifying force was simultaneously realistic and regrettable. The mouthy, media-savvy maverick and long-time Corbyn critic would have at least livened up the campaign and come closest to carrying a neo-Blair flag.

Only Continuity Corbyn candidate Rebecca Long-Bailey, with her extraordinary '10 out of 10' rating for Corbyn's leadership record would do the reverse.

Yes, given the influence of Momentum and certain powerful trade union leaders she's undoubtedly a potential victor in Labour's own election, while highly likely to meet the same fate as Corbyn himself in 2024.

If how to prevent a long Tory hegemony and save Labour from dwindling to a cult-like permanent protest movement is the question, Rebecca Long-Bailey is not the answer. She would risk a Corbynesque repeat of a leader seriously at odds with much of the parliamentary party.

For many Labour moderates, the *Mail on Sunday* article penned by Alan Johnson, once seen as a Labour leadership front runner himself and headlined '*Either we ditch the Momemtum cult—or Labour becomes a cult itself*' (December 15, 2019) rang true.

The issue of the next Labour leader is the more significant when my research sample didn't represent any great love affair with Boris Johnson. More a shoulder-shrugging, grudging 'at least he's not Jeremy Corbyn' demi-approval.

While our prime minister may share a Trumpian disregard for fact-based truth, there was, perhaps, a moment of candour the morning after the election when he acknowledged many of those captured red-wall Labour areas may only have 'lent' him their votes.

But beware that inside Number 10 both Boris and his Svengali-esque strategy chief Dominic Cummings will be counting on Long-Bailey (or 'RBL' as she's been dubbed) to prove as electorally toxic as the bearded man who privately favours her to pick up his baton, maintaining the delusion 'Labour won the argument' but merely lost the election due to Brexit and the familiar theme of the ferocity and bias of the Tory press.

So who was it wot won it?

Ongoing academic research will ultimately evaluate the impact of both the mainstream media (MSM) and social media in the story of the 2019 election. But my hunch is that the role of *The Sun*, *Mail* and *Telegraph*, influencing the outcome amid steady circulation decline will again prove as hyperbolic as that famous or infamous (take your pick) '*It was The Sun wot won it*' front page claiming credit for John Major's surprise 1992 victory over Neil Kinnock. Back in the day when *The Sun* sold 3.57m copies compared with today's 1.2m, a big shift from 6 per cent of the UK population down to 1.8 per cent.

In normal times, of course, an 80-seat landslide would guarantee the victorious party a two-term spell in power. But 2020 represents a far from normal time and, although the Leave/Remain/ second referendum argument became largely redundant after January 31, a disastrous no-deal Brexit remains on the table at year's end.

As Anand Menon, director of the UK in a Changing Europe, and professor of European politics at King's College, London, posited in an article for *The Guardian* on December 13, "traditional party loyalties seem to have been stretched to breaking point by the Leave-Remain divide. We've emerged not knowing what kind of Brexit the prime minister intends to deliver. On the one hand, pro soft Brexit Tories whisper that the kind of substantial majority the prime minister has will allow him to move to his inner one-nation Conservative. Freed from the grasp of the ERG they say, he will be able to negotiate the soft Brexit he has always secretly wanted, limiting the economic impact of Brexit, and allowing him to achieve it with minimal pain."

Not so, say critics such as former Tory cabinet ministers Philip Hammond and David Gauke, pointing out that enshrining in law that the UK will not seek a negotiating extension with the EU and leave on WTO terms at the end of 2020 if a trade deal hasn't been agreed at improbably breakneck speed, suggests Boris Johnson remains in thrall to the ERG zealots, xenophobes and climate change cynics.

Yet, to add to the confusion, Johnson also sought out some cabinet members to portray himself as an unlikely 'Brexity Hezza'—in reference to the outcast arch-Remainer Tory grandee, Lord Heseltine!

That said, those of us who've known Boris over the years and firmly believe power, and not principle or consistency, are his ultimate political aphrodisiac won't be ruling out a Johnsonian reverse ferret on that no-extension 'deadline' (more gesture than legally binding, in truth).

Research by Bloomberg Economics suggests that the cost of Brexit since the 2016 referendum could reach £200bn by the end of 2020. Some economists go as far as contending that a no-deal Brexit involving trade tariffs with the EU could surpass the entire net cost of our 47-year membership history.

And if Sajid Javid's tough 'no regulatory alignment with the EU' warning in a January 18 *Financial Times* interview holds firm, then Boris Johnson may need to cling on to one of his hero Churchill's slightly less famous quotes: 'Success is going from failure to failure without losing your enthusiasm.'

Johnson is acutely aware that Nigel Farage's grudging decision to pull Brexit Party candidates out of Tory-held seats was a major factor in the scale of his victory. By the same token, pro-Remain parties lamentable failure to forge meaningful tactical alliances was manna from electoral heaven for the Conservatives. All the more so, given more votes in total were cast for pro-Remain parties, but not in the right places under our first past the post system.

At one stage No. 10 dropped strong hints Johnson would ditch the Fixed Term Parliament Act if re-elected. No surprise that appears to have disappeared now. How easily a political philanderer like Boris is seduced by the lure of a five-year guarantee on a Downing Street boudoir!

Now, too, we know that some senior shadow cabinet figures, most notably Emily Thornberry but even, rumour has it, John McDonnell, urged Jeremy Corbyn not to bite the December election bait being desperately dangled by the prime minister. Instead, they argued, leaving Boris flapping on the hook of a minority government in a hung parliament would damage his Brexiteer credibility and electability in the longer term and strengthen the case for a second referendum over a general election.

But the Labour leader's tight circle of un-elected advisers, including Seamus Milne, had convinced themselves the Tories were 'there for the taking' and fatally won the war of Jeremy's ear.

What the Dickens....

To add to the surreal flavour of 2020's dawn, the Johnson/Dominic Cummings axis appears to be gearing up for a bruising battle with the BBC; something that should ring alarm bells among journalists and the public alike, whatever their political colours. The row over selective briefings that sparked a protest walkout by lobby journalists provides further evidence of No 10's addiction to control and resentment of press scrutiny.

The rediscovery of the 2004 study by Cummings' New Frontiers Foundation think tank on the BBC, branding it the 'mortal enemy' of the Right, in need of 'ending in its current form' and espousing the merits of a UK version of Fox News, is the harbinger of a nation-dividing cultural showdown.

It also plays into a narrative starting to trouble some more thoughtful Tory MPs; namely that, for all their formidable campaigning abilities, the prime minister and his curious strategy chief may be alarmingly clueless when it comes to converting campaigning success into coherent government. In February alone, the Johnson/ Cummings response to the floods and coronavirus crises, the Heathrow court ruling and the ugly Andrew Sabisky business compounded that suspicion.

Over Christmas, some on the Conservative side even managed to take offence at what they considered a 'politically loaded ' BBC TV version of *A Christmas Carol*.

While, sticking to the Dickens theme, Boris Johnson's seasonal message to the nation amounted to *Great Expectations'* brimful of 'oven-ready' rehashed election slogans, but as thin as Oliver Twist's gruel on how he'll juggle keeping happy the Tory party's three tribes conundrum – the traditional pro-Brexitshire support base; the Brexit-sceptic big business donors; and its new 'on-loan' hopefuls out there in the economic wasteland towns, desperate for election pledges to translate into meaningful change to their lives.

Communities where contempt for Corbyn outweighed disdain for the Tory party and suspended suspicion that *Get Brexit Done* might not turn out to be the national salvation recipe concocted by Boris, a man whose American heritage could just as easily qualify him as a snake-oil salesman as a prime minister and fall way short of matching his own hero, Churchill, whose voice and mannerisms he's increasingly echoed since becoming PM.

To take another liberty with Dickens, 2020 could well turn out a dangerous *Tale of Two Cities* – London and Brussels this time. Or, maybe, three, with Paris re-entering and President Macron the stumbling block to the kind of advantageous post-Brexit trade deal Boris Johnson is counting on to secure his legacy and maintain his No. 10 tenancy beyond 2024.

The Trump factor

Or, perhaps that should be *A Tale of Four Cities* – to include Washington? That Donald Trump didn't deign to consult or forewarn his 'pal' Boris – a man he's labelled the 'BritTrump' – before ordering the legally-dubious assassination of Iran's General Qasem Soleimani should serve as a sharp foretaste of who'll pack the real muscle power during US/UK trade negotiations, always assuming The Donald holds onto the White House after November.

Unimpeachable evidence of the Boris/Cummings axis's Trumpian approach to power came with the fate of Chancellor Sajid Javid and widely-respected Northern Ireland Secretary Julian Smith on the eve of Valentine's Day. A message that total loyalty trumps independent thought or valued principle. A common denominator between Javid and Smith? Both were recipients of lavish public praise from the PM not long before he and 'The Dom' massacred their cabinet careers. Oh, sooo like The Donald.

The irony in Javid's case was that he had incurred Cummings' Machiavellian wrath by playing a big role in swinging the PM behind the HS2 go ahead. In Smith's it was a cruel reward for skilfully restoring power sharing at Stormont. But the former chief whip paid the price for daring to continue whipping up warnings about the danger of a no-deal Brexit.

The Trump administration's threatening response to Johnson's flagship digital tax policy on the US tech Titans, the Huawei security issue and Washington's rejection of the UK's extradition request over diplomatic-immunity death-crash driver Anne Sacoolas further clouded the wondrously simple trade deal picture long painted by ardent Brexiteers. For Boris, ducking becoming The Donald's poodle represents another personal zip wire act of the first order.

To end where we began, the only certainty about 2020 is that it's going to be spectacularly uncertain. A helluva fascinating, hairy, dangerous rollercoaster ride, courtesy of Boris the unpredictable yet charismatic showman-cum-clown conductor.

Fasten your seat belts, brace yourselves, close your eyes and cross your fingers tight. Off we go. Final destination unknown. And beware the wheels falling off en route.

References

YouGov and Ipsos Mori post-election polling.

Private Eye issue 1512, Dec-January.

'Labour's lost working class voters have gone for good', Chris Bickerton, lecturer in politics at Cambridge University, published in The Guardian, Dec 19, 2019.

'What will Boris Johnson's majority mean for Brexit?', Anand Menon, professor of European politics, King's College, London and director, UK in a Changing Europe, published in *The Guardian*, December 24, 2019.

The Daily Mail, The Sun, The Daily Telegraph, The Guardian, Daily Mirror, The Times, The New European, BBC, ITV, Sky News, Talk Radio (various dates).

Tribune Magazine (January 2020)

Note on the contributor

Paul Connew is a media commentator/consultant, broadcaster, author and former editor of the *Sunday Mirror*, deputy editor of the *Daily Mirror* and a former Mirror Group US Bureau Chief and a former deputy editor of the *News of the World*. He's a regular columnist for *The New European* and *The Drum* and comments on media and political issues for the BBC, Sky News, CNN, al-Jazeera, Talk Radio and Australian broadcasting.. He's a long-standing judge at the British Press Awards and the RTS awards and has been a contributing author for three previous books in this series, *After Leveson?* (2013), *Last Words?* (2016) and *Anti-Social Media?* (2018).

How 'them' showed how out of touch 'us' were

Nigel Willmott was that rare beast – a Leave voter who worked for *The Guardian*. Here he argues that politicians (and journalists) who believe the long-held attitudes of the so-called forgotten voters will change do so at their peril

The highest-rated television programme at Christmas 2019 was a *Gavin & Stacey* special, with 11.6m viewers, the highest TV audience for a decade. It was an emphatic popular endorsement for a Britain as absent from our media over the last 10 years as the series itself.

Gavin & Stacey is set in the Essex satellite town of Billericay and Barry Island, south-west of Cardiff, both in leave-voting constituencies. The two capital cities in England and Wales maybe a bus ride away for the *Gavin & Stacey* characters, but they are effectively in other countries.

In the US they refer to the 'flyover states' between the main cities on either coast. In Britain it's the places that fly by the train or car window as city people travel from one metropolitan centre to another.

Gavin & Stacey is a warm, humorous portrayal of working-class lives centred on family, friends and community. There are quirks and eccentricities, but no Brexit traumas or social breakdown, name calling or 'calling out'.

Even so, it did run into flak for the scene where the characters bellow out *The Fairytale of New York*, including the song's reference to a 'faggot'. But as Ruth Jones, one of the writers and actors, put it: "Characters in *Gavin & Stacey* are big-hearted, I believe. So I think no one is going to be intentionally hurt. But by the same token, they're not going to be completely politically correct or be aware of political correctness."

A well-established rhetoric

The two nations rhetoric is now well established: the elite versus the 'left behind'; graduates vs non-graduates; cities vs towns; social liberals vs social conservatives; Leave vs Remain. This is mostly seen by the 'elite' side in political terms. But, as Jones points out, there is another division: between the politically engaged and the politically detached.

As many found on the doorstep in the election, the issues that concern and motivate the people 'out there' are often very different from those defined by the politicians, activists, lobbyists and commentators.

But how did two whole sections of society become so detached from each other that in the 2016 EU Referendum the country was split down the middle in an uncomprehending face-off? As the Queen asked after the 2008 financial crash: why did no one see it coming?

Or to be more precise, why did the influencers, decision-makers, the comfortably off and politically engaged not grasp the degree of disaffection among those who felt themselves excluded from that world?

Remain was supported by the three mainstream political parties, by large majorities of MPs and Lords, business, the City, trade unions and most of academia. Brexiteers were outriders in all the main institutions. Only the media was split pretty evenly.

When David Cameron called the referendum – supported by all but 50 or so MPs – it was in the expectation of a comfortable remain victory, which would finally put to bed the divisions over Europe in the Tory party and the country.

A culture shock

There is no doubt the result was a culture shock for the self-defined liberal part of the country. Until the end of 2018 I was the letters editor of *The Guardian* and one of only four staff journalists out of hundreds to write in support of a leave vote. The packed meeting of editorial staff on the day of the result revealed a level of shock bordering on trauma. But *The Guardian* clearly reflected the views of its readers; the letters of shock, denial and outrage began to pour in (and haven't really stopped).

The divisions crystallised by the Brexit vote have two elements: the real world economic and social changes in our society and the reflection, representation and understanding of these changes in the media and public debate. Deindustrialisation, chiefly caused by the opening up of global markets and increased automation, has undermined the jobs and conditions of many people, particularly in the northern and coastal towns. The media, for its part, was (and is) a mainly uncritical cheerleader for those changes.

Much of the media has also been complicit in what Professor Matthew Goodwin of Kent University has called the 'Revolt on the Right' by the way it has represented and reported – or not reported – the other side of the tracks.

After the left-wing challenge to Margaret Thatcher's marketisation of the economy faded, following the defeat of the miners' strike and 'Big Bang' in the City of London that opened up the financial markets, Labour began an accommodation with the changes, encouraged and endorsed by pretty much all of the media.

New Labour, with its 'young country' rhetoric of aspiration and opportunity, set about forging a new coalition among the winners from globilisation in the service and tech sectors, distancing itself from older, manual workers, who saw their industries privatised or closed, their jobs and status lost, and communities ravaged. In response, some of these traditional Labour voters turned in protest to far-right parties such as the BNP and Ukip in local and European elections.

The fatal disconnect talks hold

It is perhaps here that the fatal disconnect – as charted in voting patterns by Goodwin in his post-election analysis, *Labour's defeat: A long time coming* – began. Until then, the BNP had been a nasty, but fringe group; while Ukip was a vehicle for Little Englander nostalgia, and Atlanticists who wanted a post-imperial Anglosphere.

Nigel Farage, a public school City trader, forged an unlikely coalition of neoliberal finance, which wanted more and faster globalisation, and small firm owners, who saw further clampdowns on wages and workers' rights as a way of saving their businesses, threatened by those very forces of globalisation.

Both sides of this unlikely coalition were able to unite in opposition to the European Union: the neoliberals saw it as putting constraints on globalisation, while those small businesses and independent traders bridled at the EU's labour and environmental standards.

The already Eurosceptic right-wing papers – the 'billionaire press' as Labour not unfairly dubbed it – quickly saw the potential of a new partner in this alliance that could give it electoral heft: those disillusioned and angry Labour voters.

In response, the Labour Party and the liberal left media increasingly defined themselves in opposition to this new harder right, with a growing undertow of antipathy to the working-class voters who used the new parties as a vehicle for protest votes.

It was one thing to vote Green or Lib Dem or for one of the nationalist parties as a protest, but to vote in protest for parties either actually racist or perceived as such was beyond the pale, however much those voters returned to Labour in general elections.

This growing tension came at a time of change in the social composition of both the Labour Party and the press. According to Goodwin, in 1964 37 per cent of Labour MPs came from manual occupation backgrounds; by 2015 this had fallen to just 7 per cent.

This was mirrored among the individual membership and in the decline of manual trade unions. In the process, Labour became less the representative of a socio-economic interest, than a community linked by values, such as anti-racism, gay rights, diversity, internationalism and support for immigration.

Opposition to growing inequality based on income, wealth and economic power remained, but only, it often seemed, if you signed up to these 'Labour values' first. This concept of a values-based party broke with the long tradition of social democratic parties united around a programme or manifesto for reform, beginning with the inaugural 1875 Gotha Programme of the first major social democratic party, the German SPD.

The media also became more middle-class. According to the Sutton Trust, in 2019 43 per cent of senior editors and broadcasters went to private schools and 44 per cent of columnists. Alan Milburn's most recent *State of the Nation* report estimated that only 11 per cent of journalists were from working class backgrounds. As the Sutton Trust's *Elitist Britain* commented: "If journalists and others working in the media all come from a similar background and have similar experiences, there is a danger that even with the best efforts to reach out, there are likely to be important stories, nuances or angles that they simply miss."

Will the divide end?

Three and a half years of Brexit warfare has entrenched the two nations division. Does the impasse that at last ended with the formal exit of the UK from the EU on January 31, 2020 open the way to ending the divide?

Goodwin has long argued that the space in British politics is for a party that supports high public spending and more 'conservative' (i.e. non-elite) social values. A position argued for by so-called 'Red Tories' on one side and 'Blue Labour' on the other. However, Goodwin also judged that it was easier for a party of the right to move left on public spending, than for a party of the left to change its cultural values.

It could be that Johnson's Tories have moved into that space with their high-spending pledges (NHS, education, police, infrastructure), while being anti-EU and tough on crime, security and immigration. But it may be easier to tear up widely discredited fiscal rules than the ingrained small-state attitudes that underlie them.

And the Brexit right that Johnson has been able to incorporate into the Conservative orbit has never been able to develop a policy programme beyond leaving the EU.

One of the new working-class Tories, Ben Bradley, who took the formerly solid Labour seat of Mansfield in 2017 and again in 2019 made clear the challenge in an article for the Conservative Home website.

He concluded: "We have to repay the people who have put us into power. They have done so off the back of our message, our Blue Collar Conservative promises to back our public services and invest in these places that have been so often forgotten, The proof will be in the delivery; in showing whose side we are on."

For Labour, it may be even more difficult. Keir Starmer, the frontrunner for the leadership and main architect of its tilt to a second referendum on Brexit, has indicated that the battle is lost and Labour must move on and try to obtain a close relationship with the EU – ironically Jeremy Corbyn's position from 2016 to 2018. But a new Labour leader still has to show the party can credibly implement its own public spending plans and reconnect with its former heartlands voters.

The values' issue is likely to be the key to bridging the divide both for Labour and wider liberal Britain.

Can they make their stringent acceptance criteria to its republic of virtue more welcoming to the *Gavin & Stacey* world of family and community? Can the media report on and represent life outside the metropolitan centres without the judgmental presuppositions that usually colour its views – on both left and right.

The Brexit vote could be seen as an assertion that the 'left behind' would not be ignored. To use Farage's phrase: will 'they' have to tell 'us' again?

References

Gavin and Stacey Christmas special watched by 11.6 million people, Guardian, December 26, 2019

https://www.theguardian.com/tv-and-radio/2019/dec/26/gavin-and-stacey-christmas-special-watched-by-116-million-people

Wikipedia https://en.wikipedia.org/wiki/Gavin_%26_Stacey

The Fairytale of New York https://www.youtube.com/watch?v=Pv0hlbWpa1w

Gavin and Stacey Christmas special: BBC viewers complain after Nessa and Bryn sing slur in 'Fairytale of New York', The Independent, December 26, 2019

https://www.independent.co.uk/arts-entertainment/tv/news/gavin-and-stacey-christmas-special-nessa-bryn-faggot-fairytale-of-new-york-bbc-catchup-a9260281.html

The Queen asks why no one saw the credit crunch coming, Daily Telegraph, https://www.telegraph.co.uk/news/uknews/theroyalfamily/3386353/The-Queen-asks-why-no-one-saw-the-credit-crunch-coming.html

Revolt on the Right: Explaining Support for the Radical Right in Britain, Ford, Robert, Goodwin, Matthew J. (2014) Routledge

See also National Populism The Revolt Against Liberal Democracy. Roger Eatwell and Matthew Goodwin, Pelican Books, 2018

Nine lessons from the election: Boris was lucky – but he also played his hand right, Matthew Goodwin, Spectator, December 24, 2019 https://blogs.spectator.co.uk/2019/12/nine-lessons-from-the-election-boris-was-lucky-but-he-also-played-his-hand-right/

Five reasons why we don't have a free and independent press in the UK and what we can do about , Ed Jones, Open Democracy, April 18, 2019 https://www.opendemocracy.net/en/opendemocracyuk/five-reasons-why-we-don-t-have-free-and-independent-press-in-uk-and-what-we-can-do-about/

Full text of The Gotha Programme, Internet Archive https://www.archive.org/stream/GothaProgramme/726_socWrkrsParty_gothaProgram_231_djvu.txt

Elites Britain 2019, Sutton Trust https://www.suttontrust.com/wp-content/uploads/2019/12/Elitist-Britain-2019.pdf; Britain's top jobs still in hands of private school elite, study finds, Guardian, June 25, 2019

State of the Nation 2017: Social Mobility in Great Britain, Social Mobility Commision State of the Nation 2017: Social Mobility in Great Britain https://assets.publishing.service.gov.uk/government/uploads/system/uploads/attachment_data/file/662744/State_of_the_Nation_2017_-_Social_Mobility_in_Great_Britain.pdf

Pale, male and posh: the media is still in a class of its own, Jane Martinson, Media Blog, April 29, 2019 https://www.theguardian.com/media/media-blog/2018/apr/29/journalism-class-private-education

Rise of the red Tories, Philip Blond, Prospect, February 28, 2009 https://www.prospectmagazine.co.uk/magazine/riseoftheredtories

What is Blue Labour, inews, December 16, 2020 https://inews.co.uk/news/politics/blue-labour-what-twitter-party-group-culturally-conservative-policies-explained-1342190

Voters tore down the Red Wall because they were sick of Labour talking down to them and holding them back, Ben Bradley MP, Conservative Home, December 17, 2019 https://www.conservativehome.com/platform/2019/12/ben-bradley-voters-tore-down-the-red-wall-because-they-were-sick-of-labour-talking-down-to-them-and-holding-them-back.html

Sir Keir Starmer: 'The argument about leave and remain goes with Brexit', Sky TV interview, January 5, 2020 https://news.sky.com/video/labour-leadership-sir-keir-starmer-quizzed-over-brexit-position-11901593

Note on the contributor

Nigel Willmott is a journalist and writer who has worked for the *Financial Times*, *Observer*, *Independent* and *Guardian*, where he was the letters editor until the end of 2018. He is co-author of *Drama at the Palace: Victorian Heyday* (2014) and *Drama at the Palace 2: Lost and Found* (2019), a history of the Alexandra Palace Theatre.

The election and identity politics

***

How different groups were reflected by both mainstream politicians and the media

John Mair

Britain and the British electorate are now a racial, ethnic and gender patchwork. Wasps no longer rule; white is no longer right. The way in which the major parties approached the 'hyphen' groups – Jewish, British Muslim, British, Indo-British and so on determined their electoral fate.

Labour and Jeremy Corbyn had two albatrosses round their neck – the potage they presented on Brexit and their having alienated Britain's Jews. Muslims and other South Asians felt equal discontent with perceived Tory 'Islamophobia' and their representation in the mainstream media.

First the editor of editor of the *Jewish Chronicle*, Stephen Pollard, explains in *That sense of relief on December 12* why he is proud of what his newspaper did to make that happen. "Ask almost any Jew today for their reaction to the election result and they will recall the same thing – even previous die-hard Labour supporters. The word that crops up repeatedly is the sense of relief as the exit poll was published at 10pm on December 12. Not because they were celebrating a win by the Conservatives, but because they dreaded a Labour victory," he writes.

One prominent journalism academic who hides neither his Jewishness nor his Labour sympathies is Ivor Gaber; here for the first time links the two.

Professor Gaber in *Anti – Semitism – the touchstone issue for the next Labour leader* says: "Growing up as a Jew in London in the 1950s (with the Second World War only a decade away) I needed nobody to explain to me why every old and musty prayer book I came across began with the words 'Next Year in Jerusalem'. Nor did my grandmother's story of her escape from a murderous Cossack mob overrunning her village in Czarist Russia sound like an out-of-the-ordinary piece of Jewish family history".

"The Jewish community in general, and its (the Labour Party's) Jewish members and supporters in particular, have felt initially offended, then confused and finally angry at seeing what it used to regard as natural political home drifting further and further away." Not just Jews and not just Labour.

With less effect and noise Britain's 4.4 per cent of the UK population who are Muslims could be heard bemoaning their treatment by the Conservative Party.

In *First they came for the Muslims... Islamophobia and the 2019 general election,* Aaqil Ahmed, the former head of religion at both the BBC and Channel 4, sees Islamophobia set to become the new normal for the Tory Party

"It's possible to argue that the real story of the election wasn't that Muslims held the balance, but that the real power they held was the ability to be used as whipping boys and a great unifier between the mainstreaming of the politics of the far right and the average voter," he writes.

He issues a stark warning: "Unless we wake up to the consequences of constant negative stories in the press and not treating Islamophobia as a problem that needs proper investigating within the Conservative Party, then the demonisation will grow and, as we know from history, it starts with words and never stops there."

Among the Muslims there are differentiations due to place of origin, the British-Bangladeshis seen as restaurateurs and little else, for example. Niaz Alam is a foreign correspondent at home in the UK. In *'Big enough to see, too small to count,* he says: "As for the British Bangladeshi vote, it was similarly predictable, being mainly pro-Labour and concentrated in safe seats. Just as the population of Bangladesh is less than a tenth of the Indian sub-continent's population, so British Bangladeshis are just a small part of the UK's non-white, mixed and religious minorities. Big enough to see, but small enough to overlook!"

"A Venn diagram of UK media stories would show coverage of British Bangladeshis to be almost completely encircled within coverage of British Asian and British Muslim communities. Commonwealth, cricket, curry and Islamist radicals – the usual suspects".

As on the doorsteps for the political parties, so on the television screens. Professor Barnie Choudhury, a British Asian, is a gamekeeper turned poacher. He was one of the first non-white BBC News correspondents and is now a media academic. In *It'll be all white on the night (the sequel): How UK's flagship television bulletins failed south Asian viewers again during a general election,* he holds his former colleagues' feet to the fire on their coverage of British Asian issues.

"What the predominantly white broadcast editors and commissioners appear to have failed to comprehend is that after being wooed by the Leave campaign, the views of south Asians have been ignored... What programme makers failed to understand is voting intentions among south Asians are no longer homogenous, and the days of a so-called community leader or husband or father telling families how to vote are, thankfully, dying out."

So, many elements of the patchwork that is now hypen Britain came away unhappy with the major parties and with non-reflections of themselves in the media. The hypens will increasingly become a big minority and then a majority of voters.

Watch our Boris and Keir.

That sense of relief on December 12

**Jeremy Corbyn could never throw off the issue of anti-Semitism in the
Labour Party in the 2019 election campaign. Here Stephen Pollard,
editor of the *Jewish Chronicle*, explains why he is proud of what his
newspaper did to make that happen**

In August 2015, I was sitting in a cottage in Devon, enjoying my summer holiday.
The previous month, a YouGov poll of Labour members for *The Times* had put
Jeremy Corbyn ahead in the party's leadership contest. For a while there were some
who doubted its veracity. But as the weeks passed it became increasingly clear that
Corbyn would romp home.

To most people – even political journalists – Jeremy Corbyn was just a minor
backbencher whom they had almost entirely ignored throughout his time in
parliament. But to the *Jewish Chronicle (JC)* he was anything but that.

As the Jewish community's leading newspaper, we have always monitored anti-
Semitism and those who ally with anti-Semites, and the name Jeremy Corbyn was
one our readers were extremely familiar with. We had been reporting his antics for
many years.

And so, as I sat in the Devon sunshine, I started to write a leader, which I
envisaged would go on the front page of the paper. In it, the paper posed seven
questions for Corbyn to answer, asking him to explain or justify behaviour such
as his description of Hezbollah and Hamas as 'friends'; his attendance at and
donations to meetings organised by notorious Holocaust denier Paul Eisen; and
his invitation to tea in the Commons as an 'honoured citizen' to Raed Salah, a
Muslim cleric convicted of the blood libel.

The leader had one real purpose, since I never expected Corbyn to answer the
questions: it was designed to flag up to other journalists that there were a number
of deeply troubling issues around the MP for Islington North. At no point until
then in the leadership contest had any of those matters been raised.

A purpose achieved

That August 14, 2015 issue of the *JC* achieved its purpose, since from then on questions started to be asked of Corbyn by other reporters. Indeed, that edition can be seen with hindsight as the start of a four-year long crisis for Labour, as Corbyn's own views – he was described by Labour MP Margaret Hodge as an 'anti-Semite and a racist'– and his party's refusal to take serious action against anti-Semitic members combined to force anti-Semitism to the forefront of British politics for the first time.

I have been editor of the *JC* for 11 years. For the first few years, the most frequent complaint from readers was that there was too much anti-Semitism in the paper. And they were right; it felt wrong that a vibrant community should somehow be defined by the often trivial antics of a few Jew haters.

We had even come up with a plan to 'box off' anti-Semitism stories into a section marked 'Anti-Semitism watch'. But 2015 changed all that. On January 9, an Isis terrorist murdered four Jews in a kosher supermarket in Paris. There was fear in the British Jewish community of a similar outrage here. Our readers felt that anti-Semitism – which the official CST figures showed was on the rise – was no longer something to be ignored. And then, a few months later, a man known to *JC* readers as a *bete noir*, was elected Labour leader.

Over the next four years, the *JC* devoted – through force of circumstance – enormous resources to uncovering and reporting instances of Labour anti-Semitism.

Our political editor, Lee Harpin, had superb Labour contacts through his time on the *Mirror* and these proved invaluable in leading us to a series of scoops. And a new phenomenon emerged: social media investigators, who spent untold hours digging up anti-Semitic posts and videos. Their contribution to exposing Labour's Jew haters was immense.

The complaint is sometimes made that we focused on Labour while ignoring the Tories (and LibDems). The answer is straightforward: the problem in other parties is isolated and sporadic.

We have, of course, reported them. But there was an avalanche of cases in the Labour Party. There were times when we were being sent two or three examples of Labour members' anti-Semitism a day. But while it was important for us to document all instances we found, news values dictated that some were more important. And although the story was an undercurrent up to and throughout the 2017 election, it was only really in March 2018 that it started to dominate coverage of the Labour Party.

The mural emerges

In that month, Luciana Berger, than a Labour MP, asked Corbyn about his support for a mural containing anti-Semitic imagery, *Freedom for Humanity*, painted on a property near Brick Lane in London's East End. The mural was painted in 2012 and depicted a group of businessmen and bankers sitting around a Monopoly-style board and counting money.

Corbyn offered support to the artist when he reported it was to be removed by the council. He wrote on Facebook: "Why? You are in good company. Rockefeller destroyed Diego Viera's mural because it includes a picture of Lenin."

The *JC* first reported this in 2015 (before the leadership election), and asked Corbyn about his comment. He ignored us. Then, after Berger raised the issue in 2018, a Labour spokesman said: "In 2012, Jeremy was responding to concerns about the removal of public art on grounds of freedom of speech. However, the mural was offensive, used anti-Semitic imagery, which has no place in our society, and it is right that it was removed."

This statement was astonishing. It acknowledged what it could hardly deny, that the mural was anti-Semitic. But it also said that Corbyn was defending it on "grounds of freedom of speech". In other words, we were expected to accept that it was perfectly fine for the leader of the Labour Party to support the existence of a large public anti-Semitic mural.

The obvious truth was that he liked the mural and saw it as wrong that it should be destroyed. There was almost no room for ambiguity over this, despite his spokesman's attempt to create some.

Even Corbyn's office could see that its explanation made things worse. So a few hours later, a statement from Corbyn himself was issued. This was incendiary.

"In 2012 I made a general comment about the removal of public art on grounds of freedom of speech. My comment referred to the destruction of the mural *Man at the Crossroads* by Diego Rivera on the Rockefeller Center. That is in no way comparable with the mural in the original post. I sincerely regret that I did not look more closely at the image I was commenting on, the contents of which are deeply disturbing and anti-Semitic," he said.

"I wholeheartedly support its removal. I am opposed to the production of anti-Semitic material of any kind, and the defence of free speech cannot be used as a justification for the promotion of anti-Semitism in any form. That is a view I've always held."

This statement led directly to the official communal bodies of the Jewish community, the Board of Deputies and the Jewish Leadership Council (JLC), calling an 'Enough is Enough' demonstration in Parliament Square a few days later – unprecedented for British Jews who are usually (rightly) caricatured by quiescence and an unwillingness to rock the boat.

The statement was clearly untrue. Corbyn saw the image. He went out of his way to comment on it on Facebook. He knew what the mural depicted; it is not possible not to see that after even a moment's glance. The Jewish caricatures were the entire point of the mural. (And the previous week, Corbyn was revealed to have been an active member of a private Facebook group which was suffused with anti-Semitism. His excuse then was the same as his excuse for supporting the mural: that he hadn't noticed it.)

A meeting but not of minds

The following month, Corbyn, Labour Party general secretary Jennie Formby and communications director Seamus Milne met representatives of the Jewish community. Expectations from the latter were low. In the event the meeting was even worse than they had expected. As one source present at the meeting put it: "They think it's all about process, that process is all that matters. Process is what they offer and it's the excuse they give why they can't do anything."

Jonathan Goldstein of the JLC told Corbyn that his parents had attended their first ever demonstration in Parliament Square. When they were nearby they were jeered by supporters of the Labour leader. "Why won't you stop these people?", Goldstein demanded. "It's not in my name", Corbyn replied. "So why are you not saying that loud and clear, with the passion you have shown over the Windrush scandal?" Goldstein responded. Corbyn is said to have shrugged his shoulders.

These events from 2018 matter because they are the prism through which the build-up to the 2019 election must be viewed.

From March 2018 onwards, the issue gained in intensity. Most coverage of Labour in the summer of 2018, for example, was dominated – not just in the *JC* but across the media – by Labour's initial refusal to adopt the internationally recognised working definition of anti-Semitism put together by the International Holocaust Remembrance Alliance.

Even at the time, it stuck many people as bizarre that Labour should destroy all chances it had of creating a positive news agenda over the summer by such a refusal. The reason was simple: Labour refused to adopt the definition because it didn't want to. (Eventually, recognising that the issue was doing the party untold political damage, it backtracked and adopted it – although only partially.)

In July 2018, the *JC*, the *Jewish News* and the *Jewish Telegraph* – fierce competitors – published an unprecedented joint front page, headlined United We Stand above a shared leader.

The events of 2018 meant that the words Labour and anti-Semitism were now firmly fixed together in voters' minds. A YouGov poll for the *JC* in May 2019 found that 50 per cent of all voters believed Labour had a problem with anti-Jewish racism.

Only 18 per cent of voters thought that Corbyn had been honest and transparent in responding to accusations of anti-Semitism in the Labour Party, compared to 60 per cent who said he was neither honest nor transparent.

Stories continued to emerge week by week – a Labour councillor here posting an anti-Semitic tweet, a Labour parliamentary candidate there mouthing off about the Rothschilds and Jewish loyalty to Israel. On and on it went.

Refreshing voters' minds

Come the election, the issue for the *JC* was simple. What could we do to refresh voters' minds about anti-Semitism? I had spent a frustrating week at the start of the campaign watching TV discussions and silently screaming at the failure to ask Labour MPs about the notion that their leader was a racist.

I came up with a simple idea that I thought might get attention. We would devote our next front page to an appeal to non-Jewish voters. Jewish voters would have no truck with Corbyn's Labour. Polls consistently showed that fewer than 10 per cent would vote Labour. But there was real fear in the community that other voters would not regard anti-Semitism as an important issue. So we tried to get the issue back on the agenda.

In bold 100pt were the words: "To our fellow British citizens," with the sub-head: "This front page is addressed not to our usual readers – but to those who would not normally read the *Jewish Chronicle*, to non-Jews. This is why." The lower half of the front page was occupied by a leader on Labour, Corbyn and anti-Semitism.

The idea worked. The front page received huge attention – not least because of the inspired idea of our creative director, Gus Condeixa, to design it as a billboard rather than a front page – and, more to the point, the issue started to be raised again. The following week the Chief Rabbi weighed in with a devastating piece in *The Times*, accusing the Labour leader of peddling 'mendacious fiction'. This lifted the issue to another plane.

Ask almost any Jew today for their reaction to the election result and they will recall the same thing – even previous die-hard Labour supporters. The word that crops up repeatedly is the sense of relief as the exit poll was published at 10pm on December 12. Not because they were celebrating a win by the Conservatives but because they dreaded a Labour victory. As editor of the *JC*, I am proud of the part we played.

Note on the contributor

Stephen Pollard has been editor of the *Jewish Chronicle* since 2008. Previously he worked for the *Evening Standard*, the *Daily Express*, *The Times* and the *Daily Mail*.

Anti-Semitism – the touchstone issue for the next Labour leader

The Labour Party's 2020 leadership election was about many things. It was about Brexit, Jeremy Corbyn and above all the future of the party itself, which is why dealing with anti-Semitism within its ranks became a touchstone issue. Ivor Gaber, who has watched anti-Semitism within Labour's ranks fester long before it hit the headlines, takes a personal view of its roots and consequences, and recommends a possible way forward

With the intervention of the Board of Deputies of British Jews into Labour's 2020 leadership election, anti-Semitism became one of the defining issues of the campaign, as it was in the 2019 general election.

As aspirants for the top post vied to be seen either as the true torch-bearer of the Corbyn inheritance or the change-or-die candidate, their pronouncements on the party's past and future handling of anti-Semitism was seen by many as a means of sorting the continuity sheep from the change goats. On one thing all were agreed – that there was no escaping the fact that anti-Semitism had been a wholly negative issue for Labour in 2019's election campaign.

Favourite Sir Keir Starmer, even before the leadership campaign started, told *The Guardian* that he wanted to see Labour's rulebook changed so that in a clear case of anti-Semitism a member was automatically expelled; and Rebecca Long-Baily – seen as the true heir to Jeremy Corbyn – told Radio 4 that she had privately pressed for tougher action to root out anti-Semitism in the party; and the third candidate Lisa Nandy called for a completely independent disciplinary system for dealing with the issue.

All candidates must have been acutely aware of how Labour's problems with anti-Semitism had impacted so very badly on perceptions of both the party and its leader during the election campaign.

It was all painfully personified by Corbyn's inadequate response to the issue when it first broke, his continuing failure to properly address it over the past three years, and then his extreme reluctance to apologise for it during the election.

It was also a significant campaigning distraction for the party and gave the Conservatives and Liberal Democrats an easy line of attack, enabling them to avoid being questioned about their own shortcomings (notably Islamophobia in the Conservative Party). And it was a cause of deep hurt and demoralisation, not just for Labour's Jewish members and supporters, but also for many non-Jews as well.

How little Corbyn knew

For me, Corbyn's cack-handed approach to the issue was crystallised in one moment during his campaign interview with Andrew Neil on BBC TV when he said: "It is an evil within our society, it is an evil that grew in Europe in the 1920s and onwards and ultimately led to the Holocaust." The statement revealed just how little the Labour leader knew about, or really understood, anti-Semitism and why Jews reacted so strongly against its perceived prevalence within the Labour Party.

Growing up as a Jew in London in the 1950s (with the Second World War only a decade away) I needed nobody to explain to me why every old and musty prayer book I came across began with the words 'Next Year in Jerusalem'. Nor did my grandmother's story of her escape from a murderous Cossack mob overrunning her village in Czarist Russia sound like an out-of-the-ordinary piece of Jewish family history.

Anti-Semitism did not begin in the 1920s in Europe. It dates back to the expulsion of the Jews from Palestine 2000 years ago and has continued ever since 'Jews were expelled from England in 1290', I wanted to yell at the screen during Corbyn's interview with Andrew Neil.

Given the scale of the anti-Semitic backlash that had been unleashed against Labour and its leader in the years preceding the election campaign, it was, or should have been, incumbent upon Corbyn to better inform himself about the history of anti-Semitism. Had he done so he might have come to see why attacks on Zionism – as opposed to attacks on the Israeli government – are seen by many Jews as inherently anti-Semitic.

Why, they ask, should the Jews be denied what almost every other group aspires to – a national home, a place of safety? After the attempted genocide of the Jewish people it should have come as no surprise to anyone that the Holocaust still plays such a dominant role, not just in Israeli politics but in the Jewish psyche almost everywhere.

This is characterised by a 'never again' mentality, coupled with a heightened sensitivity to the re-emergence of the worst forms of anti-Semitism and an unspoken sense of shame at a perceived lack of Jewish physical resistance to the Nazi genocide.

This is the context to an understanding of why a pre-election Survation poll suggested that 39 per cent of British Jews would consider emigrating if Corbyn were to move into Downing Street (fears I did not share) and why Jewish Labour MP Margaret Hodge recalled her father's advice: "You've got to keep a packed suitcase at the door, Margaret, in case you ever have to leave in a hurry." These might be seen as over-emotional responses, but the expulsion and flight of Jews from most Arab countries following the establishment of the State of Israel in 1948 is no distant memory.

Anti-Semitism doesn't have to be expressed in particular words to be experienced as such. Indeed, obvious anti-Semitic utterances are, or should be, easily dealt with. But anti-Semitism can manifest itself as an overarching anti-Zionism (which refutes the right of Jews to their own homeland) as opposed to opposition to the current policies and practices of Israel or its government.

It can also manifest itself in something as intangible as a hostile atmosphere in meetings which makes Jews in particular, but others as well, shift uncomfortably in their seats.

As a journalist who has attended virtually every Labour conference since 1979, I have always been struck, and concerned, by the atmosphere in the hall whenever the Israel/Palestine issue has been debated. For example, I recall how at the 2017 conference in Brighton Jeremy Corbyn was applauded when he condemned the attempted genocide of the Rohingya people in Myanmar and got a similar reaction when he spoke against the Saudi atrocities perpetrated against the people of Yemen, but when it came to condemnation of Israeli bombing of Gaza, the cheers turned to visceral yelps of approval.

Similar yelps greeted any rostrum speaker who spoke against Israeli policies, particularly if they declared themselves to be Jewish. Even debates about the evils of apartheid in the 1980s never aroused the same degree of emotion. The atmosphere at Labour conferences during debates about Israel/Palestine have always been, for me, redolent of the Big Brother-induced 'hate sessions' described by George Orwell in his novel 1984.

Labour's obsession

So why is Labour, and its activist membership, so obsessed (and that's the right word) with the Israel/Palestine issue? It is certainly true that for the past two decades Israel has had a harsh right-wing government that has not hesitated to use its superior military force against those it perceived as its enemy. It is also the case that it has illegally occupied Palestinian territory for the past 50 years and more. However, none of this explains Labour's obsession and how that obsession has morphed into anti-Semitism. The explanation is, I believe, many-faceted.

On the positive side, in the post-colonial era Labour has had an honourable tradition of supporting movements of national liberation. It also has an equally honourable tradition of aspiring to be an internationalist party whose concerns have always gone beyond Britain's borders and because Palestine was a British Mandate, it's always believed that the United Kingdom has had a particular responsibility to promote justice in this area of former UK rule.

On the negative side of the ledger there is the fact that there have always been sections of the British population that have harboured, and sometimes articulated, a strain of 'polite' anti-Semitism – sometimes articulated, *sotto voce*, as 'not quite one of us'.

But there are other specific Labour perspectives. In recent times the party has been flirting with populism, the discourse of 'the many not the few' begs the question: 'Who are the few?' Are they the bankers, the financiers, the industrialists, the lawyers and so on, groups in which Jewish representation outstrips its proportion in the population at large (and was symbolised by the anti-Semitic mural that Corbyn initially approved of)?

Another factor has been the recent influx into the party of both out-and-out anti-Semites (a small minority) and also of a larger minority of mainly younger Muslims, many of whom have been brought up in households where it was common to talk about 'the Jews' in a very generalised negative way and to conflate hatred of Israel with hatred of Jews. Recent research shows that British Muslims are three times more likely to hold anti-Semitic views than non-Muslims.

Into this already heady mix one adds Britain's own Jewish population (far smaller than is commonly assumed, now between 250,000 and 300,000) that has, until recently, felt a particular historical affinity towards the Labour Party.

Impoverished refugees arriving from Eastern Europe and Russia in the early years of the 20th century naturally gravitated towards the trade union and Labour movement. As the Jewish community has become more affluent, that tie began to weaken but it still remained strong up until, and including, the Blair/Brown years when the Labour Friends of Israel reception at the annual conference was a not-to-be missed event for most, if not all, members of the Labour cabinet.

A natural home drifts away

So as Labour has drifted into becoming, if not an anti-Semitic party (which I do not believe it to be), but sadly a party that has been prepared to tolerate an unacceptable level of anti-Semitic behaviour. The Jewish community in general, and its Jewish members and supporters in particular, have felt initially offended, then confused and finally angry at seeing what it used to regard as natural political home drifting further and further away.

As to whether the issue of anti-Semitism was a crucial determinate of voting behaviour in the 2019 general election it is difficult to gauge. A seat with one of the largest Jewish populations, Bury South in the North West of England, was won by the Conservatives from Labour (and even in this seat Jews constitute just 10 per cent of electorate), but then Labour lost 12 other seats in the same region.

The other constituencies with significant Jewish populations had results that were not markedly out of line with regional swings. Even Finchley and Golders Green, where Luciana Berger, a Jewish former Labour MP who had been a victim of anti-Semitic abuse, and had recently left Labour for the Liberal Democrats, took second place from Labour behind the Tories – but many had expected her to actually win the seat.

On the other hand, media monitoring by Loughborough University of the key issues in the campaign as reported by the media, indicated that anti-Semitism might have played a significant role. They did not specifically classify the item as such but grouped it under 'Standards and Scandals' and this was the fifth most reported issue during the election. Anecdotally it was an issue that appeared to attract a high level of coverage on social media.

Eventually research should tell us about the true effects of anti-Semitism on the result but it would be difficult to believe that, given the overwhelming negativity of the issue, it did not play some role in contributing to the perception of the Labour Party and its leader as lacking in competence, empathy and common decency – hardly a profile likely to win over a sceptical electorate.

A way forward?

Winning over a sceptical non-Jewish electorate could be a relatively easy undertaking, compared to persuading those many Jews who might still feel an attachment to the Labour Party and want to continue supporting it but are currently alienated. So what should be done to achieve this?

Clearly the ending of Corbyn's time as Labour leader will help, but only to the extent that his successor is not seen as more of the same. This required that during Labour's leadership campaign it was vital that anti-Semitism was not swept under the carpet and that all the leadership candidates made unequivocal statements about where they personally stood on the issue and acknowledged that the Party, to date, had got it wrong.

Labour needed to ensure that in future it acts far more swiftly in dealing with anti-Semitic behaviour than it has done in the past and, while there might be some allegations which legitimately require further investigation, the leaked evidence from the Jewish Labour Movement to the Equality and Human Rights Commission investigation into anti-Semitism in the party revealed an appalling litany of evidence about unambiguous anti-Semitic abuse which had not led to immediate expulsion.

But the need for action was not just confined to the leadership. Labour members themselves need to be far more watchful as to the emotional content of their words and behaviour when debating the Israel/Palestine issue.

Labour's new leader needs to reach out to the Jewish community in a less defensive mode than has been the case in the past, in effect seeking advice as to how the Party can best grapple with this issue.

The ten pledges, which the Board of Deputies of British Jews succeeded in getting all the leadership candidates to sign up to, was a good starting point, indicating a constructive approach to the issue by both sides. There also needs to be a recognition that Labour's anti-Semitism problems were not a unique failing. The Conservatives' extreme reluctance to hold a full and independent investigation into Islamophobia in their ranks (as opposed to discrimination more generally) is an ongoing failure of both leadership and morality, leaving them in no position to criticise Labour's own failings.

If Labour is able to meet these challenges then the new leader of the party will have a better claim on the loyalty (and the votes) of its former Jewish supporters than has been the case in the recent past; and British politics will be the healthier for it.

Note on the contributor
Ivor Gaber is Professor of Political Journalism at the University of Sussex. As a broadcast journalist he has worked for BBC TV and Radio, ITN, Channel 4 and Sky News.

First they came for the Muslims…
Islamophobia and the 2019
general election

Negative stories about Muslims have become a regular feature in many newspapers, so there is clearly an audience. Aaqil Ahmed explores why he thinks this is the case and why its seepage into the political discourse of the Conservative Party is a worry for all of us

The 2019 election was supposed to be the election where the Muslim community held the balance of power in a number of constituencies. There really isn't a need for an over-elaborate analysis of the election to know that wasn't the case. As voters you could argue Muslims were largely irrelevant to the outcome, but as a subject matter they were definitely key to many people's votes.

It's possible to argue that the real story of the election wasn't that Muslims held the balance, but that the real power they held was the ability to be used as whipping boys and a great unifier between the mainstreaming of the politics of the far right and the average voter.

Islamophobia, or just being derogatory about Muslims, it seems is a vote winner for many and generates significant column inches and that's where any real analysis of the Muslim impact on the election should focus.

I'm a Muslim, get me out of here….
On many of my talks I ask a simple question: what is the Muslim population of the UK? Replies are often around 10-20 per cent. Journalism students often include the odd expert who gets it, but generally the figures are around these, with the odd 30 per cent thrown in. The answer is very different. Muslims make up, according to census figures, 4.4 per cent of the UK population, 5 per cent of England and around 1.5 per cent of both Wales and Scotland.

It goes without saying that in particular geographical areas those figures are more significant, with the vast majority living in London, the West Midlands, North West England and Yorkshire.

The overall numbers across the UK would suggest that this is a group that shouldn't attract the level of attention it does. But they do, and for me it is a mixture of a number of things; poor religious literacy; the inability to cope with religion in the public space; and a press that seems obsessed with them.

Poor religious literacy is a huge issue within the UK. We live in a time and a continent, often referred to as being post-Christian Europe, a period and place where religion is a spent force and irrelevant. The problem with this analysis is that Western Europe may have moved on from traditional religion, but the rest of the world hasn't. Right now, across Britain and Europe, people from around the world are living in the continent and to them religion is still important.

And those people aren't just Muslim. Britain has more than one million Hindus and many other faiths growing in numbers, such as Sikhs and Buddhists. While traditional Anglican Christianity may be in decline, through immigration and conversion Catholicism and Pentecostal Christianity are growing. Migration patterns and low birth rates amongst traditional European communities suggest that the percentage of people with faith is going to grow and by 2050 it is suggested that 40 per cent of Britain's population will have some form of ethnic minority or migrant background.

So these numbers, while not in the 10s or 20s percentages, are still significant when you factor in the religiosity of the people involved. For many of them any notion of post-Christian Europe is irrelevant: religion still means something to their daily lives and it's that intersection with the public space that makes people with no interest in religion, and no religious literacy whatsoever, uncomfortable, whether it is consciously or unconsciously.

How many times have you heard someone say that they know nothing about religion? That they think of it as a badge of honour? Compare that with if you were to say that you knew nothing about race, cared nothing about sexuality. Surely they are similar; people are often rightly or wrongly defined by characteristics such as race, sexuality or faith. Can it really be acceptable to not know or care about any one of these?

But it's not just an issue of fairness or accepting diversity because it's the right thing to do. A society that has such poor religious literacy creates a vacuum and into this vacuum it's possible to say anything about peoples beliefs and for that uninformed knowledge to lead to intolerance and prejudice.

The first chair of press regulator, the Independent Press Standards Organisation (Ipso), Sir Alan Moses said in 2019: 'I speak for myself, but I have a suspicion that [Muslims] are from time to time written about in a way that [newspapers] would simply not write about Jews or Roman Catholics'.

Most Muslims, who have heard of Ipso, would argue that Sir Alan has presided over a regulator that has allowed newspapers to print silly scare stories and, in some cases, like the now debunked *Times* story about a 'white Christian child forced into

Muslim foster care' to effectively get away with doing as they please.

There would be many journalists and commentators who would argue with this opinion, but it's a view shared by many Muslims and non-Muslims. It is easy to be able to prod Muslims and refer to them in ways you wouldn't be able to about other groups in society. Why? Because the audience and the journalists know very little and what they think they know, they often don't like.

The enemy within?

So in the election we had dossiers on Islamophobia within the Conservative Party, including social media comments suggesting that 25 Conservative councillors posted racist material, which included Muslims being described as barbarians and the enemy within.

The Enemy Within is the title of Baroness Sayeda Warsi's book about many things, including her journey in the Conservative Party. At times a one-woman crusader against Islamophobia in her party she has pushed for the Conservatives to understand the depth of the problem she feels they face and to hold an inquiry into it.

MP Sajid Javed brought this issue up in one of the Tory leadership debates, and suddenly everyone agreed – yes we need to have an enquiry. Great news, the Baroness's argument had won and everything must be ok as it was pushed over the line by someone who has been the Home Secretary and was about to become Chancellor of the Exchequer.

So far it hasn't yet worked out as many imagined. There will be an inquiry of sorts, but it won't solely focus on alleged Islamophobia and will be a general broad brush review of how the party handles discrimination complaints.

There are many who point to the fact that the party is led by someone who describes niqab wearers as resembling letterboxes or bank robbers. However, maybe a better indication as to why the lack of interest in rooting out any alleged Islamophobia is more to do with a survey held in the summer of 2019 by YouGov for the anti-racism group Hope not Hate.

The survey found that 60 per cent of Conservative Party members believe Islam is generally a threat to western civilisation; 43 per cent did not want a Muslim as Prime Minister and 40 per cent want to lower the numbers of Muslims entering Britain.

Of course, it would be unfair to say this is scientifically accurate, or necessarily a true reflection of the majority of Conservative politicians or voters, but when you add in the apparent disregard for the comments of Boris Johnson with the dossier of troubling statements by party members and politicians to this survey, then it makes it easy to understand the party's lack of interest in investigating this as well as the press's lack of desire to hold them to account.

This survey shares with many others of the general public a sense of a them and us when it comes to Muslims and the rest of society. Yes, it can be attributed to that lack of religious literacy and deep rooted mistrust of religion in the public space, but I think it is something else – a sense that this is an easy target and a group that you can be openly prejudiced about without being labelled a racist.

The Labour Party was rightly attacked for its inability to deal with accusations of anti-Semitism. Many Jewish members came forward with horror stories that seemed to suggest the sensible thing to do would be to root out this prejudice. It didn't happen, either at all or quickly enough to many people, and the party and its leadership has been chased on this relentlessly.

Compare it to the Islamophobia accusations against the Conservative Party. There are no hierarchies of intolerance and this is definitely not a moment to pit anyone against anyone else. It was right to hold Labour to account on some of its members failings and prejudice, but why not give equal treatment for the Conservatives and Islamophobia?

Double standard

Imagine a poll that suggested 43 per cent of Labour members did not want a Jewish leader or that 40 per cent of Labour members wanted to limit the Jewish population? Would it be expected to dominate the front pages and lead the news agenda for days, if not weeks?

That is the double standard that many Muslims point to when assessing how they are treated by political parties, the press or broadcasters. The secretary general of the Muslim Council of Britain (MCB), Harun Khan, has written to the Director General of the BBC on the issue of the BBC's coverage of Islamophobia in the Conservative Party, saying 'particularly during the general election, it has not given due prominence to the Conservative Party's systematic problem with Islamophobia'.

The Muslim Council of Britain has also formally complained to the Equality and Human Rights Commission over what it suggests is Islamophobia in the Conservative Party.

And now that the general election dust has settled? The Conservatives' internal investigation will no doubt uncover a few rotten apples, but no prevalence of Islamophobia; the Prime Minister will occasionally put no doubt his foot firmly in his mouth, and Baroness Warsi will continue to try to drag her party into where she thinks they need to be in the 21st century.

Why would she persevere? She is a one-nation Tory and proud of it. And like many people also realises there is not one Muslim community, but a series of multiple communities with contrasting mother country cultures, differing generational maturity in Britain, and very diverse socio economic profiles.

What is to say that within this growing mix of people that there will not be a significant number with interests that chime with those of the party?

Do the Conservatives care?

With economic prosperity you could presume that many would support the party, but the question is – if the party doesn't address these allegations of Islamophobia within, will they be able to attract enough Muslims to join or vote for them? You could mischievously ask when you hark back to the YouGov survey, do they need to care? In the short term the answer is no, but in the long term demographic change would suggest yes, they will need to address it and they will need help in doing so.

Which brings me back to those bold statements about Muslims holding the balance of power. Both the MCB and the Muslim advocacy group Mend put out separate research looking at various constituencies up and down the country and juxtaposed them with the demographic break down in each one.

If Muslims had voted as a collective for the Labour Party then in theory they would have unseated many Conservatives. One seat that was referenced in this way was that of the prime minister. He held on, as did many others, and the unseating that went on around the country was not Conservative but Labour.

The issue with the balance of power angle is it requires too many factors to go one way, for things to be almost perfect. No one votes as a block generally, some people don't even bother to vote and understanding geography is the key.

The specific areas that most Muslims live in are generally very urban and the last few elections have seen these areas in England at least, vote Labour. Of course, in 2019 we saw many seats turn blue in Labour heartlands, but Muslim votes were not really a factor in this. Hence, Muslims holding the balance theory may be way too early and may not ever deliver, as their future economic success may change the voting patterns of many.

What 2019 did do was deliver a record number of Muslim MPs. Despite allegations of Islamophobia, the Conservatives increased their number from three to five representatives and it will be interesting to observe if this will help change a few hearts and minds in the party about dealing with the Islamophobia allegations.

I haven't until now brought up Brexit, and the opinion that many have, that it's emboldened many racist views and mainstreamed language that demonises the 'other'.

In my view there is a lot in this view, but there is more to life than Brexit. It's one part of the 2019 general election story but not the only one. You would hope it won't be an issue come the next election.

My guess is that without owning up to our poor religious literacy and weak press regulation then Muslims and overt Islamophobia will be a component in the next election.

Unless we wake up to the consequences of constant negative stories in the press and not treating Islamophobia as a problem that needs proper investigating within the Conservative Party, then the demonisation will grow and, as we know from history, it starts with words and never stops there.

Note on the contributor
Aaqil Ahmed is Professor of Media at Bolton University and a non-executive director of both Ofcom and the Advertising Standards Authority. He is a media consultant and former Head of Religion at both the BBC and Channel 4.

Big enough to see, too small to count

People see what they want to see. December's vote made no difference to the UK's relationship with Bangladesh or perceptions of the British Bangladeshi community, says Niaz Alam

"Everything we see and enjoy comes from the heritage and contribution of the British Jewish community, which right now feels vulnerable."

Rushanara Ali, MP for Bethnal Green and Bow, at election hustings, Docklands and East London Advertiser, December 6, 2019

"The thing about Bangladesh was (pause)... These were our people. In West London, we grew up in a really mixed-race place... The Bangladeshis tended to work very hard, so we respected them... we wanted to help. It was a terrible tragedy. Flood wasn't it?"

Pete Townshend of The Who, speaking to the Foreign Press Association, at The Sloane Club, London, November 7, 2019

Nobody learned much new from the 2019 UK Election. Opinion polls had consistently predicted the Conservative Party would regain the majority it achieved in 2015. Its victory, therefore, should not have been a surprise. For all their parliamentary votes and wins, it was soon clear opposition parties could not and more fatally for them, would not, agree an electoral alliance that could defeat Boris Johnson.

Sadly, for journalists at least, December's result made even less difference to the UK's relationship with Bangladesh or perceptions of the British Bangladeshi community,

'Made in Bangladesh' clothing labels might be a common sight, but from the UK perspective, the size of trade with Bangladesh is not hugely significant. Unlike India which has the size and clout to make post Brexit visa demands, the mutual Bangladesh-UK interest is on keeping the current trajectory. When global media deigns to cover Bangladesh, it is far more often as a byword for climate change and disasters than for its c.8 per cent GDP growth.

As for the British Bangladeshi vote, it was similarly predictable, being mainly pro-Labour and concentrated in safe seats. Just as the population of Bangladesh is less than a tenth of the Indian sub-continent's population. so British Bangladeshis are just a small part of the UK's non-white, mixed and religious minorities. Big enough to see, but small enough to overlook.

A Venn diagram of UK media stories would show coverage of British Bangladeshis to be almost completely encircled within coverage of British Asian and British Muslim communities. Commonwealth, cricket, curry and Islamist radicals – the usual suspects.

Inevitably, jihadi bride Shamima Begum, not Rushanara Ali, the MP for Bethnal Green and Bow quoted above,[1] was 2019's most talked about British Bangladeshi in the UK media.

For most people this was just another story about transnational terrorism and Islamist radicals, not something to change prevailing images of Bangladesh. It was somewhat superfluous for the Bangladesh Ministry of Foreign Affairs to state, "It may also be mentioned that she never visited Bangladesh in the past despite her parental lineage."[2]

Speaking to the Foreign Press Association in November 2019, Pete Townshend sounded very pleased to be asked for memories of The Who's headline role in September 1971 at the all-day *Goodbye Summer* festival in aid of Bangladesh at the Oval cricket ground. Held six weeks after the more famous *Concert for Bangladesh* in New York on August 1, 1971, it drew as many people as George Harrison's groundbreaking fundraiser, but is relatively forgotten.

Historically, both concerts have political significance beyond just raising funds for the relief of refugees. Harrison himself highlighted this in his 1980 memoirs,[3] noting that "while we were setting up the concert the Americans were shipping arms to Pakistan". The Beatle reflected that using the very name Bangladesh in the midst of war, at a moment when independence was far from certain, helped to shine a light and provided a "necessary morale booster for the Bengalis."[4]

Four decades on, Pete Townshend was understandably hazy about some aspects, but still provided some classic rock star anecdotes about the event at the Oval.[5] He also waxed lyrically to the international journalists present about growing up in a multicultural part of West London, to such an extent that by the end of his reverie he could not recall the cause for which the concert was held. Naturally he asked, "Flood wasn't it?"

In the light of Rorschach's referendum
Like Rorschach's inkblot test, reactions to British politics in the aftermath of the EU referendum lie very much in the eye of the beholder: the democratic will of the people, or reaping the reward of intolerance?

Many people from ethnic minorities voted for Brexit for the same broad mixture of reasons as other Leave voters. It is ridiculous to label them all as racist or seduced by imperial nostalgia. Yet, when some people voting the other way claim the result was influenced by racism, anecdotes often support them.

While many advocates of global Britain, both sincere and disingenuous, shout loudly of their keenness to build ties beyond Europe, some Tory Brexiteers, before and after their big election victory, blow dog whistles about allegations of electoral fraud, especially involving British Muslim communities, to call for rather un-British voter ID rules at polling stations.[6]

The assumption that intolerance amplified by social media silos has made life less civil, seems to have become universal in recent years.

"Being made to feel acutely foreign again feels unacceptable."

Kavita Puri, presenter of the BBC Radio 4 series *Three Pounds in My Pocket*[7] highlights the use of the word 'again', by the daughter of Runi Sayeed, a Bangladeshi-born teacher settled in Britain since 1968.

After 50 years in the UK, Sayeed found it unsettling and unusual to hear someone shout "Why don't you go back to your country? Why are you here?" as she got off a bus. This sort of public abuse had, like the fear of random racist attacks hugely declined during her half century in the UK.

It is a paradox that, while Britain today is more diverse, more inclusive and less insular than 1968, an astonishing amount of political rhetoric has become redolent of the language that got Enoch Powell sacked from the shadow Cabinet 50 years ago, Of course, as Pete Townshend was illustrating, pre-EU Britain was not a monolithic monoculture either, so perhaps it is just the belief that time always brings improvement, which is wrong, Intolerance is always with us, it just needs to be stoked.

Anti-Semitism and identity politics

Compared to the British Pakistani community whose political leaders include Chancellor Sajed Javid and Mayor of London Sadiq Khan, the cohort of four British Bangladeshi MPs is not nationally significant, but worth listening to, nonetheless.

As the longest serving member, the advice given in December by Rushanara Ali, to fellow Labour candidate and now newly elected MP for Popular and Limehouse, Apsana Begum, to go further than just apologise after being accused of anti-Semitism, deserves wider hearing.

Not least because the failure of the Labour leadership to fully deal with cases of anti-Semitism, personified by Jeremy Corbyn's inept leadership and slowness to say sorry, was one of the most talked about issues of 2019.[8]

Begum, a well-known Momentum activist, had shared a post on Facebook criticising Saudi Arabia, which asserted the regime's actions were due to it being in thrall to 'Zionist masters', a clearly conspiratorial anti-Semitic trope, which Begum acknowledged as such when asked to apologise.

After explaining the importance of showing zero tolerance to such language and notions, Ali said: "It's for her to rebuild trust and reach out to the community she has deeply offended".[9]

Her advice is rooted in experience of supporting former MP Oona King when she was being challenged by George Galloway's campaign to wrest the Bethnal Green and Bow seat from Labour in 2005, under the Respect party banner.

While an anti-Iraq war protest vote was bound to eat into King's 10,000 majority that year, as Galloway won in the end by barely 820 votes, the margin was small enough to have been influenced by parts of the assorted left wing and Islamist factions backing Galloway, spreading untruths and attacking King's Jewish roots.

Referring to the slanders, political and racial, thrown about during the campaign, Ali said: "I know what any form of anti-Semitism and racism is like. I worked for my Labour predecessor Oona King, a Jewish MP who experienced anti-Semitism and saw what it does to people." She highlighted the Battle of Cable Street and the common history of Jewish and Muslim communities having to fight racism in the East End, a salutary reminder in an age when the zeitgeist seems to only bring forth division.

When factors like class, education, income, profession and location of constituency are taken into account, psephologists are likely to back Ali as there is not much evidence of voters who put religious identity or views on Israel/Palestine ahead of all else, swaying the outcome of UK elections, except of course in the sectarian quagmires of Northern Ireland.

Family ties

Across town, the other two British Bangladeshis in the Commons are both noted for having supported Remain and a second referendum. Both are also known for famous relatives; Ealing and East Acton MP Rupa Huq for sister and *Blue Peter* presenter Konnie; and Hampstead and Kilburn MP Tulip Siddiq for her aunt, Sheikh Hasina, the prime minister of Bangladesh.

Regularly asked by human rights groups and her aunt's political opponents alike to criticise Bangladeshi authorities for instances of state agencies kidnapping, torturing and sometimes completely 'disappearing' critics of the government, Ms Siddiq regularly desists.

For good measure she told *The Guardian* in 2019: "You don't get to be where she is by listening to your niece on national security issues. There are two words she'd say to me: 'Fuck off'."[10]

Meanwhile Huq, an experienced lecturer and academic expert on popular culture, has in brother-in-law Charlie Brooker, creator of *Black Mirror*, the perfect writer to draw upon to comment on the world in which we are living.

As 2020 dawns, Australia is burning. Coal remains its biggest export and economics deems it efficient for some of this to be burned in countries like Bangladesh, to help make goods sought by consumers in countries like the UK, which have outsourced much of their manufacturing needs and pollution.

Brexit is trivial when you look at it properly. The fact we couldn't solve it that way bodes ill for the real problems to come in the decade ahead.

Notes

¹ Election hustings report, *Docklands and East London Advertiser* 6 December 2019 https://www.eastlondonadvertiser.co.uk/seasonal/election/general-election-rushanara-at-bethnal-green-bow-hustings-1-6412479

² Shamima Begum is not a Bangladeshi citizen, says foreign minister *Daily Mail* 20 February 2019 https://www.dailymail.co.uk/news/article-6726303/Shamima-Begum-not-Bangladeshi-citizen-says-foreign-minister.html

³ I ME MINE by George Harrison — Genesis publications (1980)
Ganga Publishing Simon Schuster ISBN 0–671–42787–

⁴ As discussed by the author in All the Concerts for Bangladesh https://medium.com/@opinionmongrel/all-the-concert-s-for-bangladesh-25bb5387491a

⁵ From interview transcribed by the author see also Pete Townshend: We were honoured to have performed in 1971 Dhaka Tribune 1st December 2019 https://www.dhakatribune.com/bangladesh/2019/12/01/pete-townshend-we-were-honoured-to-be-able-to-help

⁶ George Eaton New Statesman 13 December 2019 https://www.newstatesman.com/politics/uk/2019/12/conservatives-will-use-their-triumph-ruthlessly-reshape-british-democracy

⁷ https://www.bbc.co.uk/programmes/b065z2x3

⁸ Corbyn not dealing with anti-Semitism *Financial Times* 26 November 2019 https://www.ft.com/content/5e9fb766-0fd4-11ea-a7e6-62bf4f9e548a

⁹ Hustings reported in *The Docklands and East London Advertiser* 6 December 2019 https://www.eastlondonadvertiser.co.uk/seasonal/election/general-election-rushanara-at-bethnal-green-bow-hustings-1-6412479

¹⁰ Interview with Zoe Williams The Guardian 12 February 2019 https://www.theguardian.com/lifeandstyle/2019/feb/12/tulip-siddiq-i-needed-a-caesarean-instead-i-was-at-parliament and http://camdennewjournal.com/article/tulip-siddiq-says-prime-minister-aunt-would-tell-her-to-fuck-off-if-she-tried-to-intervene-in-bangladeshi-politics

Note on the contributor

Niaz Alam is London Bureau Chief of the *Dhaka Tribune*. A qualified solicitor, he has worked on responsible business and ethical investment issues since 1992. He sat on the board of the London Pensions Fund Authority between 2001-2010 and is a former vice-chair of War on Want. During 2018 and 2019, he was honorary secretary of the Foreign Press Association in London.

It'll be all white on the night (the sequel): How UK's flagship television bulletins failed south Asian viewers again during a general election

Influential south Asian decision makers want an inquiry into why broadcasters did not cover specific issues affecting their communities, says Professor Barnie Choudhury

All national politics are local. When it comes to Leicester, one man has dominated the city politically for more than 30 years. Keith Vaz was a modern-day pioneer being one of four black Asian minority ethnic parliamentarians in the class of 1987, the first non-white MPs since World War II.[1] His suspension from the House in 2019, after a 'drug and sex inquiry',[2] and his subsequent decision to step down as an MP, warranted national television, radio and newspaper coverage. But it remains a mystery why broadcasters ignored the consequences for Labour in the 2019 General Election. It was just one example of how they might have covered the subsequent influence of, and issues affecting, south Asian voters creating a series of important and compelling national stories.

Improving times?

Those who study diversity in broadcast journalism, have criticised employers for a lack of racial representation both on and off-air. We have campaigned for decades for change, and if we are honest, we should admit broadcasters have listened and acted. By any impartial measure, and content analysis of output is probably as good a test as any, we can hear and see a greater number of non-white voices in terms of non-expert and expert contributors than, say, a decade ago. Certainly, on-air talent boasts high profile award-winning representation.

But we still need to do more. Ofcom confirmed that in a report last year.

> Last year, we reported that the people who work for the BBC are not wholly representative of the UK population. This is still the case 12 months on.[3]

And herein lies a major problem. The lack of BAME senior leaders, programme editors, commissioners and decision makers mean the BBC, and others, continue to disappoint. So, it is not surprising in the three general elections in five years, we have not seen any visible signs of improvement in terms of diverse story selection, story treatment and storytelling.

Methodology

The flagship news programme on the main broadcasters remains the nightly broadcast at 10pm. The BBC 10 O'clock News, for example, boasts a regular audience of more than four million, according to one BBC News executive. For the past two general elections I have content analysed the number of south Asian specific stories on 'The 10' for BBC, ITV and Sky News. The methodology is an adaptation of that used by Professor Steve Jones in his review into BBC's coverage of science for the Trust.[4] What I was looking for explicitly were stories driven by specific 'issues, concerns and actions' of south Asian voters or players. For example, the changing voting intentions of south Asians, especially women, over three generations or topics which specifically affected these communities in a Brexit election, such as those in business.

Performance

The Commons voted for a December 12 poll on October 29, 2019. That meant there were 44 editions of nightly news to report specifically on the general election. That meant each broadcaster had a total of 1320 minutes of airtime to fill, give or take, weekend variations included. Taking into account big, breaking or unexpected stories, such as Prince Andrew's interview with Emily Maitlis, Donald Trump's impeachment hearings, the floods in the north of England and the terror attack in London, there was still more than enough air time to spend, say, ten minutes per flagship programme, on three definitive national issues which affect south Asian communities.

How do I come up with this figure? Well, south Asians numbered more than three million people or five per cent of the UK population in the last Census in 2011, almost a decade ago. We pay a TV licence fee, and some of us subscribe to Sky. Five per cent of 1320 minutes equals 66. So why would any broadcaster begrudge a paltry ten minutes, especially when this was the Brexit election? The rise in south Asians since 2011 means this ten-minute figure is a very conservative one.

The outcome was both BBC and ITV 10 o'clock news programmes did not have a single specifically UK-south Asian report, while Sky News had one story in its 10pm slot. This bald statistic does a disservice to Sky News because it did commission one of its correspondents, Inzamam Rashid, to examine the south Asian vote.[5] Sadly, his report, a cut-down of a documentary and repeated 12 times across the day, did not make it in the flagship programme.

Why single out south Asians?

The fact is that over time south Asian voters have deserted Labour. But in 2019 it looked as if they were returning in greater numbers, according to Runnymede, the equality think-tank.[6] Simon, now Lord, Woolley, director of Operation Black Vote, urged BAMEs to get more involved in this election.

> We've now compiled a list of 100 seats in which the number of ethnic minority voters is larger than the majority held in that constituency – so they again have the chance to change the course of this election.[7]

After these elections three questions still remain unanswered. First, how did south Asians vote during Brexit? Second, how has Brexit affected them? Third, what effect did Brexit have on their voting intentions on December 12?

What the predominantly white broadcast editors and commissioners appear to have failed to comprehend is that after being wooed by the Leave campaign, the views of south Asians have been ignored.[8] They simply overlooked issues which would have shown they cared about their minority viewers, rather than approach it from a purely white lens. What programme makers failed to understand is voting intentions among south Asians are no longer homogenous, and the days of a so-called community leader or husband or father telling families how to vote are, thankfully, dying out.

In crude terms Brexit was about two things: business and immigration. For many south Asians who voted Leave, it was, again crudely, about identity and racism. They identified as British, rather than European, and fell for a false promise that our immigration rules would be better and fairer once we left the EU.[9]

But business is a big deal, and south Asians cried out for stability and decision making. 'Get us out or keep us in, one way or the other', was their cry, according to Uday Dholakia[10] from the National Asian Business Association. Mr Dholakia, a former commissioner for the Broadcasting Standards Commission and board adviser on America's Minority and Media Telecommunication Council, believes the views of south Asians are always ignored during times of big economic and political stories.

> The economic multiplier that the Asian communities create is forgotten. Brexit has been hitting Asian businesses hard over the last year, and there's been no coverage except for the BBC Asian Network. The BBC, as it is funded by the taxpayer, should have dissected this issue not just in regions, but diversity aspects as well. Their views contribute to policy and tests the politicians' commitment. My concern is this is going to get worse, because the broadcasters will say diversity is being taken care of on other digital channels.

Special perspectives

Anecdotal evidence suggests broadcasters have a set view on how general elections should be covered and there is no allowing for the changing face of Britain. South Asian newspapers, such as Eastern Eye, for which I write, know their audience. Executive editor Shailesh Solanki[11] ensured his reporters reflected south Asian opinion from across the country.

> We had an exclusive story which had impact, where 120 or so business leaders wrote to Eastern Eye in support of Boris Johnson's business policies, as opposed to Jeremy Corbyn's. We interviewed all the party leaders, except for the Lib Dems, on issues affecting south Asians. We questioned them on immigration, equality, racism and creating a level playing field, and the NHS. Few are talking about NHS staffing levels and asking where the doctors and nurses are going to come from. If south Asians left the NHS, it would collapse.

What the broadcasters failed to grasp, said Solanki, was this forensic examination of voting habits would have interested television audiences, just as how the northern white working-class man or woman switched from Labour to 'lend' the Tories their support.

> It's not difficult to engage with south Asian communities. They [broadcasters] just need to go to places which have high south Asian populations. They should have south Asian focus groups. You see them doing that generally, but why don't they get one with just south Asians, different age groups, different demographics and different professions and canvas their opinions. Broadcasters would have a host of issues to discuss, and they would be able to mine such different opinions we just don't see on mainstream television.

Solutions

All three broadcasters failed to look at how south Asian businesses were lobbying all the main parties. Two of the three simply made little or no effort to engage in any meaningful way with south Asians. Where Sky News excelled was in its commissioning of attitude polls on voters' intentions with YouGov. Since poll companies charge a little shy of £10,000 for about 20 questions to be asked of 1001 people, then this was a huge investment by Rupert Murdoch's broadcaster. But where it could have capitalised was to make sure there was an ethnic breakdown, especially targeting south Asian voters.

Sky News covered the story about Hindus using WhatsApp to persuade followers not to vote for Labour. All three failed to grasp the potential upset in Leicester East.[12] Here, British-Indian voters were angry with Labour for its criticism of Indian prime minister, Narendra Modi, and the apparent imposition of a candidate by Labour HQ. In the end, Labour retained its seat, but its majority was cut by 16,000.

Consequences

When asked about their coverage and engagement of south Asian voters, only ITV declined to comment. One ITV News insider told me, off the record, the programme missed a trick by not looking at what ITV regional programmes were doing. The BBC News at 10 editor, Paul Royall,[13] explained his strategy for his programme was to concentrate on geographical diversity.

> The Ten O'Clock News committed time and space to analysing and explaining Brexit so voters were fully informed about the choice on offer. We also focussed on substantial, in-depth analysis of the other major themes vying with Brexit – the NHS, the climate crisis, regional inequalities and trust in politics. We knew there was a real demand and desire from our audiences to have insights and understanding on these big choices. To help deliver this, the Ten O'Clock News also co-anchored the programme – at least twice a week – from towns and cities across the UK. This geographical footprint was a priority for us.

Sky News, director of content, Cristina Nicolotti Squires,[14] was clear that 'getting under the skin of modern Britain' was very important to the broadcaster.

> The 5 and 6pm News hours were presented from a different town and city each weekday evening throughout the campaign and we were very keen to ensure voters got to voice their concerns rather than simply carrying and analysing the politicians' claims and counterclaims. Many people from south Asian backgrounds appeared on those programmes. We also commissioned a series of longer form pieces looking at the changing party loyalties of various groups of voters – and Inzamam Rashid's report was one of these.

The lack of response from ITV and the BBC's decision to go for geographical diversity have raised alarm bells among some south Asian influencers and politicians. According to one Westminster insider,[15] they want Ofcom and the media select committee to investigate the coverage of these general elections from an ethnic minority, and south Asian specifically, perspective.

> The coverage for south Asians was woeful. If I was from Mars, I'd have thought that Britain was white. We ought to have written questions in the House, and the culture secretary should urge Ofcom to investigate. Otherwise why are black and Asian people paying their licence fee? This isn't just about the BBC. ITN especially needs to seriously get its programmes in order. Its coverage was shameful.

Conclusion

If Ofcom or parliament choose to examine the coverage, then they must ask one basic question: are black and Asian viewers truly and proportionately represented in meaningful ways during general elections and big political moments when compared to white viewers? Sadly, the answer currently is an overwhelming 'no'. The future for diverse broadcasting must be much better.

All the main broadcasters need to be less defensive and acknowledge they need to improve. They should consider attitude survey polls in general elections, with an ethnic breakdown and analysis, as a matter of course. To cheapen the cost, they can pool resources and ask universities to research the changing polling attitudes among BAME voters. Broadcasters can also forge partnerships with specialist publications who are more expert at connecting and engaging with south Asian and ethnic minority voters.

But above all, they need BAME commissioners, editors, producers and reporters to speak and drive through change in election coverage. Unless they do so, ordinary brown folk will stop engaging and look for of coverage which caters for them. Down that road lies the mirage of fake news dressed up as truth. Something which seems undemocratic and dangerous in the mother of democracies.

Notes

[1] Audickas, L. Bellis, A. and Cracknell, R. (2019) Social background of MPs 1979-2017, House of Commons Briefing Paper CBP 7483

[2] BBC News (2019) MP Keith Vaz suspended from Commons after drug and sex inquiry. Available online at https://www.bbc.co.uk/news/uk-politics-50252630 accessed 15 Jan 2020

[3] Ofcom (2019) Review of BBC news and current affairs. Available online at https://www.ofcom.org.uk/__data/assets/pdf_file/0025/173734/bbc-news-review.pdf accessed 16 January 2020

[4] BBC Trust (2011) BBC Trust review of impartiality and accuracy of the BBC's coverage of science. Available online at https://downloads.bbc.co.uk/bbctrust/assets/files/pdf/our_work/science_impartiality/science_impartiality.pdf accessed 16 January 2020

[5] Rashid, I. and Stylianou, N. (2019) General election: South Asians could hold balance of power in key marginal seats. Sky News. Available at https://news.sky.com/story/general-election-south-asians-could-hold-balance-of-power-in-key-marginal-seats-11879224 accessed 15 December 2019

[6] Booth, R. (2019) Loss of minority ethnic support threatens Tory power, study suggests. The Guardian. Available at https://www.theguardian.com/politics/2019/feb/26/loss-of-minority-ethnic-support-threatens-tory-power-study-suggests accessed 20 December 2019

[7] Woolley, S. (2019) Black and Asian people can change this election: it's urgent that we register now. The Guardian. Available at https://www.theguardian.com/commentisfree/2019/nov/25/black-asian-change-election-register-to-vote accessed 17 December 2019

[8] Haque, Z. (2018) Britain's eight million ethnic minorities are still being ignored over Brexit. New Statesman. Available at https://www.newstatesman.com/politics/brexit/2018/09/britain-s-eight-million-ethnic-minorities-are-still-being-ignored-over accessed 12 January 2020

[9] Eshan, R. (2017) The British Asian vote for Brexit contains a few surprises. LSE Blogs. Available at https://blogs.lse.ac.uk/brexit/2017/02/20/the-british-asian-vote-for-brexit-contains-a-few-surprises/ accessed 17 December 2019

[10] Dholakia, U. (2020) Questions on general election coverage among south Asian communities. [interview] Interviewed by Barnie Choudhury, 8 January 2020

[11] Solanki, S. (2020) Questions on general election coverage among south Asian communities. [interview] Interviewed by Barnie Choudhury, 15 January 2020

[12] Choudhury, B. (2019) Barnie Choudhury: Don't take us for granted. Eastern Eye. Available at https://www.easterneye.biz/barnie-choudhury-dont-take-us-for-granted/ accessed 15 December 2019

[13] Royall, P. (2020). South Asian general election 2019 coverage. [email]. Sent to Barnie Choudhury. 13 January 2020

[14] Nicolotti Squires, C. (2020). South Asian general election 2019 coverage. [email]. Sent to Barnie Choudhury. 20 January 2020

[15] Anonymous. (2020) Questions on general election coverage among south Asian communities. [interview] Interviewed by Barnie Choudhury, 14 January 2020

Note on the contributor

Barnie Choudhury is a professor of professional practice at the University of Buckingham. He was a BBC journalist for 24 years and won several industry awards for his reporting of diverse communities. Barnie is a communications consultant and writes for Eastern Eye, Britain's number one south Asian national newspaper.

.

This disunited kingdom

***

Different outcomes may emerge from all four nations of the union

Neil Fowler

The 2019 General Election may have been a near landslide for Boris Johnson in UK and English terms, but it produced different stories from around the nations. The SNP almost overwhelmed Scotland, the dominant unionist and nationalist parties were given a sharp rap on the knuckles in Northern Ireland, and in Wales Labour felt the Tories coming up hard in their heartlands. Are we now in a disunited kingdom?

Maurice Smith, long-time observer of Scottish political matters, in *Ageing issues may scupper the old union*, believes Boris Johnson and his government will have to raise their profiles, and their achievements in Scotland dramatically if the union is to stay secure. And it is down to demographics.

"Scotland needs more and younger workers," he writes, commenting on the plan for a Scottish visa, he adds. But, "Within an hour of (Nicola) Sturgeon's launch of the visa proposal in January 2020, Downing Street had rejected it flatly, reminding Scotland – as if it needed to – that immigration remains a 'reserved power'. In other words, Whitehall and Westminster know best."

This will lead to problems, Smith says. "We can be sure the SNP is ready with many more such proposals, many of them likely to be rejected, which they can then use to underline the claim that Tory England does not care."

Martin Shipton, another political journalist of vast experience from outside the London bubble, has long been reporting on matters Welsh. In *Pyrrhic victory for Labour in Wales as Red Wall crumbles* he says normal rules didn't apply in Wales during the 2019 General Election.

All kinds of things happened. Labour may have just kept its majority of seats, but the party was virtually wiped out in the north of the country. Leave voters stuck with it in the south Wales valleys while pro-EU voters rewarded MPs who had prominently supported the Remain cause. An electoral pact between Plaid Cymru, the Liberal Democrats and the Greens turned out to be a damp squib, while the victory of a Conservative candidate imposed from London at the last minute proved that you don't have to nurture a seat for years to get elected.

But it is in Northern Ireland that the most dramatic repercussions of both the referendum and the 2019 election may ultimately be felt.

The BBC's Noel Thompson, in *The boys and girls are back in town…* welcomes that the main political parties have had to agree to resurrect devolved government in Northern Ireland and get back to business.

"The road ahead is not clear, of course," he writes. "The agreement has to be seen to work in practice, but the politicians seem ready to allow each other some room."

But Gail Walker, editor-at-large of the *Belfast Telegraph* takes a slightly more dramatic view of what is happening in *The beginning of the end for Northern Ireland?*

It's a feat of spectacular engineering across perilous and stormy waters, she says. "The stuff of fantasy. Liable to be attacked and collapsed at any time. Routinely sneered at. All reasons, of course, why the Boris Bridge, stretching from Northern Ireland to Scotland, would appear to be a non-starter. But it could be shorthand for the current predicament of unionism too," she adds.

However, she says: "The cause is not yet lost. If the unionist parties can reach out to the defectors of their own community they may – like the old cliché of the industrious, more scientifically-minded northern protestant – rediscover the joys of civil engineering and, even, of building bridges.

And finally, Leicestershire-based political journalists Tor Clark, Dan Martin and Tim Parker, recall covering Brexit and the election in Red-Blue, town and country split Leicestershire, where on the surface nothing changed and no seats changed hands, but looking a little deeper, all sorts of political reactions were going on.

In their chapter *Reporting Brexit in an English region*, they write: "The people from the regions had spoken just as loudly as their metropolitan counterparts, who get to see more of the political action close-up but for once, perhaps, the regions had had the louder voice. Time will tell whether the December 12 election was the end, a beginning or merely a continuation of what had dominated politics for the previous five years."

Ageing issues may scupper the old union

In a post-Brexit world Boris Johnson and his government will have to raise their profiles, and their achievements, in Scotland dramatically if the union is to stay secure, argues Maurice Smith

In the week that Britain finally achieved Brexit, Scottish First Minister Nicola Sturgeon unveiled an innocent-looking proposal to help solve a long-running economic and social problem: Scotland's ageing population.

Her idea of a so-called 'Scottish visa', whereby migrant workers from outside the United Kingdom could move into Scotland, looked like a worthy means of tackling the bare fact that Scottish workers are in short supply and the situation is getting worse. Scotland needs more and younger workers, a situation experienced across most first-world economies as the baby-boom generation reaches retirement age and threatens to become a growing burden on the state.

So far, so sensible. But there is little that is very sensible in this post-referendum age. Within an hour of Sturgeon's launch of the visa proposal in January 2020, Downing Street had rejected it flatly, reminding Scotland – as if it needed to – that immigration remains a 'reserved power'. In other words, Whitehall and Westminster know best.

North of the Border, there is consensus – from business organisations to opposition parties – that immigration presents the only viable means of tackling population ageing. From the berry growers of Tayside to the care homes in every town and city, and to major sectors such as tourism, Scottish business needs young workers. During the decade until the 2016 EU poll, that need was met increasingly by incomers from eastern Europe, but not only there. Scottish society has become more diverse, a fact welcomed by most in a part of the UK that voted to remain in the European Union (EU) by 62-38 per cent in 2016.

The demographic issue has dogged policy-makers at Holyrood since devolution in 1999, and not only since the SNP took power there in 2007. One government paper published in 2010 predicted that age-related public expenditure would rise from 20.1 per cent of gross domestic product (GDP) in 2007-8 to 26.6 per cent by 2057. The number of people aged over 60 is predicted to jump by 50 per cent by 2033. Such figures are true of all of the UK, but they are highest in Scotland, and within Scotland the situation is even more acute in rural areas.

As a result, the Scottish Government was at loggerheads with the Home Office even when Brexit remained a distant gleam in the eye for Nigel Farage and his fellow-travellers on the Tory right. The Labour/ Liberal Democrat coalition which ran Holyrood before 2007 launched a public campaign to attract outsiders into Scotland, across the range of skills and activities. Everybody says they want international research scientists, but many parts of Scotland also need catering staff, hotel receptionists, farm workers and so on.

As Home Secretary Theresa May was sanctioning 'hostile environment' campaigns against illegal immigrants, the Scottish Government was trying to attract more people from EU countries and elsewhere. Much has been made of the positive economic impact of immigration. Romantics have even talked of reviving pre-union Scotland's historical links with Poland and the Baltic states. In England, meanwhile, the immigration debate diverged sharply.

Tensions brought to a head

Brexit has brought many tensions between Scotland and London to a head. The 'Scottish visa' case is one of many to be exploited by two sides as politics continues to move towards what has been dubbed – perhaps carelessly – as 'Ulsterisation'. We exist in a tit-for-tat world where politics are viewed almost exclusively in constitutional terms: Are you Yes or No? Pro-independence or 'Unionist'?

This line of chatter now infects every area of policy: education, health, industry, public spending. England is witnessing a similar division between Leave and Remain, and it will be fascinating to see whether voters there return to more familiar party lines post-Brexit, or whether we shall all continue to take political positions that are rooted in our embrace or rejection of the EU.

If we judge what's happening in Scottish public discourse by the newspapers and broadcasting bulletins, or by social media, then we have a simple breakdown: if you are pro-independence, then everything bad in Scotland is the fault of an uncaring London administration and most things can be solved by a second poll – known by the shorthand IndyRef2 – and the subsequent return of Scotland to its rightful place at the table of free nations, running its own affairs.

If you are anti-independence, or pro Union, the SNP is a single-issue party eager to exploit any possible grievance as a Scottish issue, meanwhile being content to let public services fester or fail. "Get back to your day job, Nicola," shout unionist voices who insist the First Minister would be better spending her time running her government.

The election of a Tory government with a big majority and led by an unsympathetic southern bounder in the form of Boris Johnson in December 2019 is likely to bring all that to a head, sooner or later.

Johnson has been keen to portray his approach as that of a 'One-Nation' Tory. He was elected on promises that his government would be paying lots more attention to 'the regions', especially the traditionally Labour-voting north of England, where so many seats within the so-called red wall defected to the Conservatives. Johnson must pay attention to Northern Ireland too, not least because of promises made previously as he attempted to push through Brexit, and also because of the island of Ireland's key position at the heart of negotiations with Brussels.

A belief in a different country

Scotland presents a very different but no less difficult to define problem, and there is little evidence that Johnson or his advisers know what to do about it. Some seasoned observers detect parallels with the 1980s, when hardline Thatcherites could not quite understand why so many Scots did not share their enthusiasm for privatisation or the poll tax.

Regardless of their view on independence, the vast majority of Scots do believe their country is different from the rest of the UK, which was, after all, the creation of a union way back in 1707, rather than a conquest.

By the time John Major was in power, and his Scottish secretaries of state Ian Lang and later Michael Forsyth were reduced to chasing a fast-diminishing Scottish vote, the die was cast for the Conservative Party in Scotland. If the migrant visa episode was any guide, it would suggest the new Tories in charge have learned little from the experience of their predecessors.

During the run-up to the 1997, arch right-winger and proud Thatcherite Forsyth – who now broods in the House of Lords as he watches the SNP wield power back home – had belatedly adopted a populist role in an attempt to stem the tide of votes running away from his party north of the border.

Inspired by the popularity of the Hollywood movie Braveheart, he announced a new Scottish screen agency to help boost the film industry. Acquiescing to Scottish sentiment, he arranged for the return of the Stone of Destiny from Westminster Abbey to Edinburgh Castle, where it still sits on display, an act that was accompanied by overblown pomp and ceremony.

Forsyth's belated efforts at populism were to little avail. His party collapsed in the wake of the New Labour landslide, its Scottish presence at Westminster wiped out completely. Forsyth himself lost Stirling. His party ran a vain and slightly incongruous campaign against devolution, a few months later. The irony for the Conservatives is that Scottish devolution saved the party from oblivion, because a small group arrived in the parliament whose existence it had opposed, courtesy of the proportional representation system introduced in 1999.

Politics has changed

Scottish politics has changed fundamentally in the interim period. In 1997, Labour won 56 of Scotland's 72 Westminster seats. It led a coalition with the Liberal Democrats at Holyrood through two elections in 1999 and 2003, before losing power to a minority SNP in 2007 and a majority SNP government in 2011. The SNP will have been in power for 14 years by the time of the next Holyrood election in 2021, and at the time of writing they are expected to emerge from that at least as the largest party.

The Labour vote in Scotland collapsed after the 2014 independence referendum. In December 2019, after a brief revival in 2017, Labour held just one of Scotland's now 59 Westminster seats (the total number of which has been adjusted post-devolution). The SNP held 48, the Tories just six, despite Boris Johnson's overall victory.

The more things change, the more they appear to stay the same. Just as Thatcher and to a lesser extent Major failed to get a grip with Scotland, so Theresa May and now Johnson face the same experience. Do they understand Scottish issues, or care about them? Or, in this day of spin and perception politics, do they feel the need to seem that they care?

Devolution itself was a long sought-after response to Scottish problems, principally a yearning to have more control over affairs north of the border, perhaps even the ability to attempt policy initiatives that could not win support in the south.

From London, it was seen as a concession to Scottish interests. It was followed by more such concessions, through first the Calman and then the Smith Commissions, the latter an all-party group convened after the 2014 referendum to deliver some, if not all, of the promises made by the No parties during that campaign.

The loss of Ruth Davidson

The Brexit vote changed everything within Scottish politics. Ruth Davidson, whose star had been in ascendancy since she took over the leader's role of Scottish Conservative Party in 2011, found life increasingly difficult after 2016. A prominent remainer, she had attacked Johnson publicly during that campaign. Increasingly uncomfortable in her role, she returned from maternity leave in 2019 and announced an unexpected departure from politics.

It is salutary to recall that quite recently Davidson was being tipped in London, with some enthusiasm, as a possible leader of the UK Conservatives. Unequivocally pro-EU, she ended up in an increasingly awkward position in Scotland.

Since 2014, her whole stance was one of blaming the SNP for allegedly devoting all of its time to constitutional change. Yet her party in turn had dragged the UK towards Brexit, a more seismic change, post 2016. In 2014, Tories argued that Scotland needed to remain part of a common market with its larger neighbour, yet post-2016 May was insisting 'Brexit means Brexit' and Johnson rode the wave of anti-European sentiment as he led the charge out of the enormous market that is the EU.

Davidson offered little in terms of policy, but she was greatly at ease with the media, performing well in parliament and in TV studios. With her departure, the rump of Tory representation in Scotland – in Westminster and Holyrood – remains a hotchpotch of old-school Tories and younger Brexit enthusiasts. The party is now basically the main pro-union opposition at Holyrood, but its case lacks cohesion and eloquence.

Scottish nationalists are convinced that a second referendum will come soon. Such a poll is in the gift of London rather than Edinburgh and there is no evidence that Boris Johnson will be happy to oblige. One of his predecessors, David Cameron, allowed a Scottish referendum because he was convinced that the SNP would lose heavily; the result was much closer than he had believed when he had sanctioned the poll.

Will Johnson feel under any obligation to acquiesce to the SNP's demand of a second poll just a few years later? Immediately after the December 2019 poll the briefing was that the new prime minister intended to 'love bomb' Scotland, visiting more often and backing projects that would demonstrate the value of the union to Scots voters.

Just a month later he was dismissing a policy initiative aimed at addressing Scotland's very real demographic challenge. We can be sure the SNP is ready with many more such proposals, many of them likely to be rejected, which they can then use to underline the claim that Tory England does not care. Despite denials, the SNP is indeed a party of grievance when it comes to independence; most opposition parties are the same.

There is concern too that Brexit will provide the Government with the cover to grab back some responsibilities that were devolved previously to Holyrood, principally in the farming and fishing sectors, as control returns from Brussels. A few right-wing voices who oppose devolution itself have emerged recently, and the Scottish lobby is wary that Johnson may be tempted to take a more direct approach to Scotland. They may be right to remain suspicious: how else is London likely to convince Scotland that the union can continue to work for it, if it does not raise its own profile north of the border?

Note on the contributor
Maurice Smith is a journalist, columnist and documentary producer based in Glasgow. He was previously Business Editor of BBC Scotland. He is the author of *Paper Lions: The Scottish Press and National Identity* (Polygon, 1994).

Pyrrhic victory for Labour in Wales as Red Wall crumbles

Normal rules didn't apply in Wales during the 2019 general election. Labour may have just kept its majority of seats, but the party was virtually wiped out in the north of the country. Leave voters stuck with it in the south Wales valleys while pro-EU voters rewarded MPs who had prominently supported the Remain cause. An electoral pact between Plaid Cymru, the Liberal Democrats and the Greens turned out to be a damp squib, while the victory of a Conservative candidate imposed from London at the last minute proved that you don't have to nurture a seat for years to get elected, says Martin Shipton

If the result of the 2016 EU referendum in Wales represented a case of voters biting off the hand that fed them, the outcome of the 2019 general election in the same country is not so easy to categorise.

One of the conundrums of the referendum result was why Wales backed Brexit despite billions of pounds of EU aid money having come its way since the turn of the century. The answer was complex, with different emphases according to who was passing judgment, but most agreed that it reflected a disconnect between the political class and the majority of voters.

Nevertheless, the 2017 general election had confounded those who talked up the possibility of breaking the dominance of Labour in Wales, with the party actually taking three seats from the Conservatives. The final outcome in the 40 Welsh constituencies was Labour 28, Conservative eight and Plaid Cymru four.

At the beginning of the 2017 campaign, though, there had been a shock for Labour, with an opinion poll giving the Conservatives a 10-point lead in Wales.

Things had changed, as in England, because of the unconvincing nature of Theresa May's leadership and the sense that Jeremy Corbyn was not as bad as he had been portrayed. Two years later, providing further evidence of voter volatility, the run-up to the 2019 election again saw the Conservatives leading in Wales, this time by four points.

The ambitions of Remain and Leave

At the beginning of the 2019 campaign, a huge amount of attention was devoted to the means by which supporters of the Remain and Leave causes could achieve their desired outcomes. With first past the post as entrenched as ever as the means by which MPs were elected, the focus was on tactical voting and electoral pacts.

In Wales there had already been a dry run earlier in the year during the Brecon & Radnorshire by-election, held on August 1. The circumstances were unusual. The incumbent Tory MP, Chris Davies, had been removed from office after a successful electoral petition following his conviction for making false invoices when claiming parliamentary expenses.

Rather surprisingly, Davies was re-selected by the party as its by-election candidate. This prompted the resurrection of an idea that had first been floated by Plaid Cymru's Adam Price before the Welsh Assembly election in 2016: an electoral pact between Plaid, the Liberal Democrats and the Green Party.

This came to nothing in 2016, but the seeds had been sown and there appeared good grounds for implementing such a pact in a Westminster by-election whose outcome would have a bearing on the finely balanced voting strengths in a House of Commons navigating its way through the Brexit impasse.

Plaid and the Greens stood down in the by-election, a decision seen as one of two crucial factors in the narrow victory of Welsh Liberal Democrat leader Jane Dodds over Chris Davies – the other being the decision of the Brexit Party to field a candidate and split the Leave vote. The Brexit Party candidate's 3,331 votes were well over double Dodds' majority of 1,425.

Much was made of the talks taking place between the Liberal Democrats, Plaid Cymru and the Greens before the 2019 election, as if they would deliver a significant boost to pro-Remain candidates' chances of winning seats across Wales and – so far as agreements between the Lib Dems and the Greens were concerned – in England too.

But in the event, they were something of a damp squib in Wales, covering just 11 of the 40 seats. The parties' leaders came up against parochial hostility from their own local members, who thus demonstrated that they were less interested in stopping Brexit than in preserving their right to field candidates of their own, regardless of the outcome.

There were also complaints from Lib Dem grassroots members about standing down for 'nationalist separatists', and from Plaid supporters about standing down for unionists and a party that had enabled Tory austerity between 2010 and 2015. The party that did best out of this minimalist pact was Plaid Cymru, three of whose four MPs were able to successfully present themselves as the only unambiguously Remain candidates in their constituencies.

A different stance on Brexit

In Wales the Labour Party had adopted a different stance towards Brexit since its poor showing in the European parliamentary election in May 2019, when it came third behind the Brexit Party and Plaid Cymru. While all four Labour European candidates went out of their way to assert their strongly Remain credentials, leaflets put out in their name carried the fence-sitting policy position of Jeremy Corbyn. Their most fervent opponents could not have come up with a better way of undermining their credibility.

After the European election result was announced, Welsh Labour leader and First Minister Mark Drakeford moved quickly to turn the party into one that unashamedly backed Remain. What was missing, however, was any attempt to build an electoral pact with Plaid Cymru, the Liberal Democrats and the Greens. The reality is that Labour's National Executive Committee had no appetite for a pro-Remain pact because the party's leadership did not consider stopping Brexit a priority.

In all six Welsh seats lost by Labour to the Conservatives in 2019 – with an overall result of Labour 22, the Conservatives 14 and Plaid Cymru 4 – the combined votes of the Plaid, Lib Dem and Green Party candidates exceeded the Tory majority. Of course, that doesn't mean that all six would necessarily have been retained by Labour if those three parties hadn't stood, but it is the case that Remain-backing parties – if we include Welsh Labour – won more votes in Wales (52 per cent) than pro-Leave parties (48 per cent).

Equally, it can be argued that the game was up when Nigel Farage announced that his Brexit Party would not be fielding candidates in seats won by the Tories in 2017 – thus destroying any hope that opposition parties could win because of a split in the Leave vote, and ensuring that the Lib Dems' hold on Brecon & Radnorshire was short-lived.

The pattern of voting in Wales in 2019 suggests that Brexit was, while important, not in many seats the predominant factor in determining results. Had it been, then south Wales valleys seats which voted Leave would have been captured by the Conservatives or, conceivably, the Brexit Party.

None of them were, and they all stayed with Labour. The Brexit Party achieved one of its best performances across Britain in Blaenau Gwent, which had the highest referendum Leave vote in Wales at 62.0 per cent.. But despite being runner-up to Labour's incumbent MP Nick Smith, the Brexit Party's candidate Richard Taylor only got 20.6 per cent of the vote, against 49.2 per cent for Smith.

Taylor was perhaps the most colourful candidate fielded by any party in Wales, A self-confessed thief, burglar and drug abuser when a teenager, he turned to religion and was pastor of an evangelical church in south Wales before losing his job after committing adultery – a transgression that led him to weep during a podcast as election day neared.

Border issues

Four of Labour's six seat losses in Wales were bunched around the border with England, in the north east corner of the country. They could be described collectively as the westernmost extremity of the so-called Red Wall of Labour seats across northern England, many of which fell to the Conservatives and delivered Boris Johnson his landslide victory. A perception in north Wales that the benefits of devolution hadn't spread far beyond Cardiff doubtless had a negative impact for Labour.

Realising that the seats were at risk, Labour politicians in the region called for more resources in the form of leaflets and canvassing help from party headquarters. They were frustrated when leaflets they had called for were not forthcoming before ballot papers were delivered to the homes of postal voters. And they were perplexed when party activists from the north west of England sped through the seats on their way to campaign in Plaid Cymru-held Arfon. Despite all the attention, Plaid's MP Hywel Williams' saw his majority over Labour rise from 92 to 2,781.

There were also mutterings within Welsh Labour about the appearance of Jeremy Corbyn on the promenade in Aberystwyth four days before the election. Aberystwyth is the main town in Ceredigion, in recent decades seen as a Plaid Cymru/ Liberal Democrat marginal. In 2019 it was retained by Plaid, with the Conservatives in second place, the Lib Dems third and Labour fourth.

The most extraordinary result was in Ynys Mon (Anglesey), the perennial top target seat in Wales for Plaid Cymru since it lost it to Labour in 2001. In 2019, with the popular incumbent Albert Owen standing down, Plaid thought its time had finally come. The Conservatives hadn't even picked a candidate until the day before nominations closed – and when they did it was Chris Davies, the controversial former MP for Brecon & Radnorshire. But within hours he had withdrawn, and been replaced by Virginia Crosbie, deputy chair of Kensington and Chelsea Conservatives and the director of Women2Win, an organisation that campaigns for more Tory women Parliamentarians.

Ms Crosbie's selection was anything but transparent – the constituency doesn't even have a Conservative association of its own – and she had no discernible connection with or knowledge of the seat before she was installed as the candidate. Conventional wisdom has it that to win Ynys Mon a candidate should preferably be from the island and certainly a Welsh speaker. Ms Crosbie didn't pass either test, yet she came through the middle and won. It seemed that while old rules no longer applied, new ones had yet to be established.

Substantial majorities in Cardiff

In Cardiff, a resolutely Remain city, the strongly pro-Remain stance adopted by the four Labour MPs seeking re-election was rewarded with substantial majorities for each of them.

Anna McMorrin, who had surprisingly won Cardiff North from the Conservatives in 2017, had been one of the most prominent advocates of the Remain cause in the Commons. She attracted the support of pro-EU Tories and even of the Lib Dem candidate, who days before the election advised people to vote for her rather than him – a final admission, perhaps, of the shortcomings of the Plaid/ Lib Dem/ Green pact. Ms McMorrin saw her majority more than double.

Her victory appeared to suggest that voters appreciated politicians who were clear about what they stood for, and didn't equivocate like Jeremy Corbyn. Instead of speaking from the heart, he was offering himself as a leader who had no opinion on the most important issue of the day. This, coupled with relentless attacks on his past associations with groups and individuals regarded as undesirable, cut through and was a major message for politicians of all parties on the Welsh doorstep.

Plaid Cymru MP Jonathan Edwards (Carmarthen East and Dinefwr) said during the campaign: "I have had many voters in all parts of the constituency telling me they cannot stand Jeremy Corbyn. I am losing about 20 per cent of my vote to the Conservatives because of Brexit, but I am winning the votes of former Labour supporters who won't vote for Corbyn."

Other MPs, including McMorrin in Cardiff North, said Corbyn was a hugely negative factor for voters – far more than Brexit – and that she was winning support because she had very clearly distanced herself from the party leader.

The strength of the antagonism towards Corbyn even overrode feelings of anger towards Alun Cairns, who had been forced to resign as Secretary of State for Wales at the start of the campaign, after failing to distance himself from his former office manager, whose comments in court about the complainant's alleged sexual past – denied by her – had resulted in the collapse of a rape trial. An email sent by Mr Cairns' special adviser to him showed the Cabinet Minister had been kept informed about the circumstances of the trial's collapse.

At a re-trial the former office manager's friend was convicted of rape and jailed. The victim accused Mr Cairns of putting the party's interests before her welfare. Yet despite Mr Cairns' indirect involvement in what was undoubtedly a serious scandal, his constituents gave him an increased majority and vote share. For him, the simple message 'Get Brexit Done' had worked.

Note on the contributor

Martin Shipton is chief reporter of the *Western Mail*, the national newspaper of Wales. He has written about Welsh politics for more than 25 years. He is the author of *Poor Man's Parliament: Ten Years of the Welsh Assembly* and *Political Chameleon*, a biography of George Thomas. His book on Gareth Jones, the *Western Mail* journalist who exposed the 1930s man-made famine in Ukraine that killed millions, will be published in 2020. He has been Reporter of the Year in the British Press Awards.

The boys and girls are back in town…

And so the deal has been done. Three years after the collapse of power sharing, the main political parties have agreed to resurrect devolved government in Northern Ireland and get back to business. The headline in one local paper was succinct: *About bloody time*. Noel Thompson reflects on how the general election encouraged the return to Parliament Buildings

That headline sums up the message to the political parties in Northern Ireland delivered by the voters at the December 2019 general election.

It took place against a background of industrial action in the NHS, with nurses on strike for the first time in the 100-year history of their Royal College, and general agreement that the health service was on the brink of chaos.

Teachers, too, were taking action short of a strike; their issues included excessive workloads and under investment in schools. Civil servants were unable or unwilling to take the big decisions in the absence of local ministers, so long-term planning in health, education, the economy and infrastructure was moribund.

All this because the main parties couldn't agree on an Irish Language Act? There was more to it than that, of course, but the public frustration showed itself on the campaign doorsteps and in the election results.

The Democratic Unionist Party (DUP) lost North Belfast and South Belfast and failed to win the North Down seat of the independent Unionist Lady Hermon, a constituency it felt confident of taking. It lost the Belfast seats because Nationalists joined forces, and even the Greens helped out in an unofficial election pact to topple the DUP's pro-Brexit stance.

In the 2016 referendum Northern Ireland had voted 56-44 per cent to remain in the EU. The nationalist Sinn Fein and the Social and Democratic Labour Party (SDLP) were vehemently opposed to Brexit, along with the Alliance Party, the Greens and other smaller parties.

The DUP, and the Ulster Unionist Party (UUP) voted to leave, although the UUP at the later stages changed its mind, leaving the DUP defending Brexit, but ultimately feeling betrayed by the withdrawal deals struck by Prime Ministers May and Johnson.

At the centre of Brexit

Northern Ireland had found itself at the very centre of the Brexit controversy, a likelihood few had seemed overly aware of back in 2016. But latterly English politicians, who had scarcely given Northern Ireland a thought in their parliamentary careers, were screaming about defending the Good Friday Agreement,; Norway plus or Canada double plus,; technological solutions to the problem of the border,; even bridges to Scotland. There was at least unanimity on one central point – that a no-deal Brexit would be extremely damaging to Northern Ireland, economically and politically.

For Sinn Fein this was a Brexit election. It believed Brexit posed a threat not just to Northern Ireland but to the whole island of Ireland, and it claimed the only solution was for the province to be given special status within the EU, thus allowing the whole island to remain part of the project.

Of course, any notion that considered the island of Ireland as one entity, political, economic or otherwise was anathema to Unionists. That was why they opposed the Theresa May deal with its backstop, which would have kept Northern Ireland in the single market.

And in the final analysis they were equally opposed to Boris Johnson's deal, which did away with the backstop but replaced it with what effectively would be a border in the Irish Sea, requiring checks of some kind on goods and livestock passing either way from the North to the UK. It was, said the DUP, a denial of the unfettered access Boris Johnson had promised when he spoke at its party conference in 2018.

The scene was set

And so the scene was set for electoral battle. Tactical voting and electoral pacts have long been part of the scene in NI, especially in areas where the margins between Unionist and Nationalist are tight.

In Fermanagh/South Tyrone, for example, where the parliamentary seat has passed between Orange and Green like a shuttlecock, parties have regularly lent each other their votes to keep the other side out. But in this election, pacts of a different order came in to play, not just along the traditional lines.

In North Belfast, Nigel Dodds, the DUP overall deputy leader, and its leader at Westminster, had held the seat for 18 years, taking it from the Ulster Unionists. But here, as elsewhere in the city, the demography had been changing, and Sinn Fein had been moving closer to the prize.

In what was seen as a controversial move, the SDLP decided to withdraw its candidate to give Sinn Fein a better chance of winning. Controversial because in his own constituency in Foyle, the SDLP leader Colum Eastwood was campaigning on the basis that people needed an MP who would actually go to Westminster to take their seat. Sinn Fein of course is an abstentionist party.

So Mr Eastwood faced charges of hypocrisy, which he strongly denied. He said extraordinary times demanded unprecedented moves, and he'd rather see the Sinn Fein candidate, John Finucane, sitting in his own house abstaining than see Nigel Dodds sitting in the House of Commons.

South Belfast told a similar story. Here the outgoing MP was Emma Little-Pengelly, a relatively new DUP face. South Belfast is an affluent part of the city with a religiously and politically mixed electorate. Little-Pengelly had narrowly taken the seat from the SDLP in 2017. This time round Sinn Fein held back, as did the Green Party, which held about 2,200 votes. Both Sinn Fein and the SDLP insisted there was no pact involved in these deals, just a selfless effort to maximise the Remain representation at Westminster.

North Down was interesting, but in a different way. It had been held by Lady Sylvia Hermon, originally an Ulster Unionist, since 2001. She fell out with the UUP over a pact with the Conservative Party, and had sat as an independent since 2010. She was fiercely anti Brexit. Her main opponent in recent years was the DUP. It had a well-respected candidate in Alex Easton and was confident that at last it would take the seat. But in this area, which boasts Northern Ireland's affluent 'Gold Coast', the Green Party again had some 2500 votes and it stood down to allow the Alliance Party the chance to grab Lady Hermon's votes. Once again the drive was to maximise the Remain voice.

The Betrayal Act

And so through the wintry weeks the campaign progressed, with the candidates clashing on TV and radio debate programmes. The UUP, now declaring Remain as the least bad option, hammered the DUP for lending initial support to the Johnson withdrawal agreement with its Irish Sea border.

The DUP replied that it had ultimately rejected the deal in parliament, but it was guilty as charged: the party leader Arlene Foster had said at the start of October that the Johnson proposal was a "serious and sensible way forward". Weeks later, the party said it couldn't support it, and voted against it at Westminster.

Hard-line Unionists and Loyalists condemned it as the Betrayal Act. Sinn Fein and the SDLP slugged it out over whose idea special status had been in the first place. The abstention issue also featured prominently, with Sinn Fein adamant that neither it nor the SDLP would be able to change things at Westminster, since Irish interests could never be properly represented in the British Houses of Parliament. It would rather use its influence in the EU and in the US. The SDLP held that every voice in Westminster was useful and that voters deserved to have their interests represented where the decisions affecting their lives were taken.

The polls closed and people settled down for a long night in front of their TVs, radios, and computer screens. The BBC's online results page registered an exceptionally high number of hits throughout the night. It wasn't just the political anoraks who had their eyes and ears on this contest.

And so Sinn Fein took Nigel Dodds' seat in North Belfast. The SDLP took Emma Little-Pengelly's seat in South Belfast. And the Alliance Party inherited from Lady Hermon in North Down. The SDLP's Colum Eastwood retook Foyle from Sinn Fein by a massive margin, surpassing even the majority enjoyed by the legendary John Hume.

The feeling was that Nationalists had lent Foyle briefly to Sinn Fein, as a mark of respect for the late Sinn Fein Deputy First Minister Martin McGuinness, who was a much respected Derry man. Other constituencies changed incumbent but not party, so this left the DUP with eight seats, down from 10, and for the first time gave Nationalists a majority of Northern Ireland's 18 seats in Westminster.

Both the DUP and Sinn Fein saw their overall share of the vote fall, the DUP by 6 per cent, Sinn Fein by 7 per cent. The Unionist vote seems in permanent decline, and the DUP must be aware that it needs to reach out much more confidently to Nationalists if it is to persuade them that their interests still lie in a Northern Ireland which is part of the UK.

Taking the scalp of Nigel Dodds was a coup for Sinn Fein, and holding on to Fermanagh South Tyrone by 57 votes against the Ulster Unionist challenge was a relief, but these results don't paper over the embarrassing Foyle defeat. The reduced overall vote mirrors recent electoral disappointments in the Republic.

The biggest winner

The biggest winner though was without doubt the Alliance Party. It took the North Down seat, but overall its vote rose by almost 18 per cent, and it extended its support far beyond the Belfast urban area, its traditional stronghold. This followed further good fortune in the recent local and European elections. Commentators suggested that that could lead to real success for the party in a new Assembly election, and that was precisely what was on the cards.

New Secretary of State Julian Smith opened a fresh round of talks immediately after the election. He set a deadline for success of January 13, the date on which the legislation allowing civil servants to take day-to-day decisions at Stormont ran out. If devolution was not up and running by then, there would be an Assembly election. His tough tactics won him public praise and ultimately success. Stormont was back in action three days before the deadline.

There can be no doubt that the anger and frustration of the electorate played into these talks. The outcome, with the usual constructive obfuscation of Northern Ireland politics, is an agreement in which each side can claim some kind of victory.

The road ahead is not clear, of course. The agreement has to be seen to work in practice, but the politicians seem ready to allow each other some room. As the DUP leader Arlene Foster put it, "We will never agree on much about the past, but we cannot allow society to drift backwards and allow division to grow...It's time for Stormont to move forward and show that 'together we are stronger' for the benefit of everyone."

None of the issues which frustrated the voters will be solved in the short term. A health minister cannot shorten waiting lists overnight. But at least, say the punters, the politicians are there, earning their crust, and making the effort.

Note on the contributor

Noel Thompson is a BBC broadcaster. He presents the daily *Good Morning Ulster* radio programme, and for many years anchored the influential political programme *Hearts and Minds*. He is a two-time winner of the Royal Television Society Best Regional Presenter Award, and has been honoured by the Open University and the Belfast Metropolitan College.

The beginning of the end for Northern Ireland?

A feat of spectacular engineering across perilous and stormy waters. The stuff of fantasy. Liable to be attacked and collapsed at any time. Routinely sneered at. All reasons, of course, why the Boris Bridge, stretching from Northern Ireland to Scotland, would appear to be a non-starter. But it could be short-hand for the current predicament of unionism too, writes Gail Walker

In the space of three years the main unionist party, the Democratic Unionist Party (DUP), has gone from centre stage at Westminster, as confidence and supply partner with the Conservative Party, to the infamous Boris betrayal, which saw an economic border agreed in the Irish Sea.

Neither moment was particularly edifying for the party. In the days leading up to the June 2017 deal being signed with then Prime Minister Theresa May, the DUP was subjected to excoriating abuse on social media chiefly for its opposition to same-sex marriage and abortion. Old quotes from party members were dredged up amid a word stew of 'dinosaurs', 'bigots', 'Neanderthals' and 'please not them'. Cartoons in the national press were a flavour of the vicious lampoonery to come. Cynical wags couldn't resist likening the accompanying photographs of the deal being signed by the PM, government aides and assorted DUP members to a gay wedding where the in-laws weren't at all happy. Oh how they laughed.

But even with the sweetener of an extra £1bn in spending for NI (and the DUP did strike a good deal) many unionists shuddered at the stereotypical depiction of themselves as backward people set apart from a modern metropolitan elite.

Since the 1998 Belfast (Good Friday) Agreement, the border with the Irish Republic had cast a very light shadow. Though it manifestly still existed, defining two separate and distinct jurisdictions, those traversing it barely noticed where it was.

Post-referendum it took on a huge foreboding presence. The media dug out dark and menacing photos of border posts and armed guards. Hapless reporters were sent to tramp the length of it, garnering the opinions of gnarly farmers and harried commuters who crossed it numerous times each day. It had a social media account and a bestselling book. There was a rising clamour from nationalists for a border poll set against the fracturing of unionism as business and farming interests made trips to Downing Street and expressed increasing anger at the DUP's Brexit stance.

News from the Wirral

The Wirral has been in the news on two occasions recently. It was to hospitals there that planeloads of travellers from China and Japan were transported to be placed in quarantine during the Coronavirus scare of early 2020.

But before then it had been the location for the surprise summit in October 2019 between the then beleaguered Prime Minister Boris Johnson and the Taoiseach Leo Varadkar, the outcome of which finally unlocked the possibility of a new deal between Westminster and Brussels.

In the end, the wider perplexities of EU and European politics were to come down to the premiers of the two key member states with a history going back a millennium and half. The parameters discussed there provided a new fulcrum for the future of relations between these two islands.

It was certainly the most meaningful conversation between the two states since the Belfast Agreement itself. However, it may even outstrip that accord, because its terms reflected on the possible futures awaiting two sovereign governments, in a context where both parties were fully aware of the historical moment.

For the pivotal role of the border in the Brexit negotiations had brought into play the need to begin imagining a new set of relationships between all the islands of the British Isles for the remainder of this century and beyond, including 'Irish unity' in some form and 'Scottish independence' on whatever timescale.

Whatever the outcomes for the Taoiseach, who at that time was thought to have gained everything he wanted, the first main outcome was the new deal for Johnson. The second was the beginnings of Johnson reasserting Tory control over the DUP and the confidence and supply protocol; the third was the December general election; the fourth was the revived Northern Ireland Assembly.

The implications of the Brexit referendum took all parties by surprise. Yes, there was a sense of how awkward it would be for the two jurisdictions in Ireland to be in separate blocs; and there was much wry amusement about British people suddenly acquiring Irish grandparents to avail of an EU passport via Dublin. But there was no indication at any stage that the Belfast Agreement was all along a booby trap designed to scupper any Brexit ambition in the UK as a whole or, indeed, that sinister elements would begin to find, in trade tariffs and over-bureaucratic paperwork, a renewed rationale for murdering people.

Border in abeyance?

At the time of writing, the issue of 'the border' – whether in the Irish Sea, which vexes unionists, or where it has been historically, which annoys nationalists – has gone into abeyance, through the quadruple novelties of Johnson's thumping Westminster majority; the simple curious fact of the UK departure from the EU itself; the resurrection of the Stormont Assembly; and the astonishing upturn in the fortunes of Sinn Fein (SF) in the February 2020 election in the Irish Republic, after something of a spanking in the UK general election in the North.

The DUP suffered setbacks in the December 2019 election, which no amount of deflection could mask. Nigel Dodds, the deputy leader and principal party tactician and strategist, lost his Westminster seat in Belfast North, reinforcing the character of Belfast as a nationalist city.

The short-lived SF/Social Democratic and Labour Party (SDLP) pact assisted the SDLP taking Belfast South from the DUP though the party failed to lift the seat in North Down vacated by the Independent Unionist Lady Sylvia Hermon. That went to the newly resurgent Alliance under the leadership of Naomi Long, who had herself sensationally taken a European Parliament seat in 2019. The optics were not good in terms of DUP heads rolling and seats lost, whatever the robust overall vote percentage showed.

The election results of December 2019 fit nicely into a narrative of systematic unionist decline. But little has been made of the fact that the decline in the nationalist vote was even steeper. While the DUP's share of the vote dropped by 5.4 per cent compared with the 2017 general election, the Sinn Fein vote fell by 6.7 per cent over the same period. The growth electorally of the Alliance Party, which came third in terms of vote share with around 17 per cent, shows not a rejection of unionism *per se,* but a growing disenchantment with its political and cultural representation.

The unionist community has always been a very big umbrella, encompassing the loyalism of the Shankill Road, the evangelicalism of Ballymena and rural east of the Bann, the business classes of Malone and the Gold Coast of North Down, and the more deferential mode of Fermanagh.

But where does a disenchanted middle-class unionist go to register disenchantment? The old warhorse of the Ulster Unionist Party (UUP), which the DUP displaced as the main voice of the community? There is hardly a revival likely there and even less from the fringe loyalist parties with closer ties to paramilitarism. No, the obvious way to go is straight into the welcoming arms of the Alliance Party.

The Alliance Party has made very modest gains in nationalist areas but even a casual glance shows that the greatest expansion has been within unionist constituencies. This really should raise alarm bells in DUP and UUP headquarters – being a supporter of the union is not the same as being a supporter of political unionism.

Wrong-footed loyalism?

It remains to be seen whether or not the DUP is to be held responsible by loyalism for being wrong-footed by Boris Johnson over the Irish Sea border – something for which the party's own mood music could be said to have paved the way, after it earlier had accepted some regulatory alignment with the EU, necessitating checks in the Irish Sea. Or if the party's very odd invisibility in the Brexit negotiations, during the very period when it held the balance of power in the UK, will have contributed to a sense of unionist voters' exasperation with the political system generally. One can imagine the price the Scottish National Party, for example, would have wrung out of Theresa May's bones had it held the balance of power during her period of office.

The DUP missed key opportunities during the wilderness years of the NI Assembly's self-imposed quarantine. There was an opportunity, from a position of considerable influence at Westminster, to reach out to the administration in Dublin, as that state worked through its own 'decade of centenaries', which had some overlap with the Great War and historical changes in the UK, such as women's suffrage. There was also an opportunity to build new alliances of common interest within Northern Ireland, for example on a range of traditional conservative issues in areas of social change, and perhaps help usher in change in a less chaotic way than ended up occurring.

It suited both Sinn Fein and the DUP to allow MPs at Westminster to pass legislation, which introduced equal marriage and the extension of the Abortion Act into Northern Ireland, as the Assembly passed a certain deadline of inaction in October 2019. From an intractable position of no deal then, the miracle of restoration took place just over two months later, when two of the four major issues which brought the Assembly down, had been tactfully removed bloodlessly with both parties able to blame the British.

This isn't to say that nothing was done. The DUP did make gestures. In 2018 there was an outreach programme that saw leader Arlene Foster attend a GAA match on a Sunday; a *PinkNews* LGBT event at Parliament Buildings; and a Muslim celebration, These were the basis for genuine rapprochement. The problem was that there weren't enough of them and they weren't consistent.

As far as Dublin and 'the south' was concerned, northern Protestants remained an enigma. People didn't know who they were, what they believed, where they lived or what they were like. Instead, the stereotype is either of Nice Prods Who Think Like Us – who might be in the Alliance – or red-faced screaming harridans draped in the union flag.

Of course, there were some with more shaded opinions. But for a government to pursue ambitions to administer a portion of a shared island not to be making regular, if not daily, visits to the hard-core population, which would have most to fear from such a change in jurisdiction, is in fact negligent. This may yet be exposed as such as the rhetoric in favour of a border poll, with the end desired point of Irish unity really as the only acceptable outcome, increasingly ratchets up, with even more fervour after the success of Sinn Fein in the Republic's election of February 2020.

What Irish unity is; what changes the current state is considering making to accommodate one million people to whom its norms are unusual at best, hostile at worst; what representational systems may be put in place to facilitate such change; what the criminal justice system will look like; or the police; or the army – none of these questions have perhaps even been asked, let alone tested, trialed, focus-grouped or explored. Certainly Ulster Protestants have not been engaged in any serious or systematic way.

The charge may be validly put – what have the Prods done for us, in this light? But the response equally validly would be – but you are the state that wants to run us, we don't want to run you. The onus, for better or worse, rests with the Irish Government principally. It does, ultimately, claim the Ulster Protestant – unionist and all as they are – as being, in fact, 'Irish' and part of the people its constitution describes as wishing to cherish equally.

In any case, it is highly unlikely there will be any appetite for re-opening the border question, once and if there is a final determination in a trade agreement between the UK and EU, unless the Northern Ireland Assembly is able to prove itself a viable, working model of collaborative co-existence. Oddly, any hope of a united Ireland, to put it crudely, depends on Northern Ireland not being, as Sinn Fein for generations termed it, a 'failed statelet'.

Paradoxically, the more successful Northern Ireland becomes as a working economy, secure, settled, and co-operative, the better the prospects are of Ireland's voters countenancing some manner of unified dispensation.

No one wants a basket case. The deterioration of civic life; the running down of public services; the rearing up of paramilitary ghouls (some in their teens, some in their 50s); the inability to imagine an exit from the impasse; the risk to all the booming elements of the economy from tourism to a skilled 21st-century workforce ready for action – all this was the steady daily diet in Northern Ireland for more than three years as elected representatives refused to govern. There was a sequence of lines in the sand – such as the RHI heating scandal; a stand-alone Irish Language Act; Troubles' legacy issues; marriage reform and abortion legislation – each of which proved in the end (only a month ago as I write!) to be amazingly porous and erasable after all.

The stubborn and recalcitrant option simply not to work together is now off the table for good, because voters – nationalist and unionist alike – made their unhappiness with their own and their children's standards of living clear on the doorsteps, something which had not happened in Northern Ireland since a brief period in the 1930s. The message from republican voters also, as reported by SF candidates over and over, for the first time ever in my experience, was exactly the same – get back in and stay in. The next Assembly election is to be held on or before May 5, 2022.

What can Sinn Fein do?

It remains to be seen also what purchase Sinn Fein actually has on the Irish electoral imagination as a party of government as opposed to a party of complaint. The Irish Republic's election results from February 2020 were sensational from that perspective, but not genuinely unanticipated.

The very moribund character of the Fine Gael/Fianna Fail coalition, which had led Leo Varadkar to seek the best time to call the poll, took its toll in the booths across Ireland. There was much disaffection with the old truisms of the old two centre parties; also, visible inequalities on the streets and in hospitals, for example, led to increasing disdain for them. There had been a rising popularity for independent representatives over the decade; but their ineffectual performance as individuals in the Dáil, led the electorate to weigh in its disaffection behind a party with brand recognition and a working-class demographic with a record of calling for a plague on both the centre houses. That's one plausible narrative.

Another is the prophetic one of 'Wrap the Green Flag Round Me, Boys' and 'A Nation Once Again', which may be the preferred story among long-term Sinn Fein activists for whom the nation has finally come to its senses and thrown off the yoke of the oppressor. In any case, political realities shift with amazing speed nowadays and there is no knowing whether or not Mary-Lou McDonald can forge a coalition of the Left in government, or whether SF will enter government with one of the centre parties as prop, or whether it will be back to the booths for everyone.

Will the Ulster question be resolved?

Mary Lou McDonald, Arlene Foster, Michelle O'Neill, Naomi Long. Perhaps these are the leaders upon whom history will reflect upon in the end as assisting critically in the resolution of the Ulster question. A decade ago, the key players were very, very different. It is absolutely true that the fact these leaders are women has had a profound effect on the direction politics on the island of Ireland has taken. The obstacles they have overcome have included thinly-veiled misogyny from within and without their own parties.

That matters. And it matters that it is recognised and described, which it has been. For the first time in our shared history, there are issues now which won't 'wait until the border or union question is resolved' to be tackled and fixed. Domestic violence, bodily autonomy, legacy issues from both the Troubles and institutional abuse, and the resistance to forms of hate speech – these are shared insights and the solutions, from a variety of perspectives, which need to be negotiated and agreed.

It is certain that Sinn Fein has, under McDonald, managed to detoxify its brand among a large number of southern voters and that is an achievement which proved beyond Gerry Adams as president and even left the late Martin McGuinness in its wake.

In April 2019, a young journalist was murdered by a gunshot in the head by dissident republicans in Londonderry. A few days later, Foster appeared on a platform in the Creggan in solidarity not only with the murdered writer but also with the people of that area. She was barracked a little; she was challenged more than a bit; but largely she was welcomed and the visit was recognised. She came under some extreme criticism. But it is worth noting that, of all the people on the platform that day, she was the only one who was risking her life to be there.

It is also worth recognising that, slow to their feet as they may all have been, McDonald, Foster and O'Neill were shoulder to shoulder in St Anne's Cathedral in Belfast at Lyra McKee's funeral, as the officiating priest rebuked them all for the collapse of the Assembly.

The sense of a solidarity that went beyond the shouting binary politics of the constitution, the border, identity and vetoes, was palpable. It takes a certain frame of mind not to recognise the real potential of that solidarity. Just as it takes a certain frame of mind not to recognise that being together, standing together, living together, is the only unity that matters a damn.

Gerry Adams's stepping away from the presidency of SF in 2017, for whatever reason, even if part of a strategy articulated by the late Martin McGuinness, has paid dividends that it would have been hard for even the most optimistic to foresee. Overnight, almost, the character of the party changed. A visible, tangible, always unsettling link with its IRA past, was removed from public view, and a whole new set of personalities and emphases came forward, north and south.

The point is, though, that the feminisation of both the DUP – see Foster, Diane Dodds, Emma Little-Pengelly and Pam Cameron – and SF, with McDonald, O'Neill, and Elisha McCallion – hasn't just meant that figureheads have changed.

It could be said that had Peter Robinson and Martin McGuinness still been First Minister and Deputy First Minister, the paralysis of the last three years simply wouldn't have happened. They wouldn't have risked any return to the ghastly past by allowing domestic matters, such as equal marriage, or cultural issues ,such as language, to threaten hard-core political and constitutional progress and accommodation. A way would have been found.

But by the same token the new leaderships, gauche and hesitant and clumsy at times as they were, and seemingly unable to agree the set of simple effective priorities, which had driven the blokish years of Paisley, Robinson, Adams and McGuinness, did and do reflect another key fact.

Society has changed utterly
The culture which presented both Foster and McDonald as political leaders had already changed its own priorities, almost without anyone noticing. Discussions with the leaders show that they are very aware that their gender has a part to play. These leaders reflect the change in the broader culture. And, though some (maybe,

many) of their members and supporters are uncomfortable with it, the parties they lead now reflect that change also.

The presence of Foster, O'Neill and McDonald at the funeral of Lyra McKee was a powerful image; but it was much more than that. Just as Foster's arrival at McGuinness's funeral in 2018 was greeted by applause by the congregation, these were not simply local events. They had deep significance because they reflected change at levels of social and family life the two parties historically rarely touched upon.

In short, a vast gulf had opened between the values now coming to be represented by Foster and McDonald as modern, professional, political women of power and those of the armed goblin, the brute sectarian, the inhumane punishment beater, the indiscriminate partisan. The gulf is not only in image and tone and demeanour and lifestyle, it is also in substance. Coercion has become a dirty word everywhere, north and south, east and west.

What is a unionist?

The unionist is a creature of caricature – a squat dour fire-and-brimstone bigot whose favourite word is no and whose emotional watch is stuck either at the Glorious Revolution or, even worse, the Reformation. Loyalists are just tattooed thugs.

All the old binaries follow from that. Unionists/Protestants are humourless literalists having a great suspicion of the imagination and the arts. Nationalists by contrast are outgoing, charming, social, a dab hand at the yarn and possessing the souls of poets and dreamers.

But, in times of peace, simplicities and near theological certainties simply do not reflect the lives of their own electorates.

Regardless of the rights and wrongs of same-sex marriage, divorce and abortion *per se*, gay people can be unionists, unionist families have gay children, unionist fathers and mothers are divorced, unionist sisters and daughters have had abortions. That is the reality of modern life and it doesn't take too well to the implicit criticism of absolutists.

The cause is not yet lost. If the unionist parties can reach out to the defectors of their own community they may – like the old cliché of the industrious, more scientifically-minded northern Protestant – rediscover the joys of civil engineering and, even, of building bridges.

After that, who knows? Bridges to Catholic unionists? To nationalists of all hues? To their southern neighbours? To a post-Brexit Great Britain in danger of simply forgetting about Northern Ireland.

Note on the contributor
Gail Walker is Editor of the *Belfast Telegraph*, a post she has held since 2015. She will shortly take up the new role of Editor-at-Large.

Reporting Brexit and the election in an English region

Brexit and the 2019 General Election are mostly viewed through the lens of national news, but a vast amount of coverage takes place on the ground, locally, all over the country. Tor Clark has covered eight general elections in the regions, for newspapers and radio. Dan Martin has been covering Leicestershire politics for 20 years with the *Leicester Mercury* newspaper and *LeicestershireLive* news website. Tim Parker has been pointing his microphone at all things political in Leicestershire and Rutland for a decade or more. What follows is a snapshot of how Brexit and the election panned out in a fairly typical English region

Leicestershire is as good an example of middle England as you're likely to get. Its politics is nicely divided red and blue, Leave and Remain. Its landscape, people and industry are incredibly diverse. So if we need to choose a place to look at how Brexit and the election played out at ground level, Leicestershire is as good a place as any.

The city of Leicester sits like a spider at the centre of its county. It has around 400,000 residents, half of them white, with a large Asian population. It has a compact city centre, dense Victorian neighbourhoods, post-war estates and leafy suburbs. It contains a thriving retail centre, traditional and new industries and of course three famous sporting teams.

Politically the city of Leicester votes Labour, electing more than 50 Labour councillors at the last few city council elections and returning three Labour MPs solidly since 1983 (apart from a Leicester South by-election blip in 2004 when a Lib Dem slipped in temporarily). The three city Westminster constituencies, together just voted for Remain in the 2016 EU Referendum, though the Leicester East and West seats were split virtually 50:50 and it was only the strong Remain vote in the more affluent Leicester South seat, which tipped the city over into Remain.

The rest of Leicestershire and its associated county of Rutland are about as solidly Conservative as you could ever see. Leicestershire and Rutland has beautiful countryside, dotted with pretty market towns. It had heavy industry and mining in the past, but that is now largely gone. Leicestershire and Rutland votes Conservative and was very heavily pro-Leave. It's what you might call 'traditional'.

Dan Martin and Tim Parker spent the last three months of 2019 covering the endgame to the previous three years of political excitement. This is their story.

Online and in print – the *LeicestershireLive* website and the *Leicester Mercury*…

LeicestershireLive is the latest iteration of the *Leicester Mercury* newspaper website. But in the days of digital first production, it is now the most important arm of news publishing in Leicestershire. Journalists still produce the *Leicester Mercury* newspaper every day, but it is *LeicestershireLive* where its huge audiences now reside. In its heyday in the early 1970s, the *Leicester Mercury* sold more than 180,000 newspapers every night and was one of the top ten biggest-selling regional newspapers in the UK. Now it claims audiences of a similar size for its website.

Unlucky for some?

Sometime in the summer of 2019 the *LeicestershireLive* newsroom got its collective act together to arrange its Christmas party. The date was agreed and inked in the diary for Friday December 13 – unlucky as it turns out for those who would be spending the early hours of that morning in leisure centres across Leicestershire covering the overnight general election counts and complaining loudly about poor wi-fi access.

The calendar clash meant all of the reporters who volunteered to cover a count would be stumbling into the following night's festivities on at best a few hours' sleep, stolen once an awful lot of live blog updates had been posted and thousands of hastily assembled words for the print edition had been filed. Not one of those hardy reporters flinched from the challenge and they turned in another proper 18-hour plus journalism shift of the sort that begins at the news coalface and terminates in the pub.

Looking back at what was produced at the end of it, the coverage of election night was the most in-depth people in Leicestershire could get and gave them a true taste of election night drama. The organisation had reporters at all 10 of the constituency counts in its patch offering up every political cough and spit as the results came in. The payback was clear to see instantly through the main currency that counts for regional publishers these days – website page views. Readers dropped in in their tens of thousands to see what the reporters – and the candidates – had had to say as the night unfolded.

It was satisfying because it answered a question that had been at the back of journalists' minds in the weeks running up to polling day. Did readers care really about this election? The website had covered the 'big' political stories local candidates became embroiled in during the campaign – Leicester South MP Jon Ashworth's 'Labour can't win' leak or North West Leicestershire MP Andrew

Bridgen apologising for ill-judged comments about the Grenfell tragedy for example. Yet those stories barely sped up online figures and the reporting team had to ask why the 'gotcha' stories political pundits loved writing were just not resonating with readers and adjusted their approach accordingly.

Changing the message

There was a sense of fatigue among some readers, who felt bombarded with 24/7 coverage, online political adverts and eternal social media spatting. They just seemed to want it all to be over. The same downbeat attitude was present among many of the party activists and canvassers who, Tories included, thought they were heading for certain defeat. Many longed for a sunny May election rather than endless cold December street trudging. And reporters feared they were struggling to get to their core audience with some major breaking stories because they were competing online with the blanket coverage from the nationals and rolling TV and radio news.

But local coverage did prosper with a focus on the local battles that took place, often in council chambers where the election had upped the temperature of debate. As polling day approached the journalists found more and more sources wanted to tip them off about, say a Labour councillor suspended for anti-Semitism or a Tory in trouble over old Islamophobic remarks. They did better when local coverage drowned out much the noise from Westminster and chose to resist the temptation to follow up national headlines by seeking local angles on them.

The urge to rush out and cover the 'big beasts' shooting up to our patch for a quick photo opportunity was resisted. These visits are a great tool for motivating the party faithful but hardly a turn on the readers. Sometimes journalists weren't informed about them but were optimistically sent iPhone-quality pictures and five line press releases after the event in the hope they would regurgitate the message. These offerings largely ended up on the spike – if campaigning politicians don't want to talk to local journalists it shouldn't be surprising when those journalists don't have anything to write about them.

No-score draw

LeicestershireLive only really covered one big set piece political event in the whole campaign – a Marmite Jeremy Corbyn campaign rally. Online metrics instantly showed people were desperate to read about him, even if they didn't then go out and vote for him. Hustings are a usual staple for campaign coverage, but they were thin on the ground and, in some cases, organisers struggled to get candidates to agree to take part.

LeicestershireLive covers parliamentary seats which rarely change hands or throw up shocks. Boiling down local results to the extreme, Leicestershire and Rutland entered the election with seven Tory MPs and three Labour MPs and came out the other side with the same political maths.

"How the hell," remarked a tired sub-editor pulling together our election coverage on the morning after the count, "are we supposed to make an interesting front page out of that? It's a 0-0 draw." His summary was fair to a point but belied much of the energy and excitement of the weeks running up to polling day where high profile and long-serving MPs had been dropping like flies. This had turbo-charged the campaign and coverage of it.

Keith Vaz, the veteran Labour Leicester East MP, was poised for a comfortable victory until weeks before polling day when he was suspended from parliament for six months having being said to have offered to buy class A drugs for two male prostitutes in an encounter uncovered by a national newspaper sting. There were tremendous rows and great copy to be had over the eventual selection of an Islington borough councillor and Corbyn supporter Claudia Webbe in his place. She defended the 'safe' seat but saw Labour's 22,000 majority shrink to 6,000.

Outspoken Rutland and Melton MP Sir Alan Duncan departed Parliament before the election with the stinging declaration it was a 'muppet show'. It was briefly rumoured Tory leader Boris Johnson was looking to be parachuted in there as guaranteed route back into Parliament. This provided so much fresh meat for the politics pages locally. It wasn't to be, but the 'will he, won't he' uncertainty lasted right up to the minutes before the selection meeting at Melton Cattle Market, where some local Tories were still hoping Boris would breeze in at the last moment as their candidate.

Loughborough was the closest thing to a marginal seat and Conservative MP Nicky Morgan stepped down giving Labour some hope of pinching it. She cited online trolling, appalling abuse and threats over Brexit, which she had vehemently opposed but was now passionately supporting, as a reason for not standing again. She also, quite reasonably, said she wanted to spend more time with her family, though was promptly returned, albeit temporarily, to the Government post-election via the House of Lords. Many readers were quick to point out that it was this sort of Westminster manoeuvring that was turning people off politics in the round.

Serial election winner and advocate of astrology and homeopathy David Tredinnick stepped aside in Bosworth and was replaced by a GP from Oxfordshire, who it is understood does not share his predecessor's high-profile enthusiasm for alternative medicines.

But that is the point and the challenge for regional newspaper politics reporters now. Many familiar contacts in Westminster have now gone and that includes not just the former MPs themselves but their staff who would try to feed political stories through.

So as 2020 develops, journalists are still trying to see what kind of relationship they can develop with the four fresh faces *LeicestershireLive* readers sent back down to the House of Commons to represent them. They are trying to find out what their ambitions are, what motivates them, even irritates them, and what they think of what's already been written about them. It's very much a work in progress.

...while on the radio, how BBC Leicester covered the campaign

The run-up to the 2019 election was short and dramatic, replacing the constant drama of Brexit in Parliament, that had dominated politics for much of the preceding year. Before the election was called, most of Leicestershire's Conservative MPs loyally followed their leader, in a time when loyal Conservatives were increasingly fewer to come by.

North West Leicestershire MP Andrew Bridgen, among other big Brexit beasts, kept himself in the limelight by insisting a clear, immediate resolution was what business owners and the economy needed. And business owners did want that, but not at any cost. Alberto Costa, the South Leicestershire MP, not the most likely MP to cause a stir, stood up in February to defend UK and EU citizens' rights here and abroad, thereby losing his first footing on the Westminster ministerial career path.

But his rebel streak soon faded in a government that quickly agreed with him and assimilated his views. He stuck to his guns on a matter that was clearly of great personal as well as political importance. But there were few other distinct local voices on the nitty gritty of Brexit.

Melton and Rutland MP Sir Alan Duncan briefly stole the headlines in July, in an attempt to derail Boris Johnson's rise to the top of the Conservative Party. Three months later, as the election was called, he indicated he wouldn't be standing, and so did Loughborough MP, then Culture Secretary, Nicky Morgan. Suddenly, this election promised quite a bit more local change than we'd been expected when David Tredinnick said he'd bow out the previous February.

Then Leicester East MP Keith Vaz was back at the top of the local political news agenda. In the last session of the last parliament in the Commons, a six-month parliamentary suspension was approved after he was said to have 'expressed willingness' to purchase cocaine for male prostitutes. Surely, he couldn't fight another election, knowing he'd probably have to start a new term without setting foot in the Commons chamber? Debate erupted in Leicester East, as elsewhere, about his political and personal past and future.

The local narrative of the popular, hard-working constituency MP who would help anyone and 'got things done', jarred with the tabloid tales. Gujarati grannies appeared on social media streams to endorse him while almost every political opponent and national commentator had another gleeful go at pushing his reputation off the cliff. Only when his own friends in Labour publicly suggested he should go, did the city's then longest-serving MP (by quite a margin) finally quit, leaving barely a four-day window for his colleagues to unveil a replacement.

And then those same social media streams seemed to turn on his replacement. In this hugely diverse constituency, Whatsapp and Facebook discourse quickly became racially provocative and divisive, painting the 'unifying, stabilising' previous MP, against the 'unwelcome newcomer' candidate, Claudia Webbe. It emerged she'd overseen a national Labour Party emergency motion on Kashmir, which many saw as unwelcome interference in Indian politics.

It was an unpleasant episode locally, not entirely contained by the tight duration of the election campaign. As nominations closed on November 14, four out of the ten local MPs would be leaving parliament. Although, in a final twist following the election, former Loughborough MP Nicky Morgan stayed on short-term as Culture Secretary, in the sanctuary of the House of Lords.

As you were in Leicestershire

Leicestershire and Rutland finished 2019 with exactly the same electoral maths as it had started the year. It had seven Conservative MPs and three Labour MPs, but there were interesting stories to tell behind those headlines. Red Leicester, despite being fairly evenly split on the UK's membership of the EU had once again returned three Labour MPs. It had not gone the way of the northern red wall Labour seats or those midlands Brexit-voting Labour seats. Leicester's Labour attachment was weakened but not broken. Was this a result of all the students in the city, perhaps 40,000 out of a population of up to 400,000? All of them with the franchise. What about the impact of the large number of non-white voters in the city? Did that preserve a link with Labour which was eroding elsewhere in the midlands?

In the county, the Conservative majorities were nothing short of huge. The journalists covering the counts did quick maths and found Tory MPs going off to Westminster with majorities of around 30,000 votes. Rural Leicestershire and Rutland was a sea of unassailable blue.

But overall, having covered Brexit and various elections over the previous five years, there was a feeling as December 13 dawned, that this debate was conclusively now all over. A line had been drawn. For better or worse the political landscape had been redesigned and we were entering a new era without Leave-Remain, but with that argument settled by the relatively inefficient method of a first-past-the-post general election.

The people from the regions had spoken just as loudly as their metropolitan counterparts who get to see more of the political action close-up but for once, perhaps, the regions had had the louder voice. Time will tell whether the December 12 election was the end, a beginning or merely a continuation of what had dominated politics for the previous five years.

Note on the contributors

Tor Clark is Associate Professor in Journalism and BA Journalism programme director at the University of Leicester. Previously he was editor of two UK regional newspapers. He has been a political journalist for more than 30 years and in that time has covered eight UK general elections, the last four for BBC Leicester. He is co-editor of this book.

Dan Martin has been the political correspondent of the *Leicester Mercury* newspaper for 20 years. He now works across all his organisation's platform's including *Leicestershire Live*. Dan is an authority on Leicestershire politics. He began his career on the *Harborough Mail* newspaper.

Tim Parker has been BBC Radio Leicester's political reporter for eight years. He is an expert on Leicestershire politics and organises the station's legendary all-night general election broadcasts. He also regularly contributes political news to the BBC *East Midlands Today* and *Sunday Politics* East Midlands TV programmes. Previously he worked for BBC Stoke and BBC Nottingham. He is a graduate of the University of Leicester.

External perspectives on Brexit

***

Do they mean us? Or do they think we are mad? What foreign correspondents think of it all

John Mair

They are the outsiders who are insiders – the foreign correspondents who report Britain. They, especially those from what we used to call Europe, are perplexed at best by Brexit. Some are mad at the decision and at least one has taken the move of emigrating from Brexit Britain.

Diana Zimmermann reports for ZDF, the German broadcaster. In our previous book, *Brexit, Trump and the Media,* she told how going out of London to report in 2016 allowed her to forecast and understand the referendum decision. Today, four years later in *The year Johnson came – and the truth went elsewhere* she is rather Ungermanic in calling out our prime minister.

"We on the continent now know that even in the safe cradle of modern democracy, a person who speaks obvious falsehoods – such as over NHS spending in the referendum campaign in 2016 – can not only win campaigns but even become Her Majesty's Prime Minister." Put into plain English, she is saying Boris (and others) have lied their way to high office.

Angela Antetomaso works (or worked) for Italian TV from London. Just after the referendum she was advised on the top of a London bus to "F**k off back to where you came from!" So she has, but not to Italy. In *How Brexit changed Britain… and my life* she recalls her moment of truth on the day after the 2019 general election.

"On December 13, 2019, while reporting from Westminster about the results of the general election, I had my epiphany. In the end, we all got what we wanted, the UK was getting its Brexit done, and I was getting far from it all. After years of disappointment and sadness about what was happening around me, I finally got to the point of being completely detached. For the first time in ages, I was for once simply 'reporting', just coldheartedly giving the facts, without having to hide what I was feeling inside. Hey, that was a first. I was finally emotionally free."

She and her husband are in the process of moving to the USA.

Tonje Iversen is a generation below the other two distinguished correspondents. She reports from London for the Norwegians. In *A little quiet may soon inhabit what once was a very noisy place, possibly…* she recalls with horror the sheer bedlam that descended on College Green outside the UK parliament in recent years. A cacophony of competing voices, pro and anti Brexit – "An absolute belief in it as a necessity or as an absolute evil. People on both sides of the argument seem to be very certain about what Brexit entails and what it will mean for the future of Britain," she writes.

And just before the Johnson victory she was able to look back in sorrow at the little green bearpit: "One of the last times I walked out of College Green, I was met by a happy man with a big smile waving at me shouting 'smile, smile' while handing me a leaflet. Printed on it were the predictions of the end of the world in the near future, not because of Brexit, but because of a religious belief."

Finally, from a young professional to a very wizened old hand. Alan Geere is a British journalism institution. Head of journalism at more universities than you can shake a stick it and a very successful local newspaper editor. Now he is in China teaching and in *Boris, Brexit…and the view from Beijing* he reports the puzzlement of the Chinese at the British demonstration of democracy and the surprising (to some) result.

"Into this everyday story of Chinese folk enter Brexit, Boris and the concept of an election that has many people bamboozled. There is no universal suffrage in China, but an arcane system of 'elections' whereby a nominated party official is appointed to a pre-determined role. The Communist Party of China (CPC) effectively rules a one-party state so the cut and thrust of adversarial party politics is beyond the knowledge and appreciation of the man on the Shanghai omnibus."

So the views from the outsider/insiders. A very sharp lens from which to observe recent, turbulent, British political history. One is left with the question of this section: Do they mean us? Or do they simply think Britain has gone bonkers?

The year Johnson came – and the truth went elsewhere

As a European foreign correspondent in a Britain leaving the EU, Diana Zimmermann was neatly placed to observe the 2019 election. Here are her observations in which she wonders: where will it all end? Translated by Elisabeth Moseley

The election campaign was only how 2019 ended. For it was the denouement, you could say, to a busy year: when we realised Brexit was really happening; and when we saw the British parliament vote three times against Theresa May's exit agreement, only to end up accepting Boris Johnson's much worse deal.

It was the year when a prime minister tried to suspend the mother of all parliaments and then won an absolute majority in the general election. It was the year when the Liberal Democrats briefly thought their leader could become prime minister, only to end up back at square one with a miserable election result.

It was the year when the Labour Party almost found a position on Europe (finally); when nine of its MPs left the party because they could not support their leader's Brexit strategy; and because they saw the party as a haven of anti-Semitism; it was the year Jeremy Corbyn remained in office despite his devastating defeat in the December 12 election.

And it was the year of a Western European election campaign which reached, some say, new levels of mendacity. We on the continent now know that even in the safe cradle of modern democracy, a person who speaks obvious falsehoods – such as over NHS spending in the referendum campaign in 2016 – can not only win campaigns but even become Her Majesty's Prime Minister.

If you come from a country, as I do, where the last election campaign completely lacked any kind of excitement or climax and the only (albeit truly shocking) new development was the entry of the AfD into the Bundestag, you could only be amazed.

A new low

The Conservative Party reached a new low with this campaign.[1] Yes, Labour also spread half-truths, in a manifesto that seemed too good to be true for most Britons. It was evasive and not open to the allegations of anti-Semitism, but no other party came anywhere close to the amount of untruths told by the ruling Tory party.[2]

The willingness of this age-old party to throw all rules of political decency overboard and model its actions on those of the US Republicans is quite surprising, even in the context of a tough election campaign.

The Conservative headquarters edited an interview with Keir Starmer so that he came across as completely clueless, while in reality he provided fluent answers.[3] When one of the Conservative Party Twitter accounts was suddenly rebranded as a fact-checking service during the TV debate between Jeremy Corbyn and Boris Johnson, even Twitter criticised this for being 'misleading'.[4]

Tory politicians released totally unrealistic and inexplicable figures. Citizens were promised 50,000 more nurses, but on closer inspection it only turned out to be 31,000 – and there was no explanation of where they would come from, especially since there were already 40,000 vacancies in the NHS. Forty new hospitals were also announced, but in fact only six are being refurbished.[5] All of this was known before the election.

The Supreme Court verdict made it clear to the public that it had been Boris Johnson's intention to block Parliament and that he had misled the Queen. The public also knew that Johnson was suspected of having had a relationship with an American businesswoman, who he had allegedly supplied with government grants and taken on delegation trips without reporting the conflict of interest.[6]

If we lived in different times, or in other countries, these incidents would all have been severely damaging for someone aiming for the highest office in the country. Nevertheless, Boris Johnson was still elected. If many people didn't care that he broke the rules or even worse, they thought it was high time he did so, then it raises the question: Why?

Rules are generally there to protect the weak from the whims of the strong. But this belief seems to be becoming less and less significant in many western democracies. Brexit and the rise of right-wing populism in Europe are partly a result of the financial crisis. Decency is not worth much anymore. We learned this lesson at the time.

The three-word slogan works wonders

It is no coincidence that Jeremy Corbyn, who constantly tried to remind society of this, appealing to our sense of responsibility towards the weak, was perceived himself as weak, and was outdone by a candidate whose moral compass always directed him towards the highest reachable point in his career. The French phrase *'il ne perd pas le nord'* (he will always find the way which leads him upwards) is in Johnson's case satisfyingly fitting.

The British didn't want Jeremy Corbyn or a hung parliament and, as it had in the 'Take Back Control' referendum, a three-word slogan 'Get Brexit Done' worked wonders. Voters found the promise of not having to hear about Brexit anymore simply irresistible, despite it being entirely unrealistic.[7] Even Brussels began crossing its fingers that the election would result in a stable majority, in the hope that it would put an end to the frustration of its parliamentary stalemate.

Brexit has now become a reality – even though the majority of the population voted for parties that did not want it, or want a much softer version of it than Johnson.

Many people in the UK barely recognised their country after the referendum; others turned their back on the following three years of the political horror show in disgust; and many of the 48 per cent are seriously concerned about the country's political culture. Simple slogans; cheap attacks on the opponent; the choice between two unappealing party leaders; and, above all, the sheer number of obvious falsehoods have caused widespread unease. Faith in politics is at an all-time low.

After Boris Johnson played a major role in exacerbating this (only 25 per cent of the British public consider him trustworthy[8]), he is now apparently determined to change it. But he is not the first. If you look back at the last three prime ministers and their inaugural speeches, it is easy to see that the promises being made have been broken before.

As new prime minister, David Cameron said in 2010 that he wanted to restore confidence in the political system[9]. Almost word for word, Johnson repeated in July 2019: "We will restore confidence in our democracy".[10] After his election success in December, he now aims to convince, above all, traditional Labour voters, who voted Conservative for the first time in their lives, that they have done the right thing.[11]

The second problem area that appears in the prime minister's speeches is inequality in the country – between north and south, Wales and London, black and white, homeowners and tenants. But Theresa May and David Cameron both stood on the Downing Street steps and promised 'working people' (which almost sounds like they could mean 'working class', but not really) that everything will change for the better. Theresa May vowed to eliminate 'burning injustice' in the country.[12] She did not succeed. Johnson now promises to work around the clock to ensure that voters from the former industrial regions keep voting for him.

The third issue that Cameron, May, and Johnson all mentioned in their inaugural speeches, is the unity of the country. This now seems more endangered than ever.

Nationalist parties boosted

Nationalist parties have won the majority in Scotland and for the first time in Northern Ireland. Nicola Sturgeon is calling for a second independence referendum for Scotland; the nationalists in Northern Ireland have long dreamed of a referendum on reunification with the Republic. All of this has been revived by Brexit and now hangs like a dark cloud over the union.

In her Christmas speech the Queen described 2019 as a 'bumpy' year. The following 12 months of 2020 is not likely to be much easier.

However, the year at least began with a clear distribution of power. The excitement about Brexit will likely subside, now that it has happened. What form it takes, which will be negotiated from March and should be clarified by the end of the year, may seem secondary, but is of the utmost importance for Great Britain and the EU.

There is still a choice between a hard break or full alignment. The outcome of these negotiations and their economic consequences will determine not only Boris Johnson's political survival, but also the future of the United Kingdom and Europe.

Amongst all the chaos of the past three and a half years, we have often looked on, shaking our heads, and wondered: what has happened to the dignified, stiff upper lip, terribly polite Britain we once knew? But it is important to bear in mind that other European nations are not immune to following the same course.

One of the lessons that can be learned from the last few years of British politics is very clear: if political disenchantment is ignored, more justice is promised and not delivered, and whole parts of the country feel deprived, old assurances can quickly become null and void.

Angela Merkel recently said, that Brexit was a 'wake-up call' for the European Union. She was referring to the fact that the EU had to up its game, especially with regard to research and education. But it is even more necessary for the EU27 to focus on making their citizens understand how important it is to abide by societal rules, and to make sure that said rules really help those in society who need protection.

At least Johnson has started his second term in office, without breaking his key promise: the United Kingdom was no longer a member of the EU from January 31, 2020.

A new Johnson?

So perhaps we are now seeing a new Johnson who has used populism as a means to come to power, but who is now becoming a wise, honest country father intent on reunifying the country? One who, once established, abides by the rules of political coexistence – i.e. speaking the truth?

Can his right-wing regulatory policies coupled with market liberalism and more social spending satisfy voters? Will he be able to turn his energetic optimism into tangible improvements for the British? Or did the means of populism just work so well for him that he just cannot resist holding on to them?

Johnson wants to restore trust in politics (which for him means trust in him). Maybe he will surprise us. Of course, every politician who is untrustworthy fights for the credibility of his status.

Though judging by his first actions there is not much cause for hope. In typically populist and otherwise authoritarian fashion, one of his first attacks was on public service broadcasting, in this case the BBC.

Yet another public service under fire, while his special adviser takes aim at the civil service. He still maintains the fiction that a loose deal with the EU is possible without tariffs and different rules and standards stopping the free flow of goods. [13]

Experts deny this, unless the prime minister agrees to full alignment. He refused to do so at his meeting with European Commission President Ursula von der Leyen in early January 2020. But even if he doesn't one of his two claims will have to be wrong, and then the question is which one he will withdraw. And when will he finally admit that every Brexit deal will contain bitter truths?

There is a great danger that this blonde unicorn may be a gifted campaign leader, entertaining his potential voters countrywide, and seeming terribly down to earth, but that the reality of the job will catch up with him.

This would certainly leave the United Kingdom poorer than before, and with no funding for its grand, ambitious projects. There will then be the search for whose fault it all is – someone who lied, who cheated, who played unfairly. Johnson is unlikely to offer himself as the guilty party. He'll find one somewhere else – most likely in Brussels, or Remainers and immigrants in his own country.

Notes

[1] As a result of this election, a group called for future election campaigns of political parties to be checked for accuracy, referring to a study by YouGov:
-"…for the Conservatives, it said that 88 per cent (5,952) of the party's most widely promoted ads either featured claims which had been flagged by independent fact-checking organisations (including BBC Reality Check) as not correct or not entirely correct.
– For Labour, it initially said that it could not find any misleading claims in ads run over the four-day period. Subsequently, First Draft issued an update, saying a bug in Facebook's ad library meant their analysis was missing some data. In fact, according to their methodology, 7 per cent of ads published by Labour over that time contained inaccurate or misleading claims. Again, this is only over a four-day period and does not necessarily represent the whole campaign."

[2] https://members.tortoisemedia.com/2019/12/11/lies-191211/content.html
Chapter: Who was the most deceitful?

[3] https://www.irishtimes.com/news/politics/edited-v-original-tories-release-doctored-clip-of-labour-s-keir-starmer-1.4074197

[4] https://www.theguardian.com/politics/2019/nov/20/twitter-accuses-tories-of-misleading-public-in-factcheck-row

[5] https://fullfact.org/election-2019/50000-more-nurses-claim-conservative-manifesto-accurate/

https://www.bbc.co.uk/news/50544033

https://fullfact.org/health/six-hospitals-not-forty/

https://www.bbc.co.uk/news/uk-politics-50240221

[6] When Labour published its manifesto, a website suddenly appeared that was made to look like a Labour webpage, but which denounced every point put forward in their manifesto. https://www.euronews.com/2019/11/21/uk-snap-general-election-2019-conservatives-launch-fake-manifesto-website-for-rivals-labou

[7] https://yougov.co.uk/topics/politics/articles-reports/2019/12/23/their-own-words-why-voters-abandoned-labour

[8] Only 25 per cent of the British believe that Johnson is trustworthy, 53 per cent stated at the end of October 2019 that he was not "trustworthy" (YouGov). Only 23 per cent of the British consider him "honest". YouGov, polling October 29-30

[9] https://www.gov.uk/government/speeches/david-camerons-speech-outside-10-downing-street-as-prime-minister

[10] https://www.gov.uk/government/speeches/boris-johnsons-first-speech-as-prime-minister-24-july-2019

[11] https://www.gov.uk/government/speeches/pm-statement-in-downing-street-13-december-2019

[12] https://www.gov.uk/government/speeches/statement-from-the-new-prime-minister-theresa-may

[13] He repeated this on his visit to Northern Ireland on January 13, 2020.

Note on the contributor

Diana Zimmermann was born in 1971 in Frankfurt/Main and is the ZDF correspondent for the UK and Ireland. She studied comparative literature, sinology and history in Berlin, Paris and Kunming. She was a reporter for ARTE in Strasbourg and Berlin and a correspondent for ARD in Beijing. She worked as the East Asia correspondent for ZDF from 2007-2011 and headed ZDF's foreign affairs magazine *auslandsjournal* before moving to London in 2015.

How Brexit changed Britain…
and my life

Disheartened at the outcome of the EU Referendum, Italian journalist Angela Antetomaso wanted to play her part and stepped into politics trying to oppose it. With Brexit now a certainty, she turned page and seized to opportunity to leave the UK for a new beginning in the USA. She explains her journey…

I remember very well the night between June 23 and 24, 2016. It was around 2 o'clock in the morning. The EU Referendum results were being read out on TV and it was clear the United Kingdom had voted to get out of the European Union. A dismal feeling hovered over me and I felt completely hopeless. As a European citizen, and an Italian correspondent in London, I knew things were going to change for me as well. I was right.

'Go back home, you're not welcome here'
Almost four years have gone by and many unexpected things have happened since.

Not all of them good. A few months after the referendum, I was verbally attacked in a bus and angrily shouted at: "Get out of this country – go back home, you're not welcome here."

That left me in shock. This *was* home though, why should I go? So I stayed. And stayed in the hope things would change and the UK would go back to being the tolerant, welcoming country it once was. I'm afraid it didn't happen. At least not in my experience. The United Kingdom seemed to be less and less 'united'. People started to become more and more angry at each other, there were endless protests, demonstrations, petitions… basically an undercurrent of hope and despair going on, both in the streets of London and on social media. It didn't matter how sad it was to see this happening, I had to keep on smiling and had to keep on reporting about it on TV. It wasn't easy.

From journalist to candidate

In all of this – or actually exactly because of this – I even had a stint at politics. It was definitely connected to the attack on the bus and to what was going on around me. I started feeling the urge to get involved. I wanted to do my bit to try to change things. So when I received an email from this new pro-European party saying they were looking for candidates, I didn't think twice.

Everything happened very fast. After a short initial chat with them I found myself hastily putting together the paperwork. We were running against time in order to meet the deadline and finally be on the list of candidates for the upcoming European Parliamentary Elections.

Not only did I have to be approved but they also had to run a background check on me for security purposes. Time was short but I did get through. A few hours after my name was submitted, the Electoral Commissioner called to confirm I had been accepted. What a thrill. I was in. From that moment onwards, things moved very quickly. With less than one month to the elections, life for me got very hectic indeed. I had never actually been one for politics, but that was probably why I put myself fully into it – without looking back or thinking twice.

I found myself in the streets of London, in the most crowded spots of the capital, distributing pro-European flyers and talking to people. I started speaking at hustings, debating candidates of other parties and other political beliefs. It was new for me, but it wasn't really hard. After 20 years of daily anchoring and reporting on live TV, talking came easy. People started being curious, many were wondering why an Italian TV presenter was now putting her career on hold and moving to the other side of the fence. Mostly, they were wondering why she would want to get into UK politics. So I told them. I was now the one being interviewed. I was publicly making my point and openly telling my story on TV, radio and newspapers. It was fun. And it was worth it.

The interest was great, and the party was nicely supporting me in those first steps. I wasn't elected in the end and I honestly didn't expect to be. A couple of parties harvested all of the votes and there was no much chance for anyone else to get in, let alone for someone who was, in the end, a 'foreigner'. It was, though, a very fulfilling and gratifying experience and without any doubt, a really inspiring time of my life. Not only did I get a good number of personal votes, but I certainly learned a lot. More importantly, if I didn't make it to Brussels to change things, I felt I tried at least and this made me feel definitely less concerned about the Brexit situation, and much more detached about it.

A mere few days after the European Elections, the party even started considering the option of having me standing as a candidate in the 2020 race for London Mayor. Wow. I was absolutely flattered, but I knew it would be too much. I had the exciting out-of-my-world experience, now it was time to return to my life. So I happily went back to broadcasting and reporting about Brexit. 'Happily' not because I was now more optimistic or hopeful about Brexit, but simply because I soon realised I was no longer as emotionally involved as I had been in the past. That was quite an achievement for me. A powerful first step, with more to follow.

Brexit becomes a reality

Fast forward a few months and a new challenge was around the corner. The result of the General Elections held on December 12, 2019, made Brexit a new tangible reality. 'The people have spoken, they want out' chimed the TV. 'We are out' said the tabloids. It was true. The majority Boris Johnson got on election day was a clear sign the country was actually going to 'get on with business and get out of the EU'. That was it. No matter the United Kingdom on the edge of splitting up, the crisis looming, multinationals leaving the country, jobs being lost. Nothing mattered anymore. The UK was getting out of the EU, deal or no deal.

It felt kind of numb, but that's when I clearly realised. I wasn't bothered anymore. At that point I just felt simply very lucky. My husband had recently got a work opportunity in the United States and we were both given a chance to start afresh somewhere else. It wasn't going to be easy, but there it was. A one way ticket to thriving America. And all this while the UK was in a mess. 'Shall we go?' we asked ourselves. We knew the answer straight away. Yes, we shall.

Once again, I didn't think twice. Before the 2016 referendum, it would never have crossed my mind to leave London. I made this my home and I loved it here. In the past few years though, ever since the attack on the bus, I had to open my eyes and face reality. I had to see it for what it was, an increasingly difficult situation for everyone, but mostly for non-UK-born people like me. Daily life here was gradually becoming less pleasant and consequently less safe.

We decided to leap at the chance. I could even keep on doing my job, the company I was working for was happy to have me as a correspondent from New York rather than London, and that helped immensely. Yes, we could surely do it. I knew leaving London was not going to be a walk in the park. Not much from a logistic point of view, rather on an emotional level. After over 20 years, this was home. But I was being offered the opportunity to nicely step out of this mess and start anew somewhere great, and I intended to seize it.

We decided to split our time (or mine, mostly) between New York and London, where I could also keep on working for other media outlets. I could get the best of both worlds. I would at least try.

An election epiphany

On December 13, 2019, while reporting from Westminster about the results of the General Election, I had my epiphany. In the end, we all got what we wanted, the UK was getting its Brexit done, and I was getting far from it all. After years of disappointment and sadness about what was happening around me, I finally got to the point of being completely detached. For the first time in ages, I was for once simply 'reporting', just coldheartedly giving the facts, without having to hide what I was feeling inside. Hey, that was a first. I was finally emotionally free.

'Landslide for Johnson' … 'Brexit on its way' … 'Crashing out with no deal' … the words kept on coming out of my mouth on an automated roll. Everything that was going on, the pain, the uncertainty, the crisis, it didn't touch me anymore. It took a while and a few unforeseen turns, but I was eventually out of this. I was healed.

I always thought: "If we ever leave the UK, there are another 27 countries to choose from." Strange how things then work out. Sometimes life decides for you and serves you the unexpected on a plate. And at times there is also the lucky chance that reality surpasses your imagination.

Note on the contributor

Angela Antetomaso is a TV presenter and host with two decades of daily on-air experience. She has worked for CNN International, Bloomberg Television and CNBC. For many years Angela has presented her own daily show hosting a large variety of high-profile guests, while at the same time also contributing with in-depth analysis and commentaries to various international TV channels including CNBC International, Sky and Mediaset. She now lives between London and New York, working at Forbes as a correspondent for its Italian magazine. For Forbes' new TV channel, she also hosts her own weekly show *Asset and the City*.

A little quiet may soon inhabit what once was a very noisy place, possibly…

Tonje Iversen stood outside the House of Parliament for much of 2019. Here she reflects on what she saw and what she thinks may now happen in the changed world of a hefty Johnson majority

The year of 2019 was noisy. It was a year where everything was defined as being or becoming broken. Politics; democracy; the Union; the relationship with Europe.

People were parading their anxiety; constantly addressing their worries for the future and their longing for the past; how things were before the referendum; or how things were before Britain became a part of the EU.

The present seemed to be lost in dreams about the past or predictions about the future, and so the present was dominated by anger, anxiety and fear – or, at least, for most of the time.

Watching the drama

I have spent many hours outside parliament on College Green, in the cold, in the heat, in the rain and in the wind. Behind me, the perfect backdrop, The Houses of Parliament, where all the important decisions are made, or at least where MPs were trying to make them.

Watching the drama unfolding from this little spot on the Green, were broadcasters from around the world, setting up their tents and finding their live spots. Journalists glued to their phones; photographers making sure everything was working until the moment was there; the moment when you are going to tell the audience exactly what is going on in there, in the building behind you.

Explain it in a simple, clear, understandable and interesting way, so no one misses out on all the twists and turns, or the unknown juridical waters, or the complexities of the process.

But this little grassy spot in the heart of Westminster was not only reserved for the media; activists spent a lot of time here too. Eager to tell those who wanted to listen, about their fears, their worries and how they felt about politicians and the Brexit process. Many of them convinced that Brexit was a terrible idea that must never be allowed to happen; many others convinced that politicians were about to ignore the will of the people and treat them with contempt. These passionate people often found themselves in a heated debate with others, just as committed as them. Often conversations turned into shouting, and sometimes the words became abusive.

A febrile atmosphere

The atmosphere around this little place was febrile. A circle of flags, posters and disruptive noise. This was the place where you really could look at frustration unfolding, not just between protesters outside the fence, or politicians giving interviews on the inside, but also where contempt for the press came up close. Many insults and disruptive shouts were directed at broadcasters, many carrying accusations of biased news and suspicions of a hidden agenda. Some wanted to sabotage and disturb, others to be heard, loud and clear.

After more than three years of tumult, it is not surprising that the word Brexit has been loaded with tension. It has been a vessel of anger and frustration as the debate has mostly been focused on blame, guilt and shame. Who is responsible for the mess? Who is to blame for Brexit being delayed and deferred? Who should be ashamed because it is happening at all? In order to be right you need to make someone else wrong.

In 2020 College Green could be a quieter place.

There is a sense of relief that Brexit now is certain to happen, that there is a majority government in Westminster, that the stalemate is gone. The relief is of course mostly felt by those who voted to leave, and feared Brexit would never happen, but there is also relief among Remainers. If something is certain, if you can't prevent it, then there is no need to resist it anymore.

Things are slowly taking shape.

The timeline after the referendum has been a bit like finding yourself in a dark room unable to find the light switch. Slowly your eyes are getting used to the dark and you can see the shape of things, but the switch is still to be found. The impact of Brexit is far from clear.

But at least one question is silenced. It is the end of the 'never ending' debate of last year, centred around whether Brexit would happen or not.

The hope of it being sorted

As so many voters said in December, they can only hope that Brexit will get sorted, that things will calm down. They believe that Boris Johnson might be the prime minster who can swiftly close the chapter of Brexit, heal the division in Britain and turn on the light so one can see what the future holds and plan for it.

But we are still fumbling around in the dark. Not much is clear and many questions are still to be raised and to be answered. The protesters outside College Green might be gone, for now. There won't be a new referendum. But the noise in the media is still there. A devious cocktail made of worries, fears, prejudices and absolutes.

Brexit has somehow been fueled them. An absolute belief in it as a necessity or as an absolute evil. People on both side of the argument seem to be very certain about what Brexit entails and what it will mean for the future of Britain.

One of the last times I walked out of College Green, I was met by a happy man with a big smile waving at me shouting 'smile, smile' while handing me a leaflet. Printed on it were the predictions of the end of the world in the near future, not because of Brexit, but because of a religious belief.

Whether Brexit will prove to be a new golden age, or if it's downhill from this coming December, no one really knows. We can only believe, hope or guess. Maybe both scenarios will prove to be an exaggeration.

Regardless, any relief may be short lived as Britain is about to embark on demanding trade negotiations with the EU. Maybe we all just need to be comfortable with not knowing for a while. That is if we, at least, want our minds to be a quiet place.

Note on the contributor

Tonje Iversen is a journalist from Norway based in London. She mainly contributes to TV2, Norway's biggest commercial broadcaster, providing live analysis pieces, comments and reports on current affairs, politics and society in the United Kingdom. She has a Master's degree in political journalism from City, University of London and a Bachelor's degree in broadcast journalism from Gimlekollen in Kristiansand.

Boris, Brexit…and the view from Beijing

The world watched as Boris Johnson made his audacious, and ultimately successful, grab for power. But what did people in China, the most populous country on earth, get to see, read and hear? Alan Geere was there to find out

The world map hanging on the lecture room wall tells its own story. China is right in the middle, glowing pink, and over on the far left, barely visible, is the United Kingdom scrunched up against the curvature of the earth close to a very small Atlantic Ocean and a slimmed down America that looks like a reflection in one of those wacky fairground mirrors.

This is a buoyant, self-assured nation confident in its own position at the centre of the world, even if the world doesn't much care for China and its reported affronts to human rights and attempts to use world-leading technology to wrestle information and control.

So why should we care what China thinks about Boris, Brexit and the UK's position on the global stage?

The facts and figures speak for themselves. By current recognised estimates, China has a population of 1.4bn, meaning that one in every five people on earth is Chinese. It has six cities in the world's top 10, including at number one, Chongqing, a place most people have never heard of, let alone visited.

The chapter is written from Guangzhou – formerly Canton – which sneaks in at number nine, with a population in excess of 13m. This is a place not just of conspicuous wealth – expensive cars, designer clothes, lavish restaurants – but also ubiquitous technology with the smart phone in charge of every moment of your life from travelling on a bus, buying a bag of roasted chestnuts from the side of the street or even giving some spare digital change to a beggar, who is trawling a metro train displaying his QR code.

The smartphone is not a tiresome adjunct that is keeping children away from real life. It is an everyday essential.

There are more traditional scenes, such as old ladies wheeling handcarts laden with rubbish along a four-lane highway or cleaners sweeping up fallen leaves into their straw hats, but everyone seems industrious, well-fed, reasonably clothed and, dare it be said, happy.

Into this everyday story of Chinese folk enter Brexit, Boris and the concept of an election that has many people bamboozled. There is no universal suffrage in China, but an arcane system of 'elections' whereby a nominated party official is appointed to a pre-determined role. The Communist Party of China (CPC) effectively rules a one-party state so the cut and thrust of adversarial party politics is beyond the knowledge and appreciation of the man on the Shanghai omnibus.

'The Brexit farce and a test for Western democracy'

Reporting before, during and after the election was timely, straightforward and either supplied by western agencies (AP, Reuters) and from correspondents based in the UK, who were British freelancers. Coverage in the printed papers was sporadic, but online versions reported what had happened in a timely manner but without much fanfare.

China Daily is an English-language daily newspaper, established in June 1981 and owned by the publicity department of the Communist Party of China. It claims it has the widest print circulation of any English-language newspaper in China – more than 900,000 copies globally, of which 600,000 are distributed outside of China.

It has a comprehensive website in English – http://global.chinadaily.com.cn/ – with links to Facebook (84.7m likes), Twitter (4.3m followers) and a YouTube channel with videos of cute pandas and dramatic landscapes, which all feels somewhat perverse given that these social media outlets are blocked by the Chinese authorities along with Blogspot, WordPress, WhatsApp plus anything to do with Google, like Gmail and Dropbox and, of course, the search engine.

China Daily prefaced the election with an opinion piece headlined 'The Brexit farce and a test for Western democracy'. Telling it straight the author, director of the Center for European Studies at Fudan University, says: "For people in the UK and those in the rest of the world, Brexit has become a farce, not least because the Brexit process has lingered for more than three years."

This is, however, an opportunity to cast aspersions at democracy rather than analyse one of the biggest political events of the decade. "That the UK, despite being a pioneer of representative democracy, has not been able to complete the Brexit process even after more than three years shows Western democracy is neither as representative nor as efficient as is claimed."

Between baby animal videos and party pronouncements *China Daily* posted a four-minute video on Twitter fronted by London correspondent Julian Shea outside No 10. "As Britain adjusts to a new political reality after a dramatic general election, this *China Daily* explainer looks at what happened and why," says the tease and Bray kicks off the broadcast with the words: "Well, who saw that coming?"

The film had 1,800 views in the month since it was posted on December 12, not a huge return for the effort that went into it given the millions of followers.

Xinhua News Agency or New China News Agency is the official state-run press agency of the People's Republic of China, a sort of Government-run Press Association or Associated Press. It describes itself as "the biggest and most influential media organisation in China, as well as the largest news agency in the world in terms of correspondents worldwide". It is the highest-ranking state media in the country alongside the *People's Daily.* As well as providing material for media outlets worldwide it has its own website (www.xinhuanet.com) with updated content.

Xinhua reported that Chinese Premier Li Keqiang sent a congratulatory message to Boris Johnson on his election. Without quoting the Chinese Premier directly the story revealed that in his message, Li said that "China-Britain relations have generally maintained development momentum in recent years, and bilateral exchanges and co-operation in various fields enjoy huge potential". Diplomatic speak for let's be friends, please.

Meanwhile, in Hong Kong…

The South China Morning Post has been Hong Kong's 'newspaper of record' for more than 100 years. Founded by Australian-born anti-Qing dynasty revolutionary Tse Tsan-tai and British journalist Alfred Cunningham it has had a succession of high-profile proprietors, including Rupert Murdoch, and is now owned by Alibaba Group, China's answer to Amazon run by Jack Ma, the richest man in China.

Its authoritative western-style of journalism has always found a ready market among Hong Kong's upwardly mobile elite, plus readers wanting to improve their English and also appreciate content that doesn't automatically follow the Chinese party line. Perhaps most telling is the fact that its website is not available inside mainland China.

The Post published a story in the week after the election, headlined 'After Brexit, can Boris Johnson make Britain greater?' Written by correspondent Hilary Clark in London it explored the potential relationship between China and a buoyant Boris Johnson. "The new majority enables the government to stand back from the simplistic 'Golden Era' view of China, while also avoiding the easy error of adopting an overly confrontational approach," it quoted Matthew Henderson, Director of the Asia Studies Centre at Henry Jackson Society, one of the more China-hawkish of the UK's foreign policy think tanks jostling to be heard by the new government.

"Instead it can devise and implement a resilient new China policy based on a proper risk/gain assessment and clarity about Britain's lasting interests."

Yu Jie, a China analyst with the more dovish Chatham House said: "China's rise in the last 10 years or so has shown it could potentially be of enormous benefit economically and financially to the UK."

The Post also found room for a sidebar headlined 'Boris Johnson uses Huawei phone for selfie after hinting at UK ban', which reports that a day after prime minister Boris Johnson hinted that Britain could restrict or ban Huawei Technologies telecoms equipment, he was seen using what appeared to be a Huawei P20 Pro smartphone – "with a shimmering Twilight colour scheme" – for the infamous selfie with ITV's This Morning programme.

'Say no to Western media's double standards'

It is the perceived criticism, justified or otherwise, from the West about their human rights record and attempts by Huawei for world domination via 5G that is exercising Chinese media the most.

"Say no to Western media's double standards" thundered a headline *in Global Times*, which is run by the *People's Daily*, China's largest newspaper group.

Another editorial in *Global Times* headlined 'Western divisions lead to biased mentality' cited both Brexit and the Trump impeachment hearings as examples of 'ideological polarisation'.

"Western media are deeply involved in party struggles," says the piece. "Their selective reports and comments serve viewpoints. Western society's perception and judgment of right and wrong has been chaotic."

Clearly, in a country where there is no party politics, the goings on at Westminster and Capitol Hill hold some fascination but they can't let the moment pass without casting judgment on what they openly call 'Sinophobia'. "The latest round of attacks on China by some political and public opinion elites has deepened the value gap between the Western public and Chinese society. Sinophobia is being encouraged in the West," says the editorial.

Immediately after the election the *China Daily* columnists were in reflective mood. In a piece called 'UK election result only adds to country's problems' it posed questions for the new administration including 'Can a powerful extra-parliamentary alliance be constructed to challenge right-wing policies in workplaces and working-class communities across Britain?'

An opinion piece by Ding Gang, a senior editor with *People's Daily*, neatly juxtaposed two topical issues – Brexit and technology – under the headline 'How will Europe respond to China's rise?'

"Two recent events in Europe have been extensively followed by Chinese media. First, as UK's general election was held on December 12 amid a volatile political climate, Brexit became a foregone conclusion," he wrote.

"Second, the 5G technology of Chinese tech giant Huawei is facing resistance in Europe. The two events are landmarks in China-Europe and Asia-Europe relations in the 21st century." Evoking a history lesson on colonial rule the piece acknowledges that "even as its imperial power has eroded and the UK has cut its links with the European integration process, Britain's impact on Asia is still ubiquitous".

Reflecting that the looming ethnic conflicts and border disputes in Asian countries are still closely related to British or European colonial rule the piece concludes: "More importantly, the ideas for resolving these problems have not yet emerged from the outdated mind-set."

Censorship and information control

China is a champion of censorship and information control, says the Committee to Protect Journalists (CPJ), an independent, non-profit organisation that promotes press freedom worldwide.

While Article 35 of China's constitution states: "Citizens of the People's Republic of China enjoy freedom of speech, of the press, of assembly, of association, of procession and of demonstration." CPJ argues that Chinese people do not enjoy these rights. At the end of 2019, China had 48 journalists in prison more than any other nation, according to CPJ research.

"China has faced a progressively more restrictive media environment since Xi Jinping became president in 2013," says a report written by CPJ Asia Program Coordinator Steven Butler and published in the week after the UK election.

The report goes on: "Whatever the constitution says, Xi and China have made no secret about what's expected from the media. Xi outlined his expectations for media standards during a visit to news establishments in February 2016, as reported by Xinhua: 'All news media run by the Party must work to speak for the Party's will and its propositions and protect the Party's authority and unity,' Xi said."

With access to international media like the BBC, the *Guardian*, *New York Times* and *Washington Post* not available to the Chinese public, the state media has a dominant, no domineering, position as opinion formers.

So, while the information war has a distinctly one-sided feel inside China, outside the country the state media is clearly part of the battle for soft power. The social media feeds are an eclectic mix of baby animals (giraffes, pandas, take your pick), sweeping landscapes worthy of *National Geographic*, party dignitaries of official visits and even the occasional bite of foreign news. Take a bow Boris, Brexit and events in a land far, far away.

Note on the contributor

Alan Geere is a journalist, academic and media development specialist. He is currently on sabbatical in Guangzhou, southern China, teaching international journalism.

九州　责编:彭奕菲　版式:刘桂娜　校对:黄黎繁
2019/12/15 · 星期日

欧盟敦促英国尽快批准
并有效执行"脱欧"协议

留给双方的
时间不多了

为期两天的欧盟峰会13日在布鲁塞尔落下帷幕。会议期间,欧盟领导人集中讨论了"脱欧"和"欧洲绿色协议"、世贸组织改革等议题,敦促英国尽快批准并有效执行双方此前达成的"脱欧"协议。

新就任的英国首相鲍里斯·约翰逊在唐宁街10号首相府发表演讲。

无悬念"。

发布会前,欧盟27国领导人还举行了"脱欧"峰会,会后发布的公报说,欧盟将继续以"脱欧"协议为蓝本推动有序"脱欧",任命米歇尔·巴涅继续担任欧盟"脱欧"谈判首席代表。

英国保守党领袖鲍里斯·约翰逊13日在赢得下院选举后,正式就任英国首相的约翰逊表示,英国将在明年1月31日正式退盟,"没有'如果',也没有'但是'"。

易谈判是关键

英国"脱欧"期限为2020年1月31日。正式

"脱欧"后,英国将进入"脱欧"过渡期,其间需要与欧盟谈判更新贸易协议。

"脱欧"过渡期限截止至2020年底,可在英国要求下延长,英国最迟明年6月底提出延期要求。不过,保守党竞选时承诺,"脱欧"过渡期将在2020年底如期结束。

贸易谈判将涉及环境、劳工、补贴、农产品和食品标准、渔业配额、产品原产地标注等多方面问题,路透社报道,欧盟类似谈判通常耗时数年,英国想在2020年底前与欧盟达成新贸易协议并不现实。

山"。如果双方未能在2020年底前达成协定,英国又拒绝延长过渡期,就只能依照世界贸易组织规定与欧盟开展贸易活动。

路透社援引分析人士的话报道,如果出现这一状况,英国将在2020年底彻底退出欧盟单一市场和关税同盟,英国经济预期2021年出现"温和衰退"。

加拿大皇家银行资本市场经济学家认为,新一届英国政府可能只是把彻底退出欧盟单一市场和关税同盟用作与欧盟谈判的筹码,不排除申请"一定程度上"延长过渡期。

本栏文图均据新华社

'There's not much time left for both sides' says this headline in a Chinese regional daily reflecting on newly-elected Boris Johnson's pledge to 'Get Brexit Done'

Boris Johnson's thumping election victory made prime time TV news across China

Minefields?

***

Journalism: there may be trouble ahead…

Raymond Snoddy

If the EU Referendum, the years since, and the 2019 general election were difficult times for journalists in both broadcasting and newspapers, the worst may yet be to come.

The government of Boris Johnson with its 80-seat majority seems hell bent on decriminalising the BBC licence fee, something that would almost certainly result in the loss to the BBC of several hundreds of millions of pounds a year, adding to the £250m a year it will lose providing free access to all over 75-year-olds on income support.

Worse still the UK Government seems determined to try to replace the licence fee entirely by 2027 and replace it with a form of voluntary subscription – a move that would destroy the concept of the BBC as a national public service broadcaster paid for by all households. At the same time there is little sign of the Government moving to help the press financially –particularly the struggling regional sector.

And, as journalists mainly failed yet again to appreciate what was happening across the country, or predict the move to the Conservatives in what used to be Labour's northern heartlands, hard questions were once again being asked about what it means to be a journalist and how they should report an increasing complex world.

Curiously a clarion call on what journalism should be, and what it has to become once again, came not from a journalist at all, but from the pulpit of St Martin's-in-the-Fields, London.

In his funeral oration for Richard Lindley, a journalist who exemplified what difficult and dangerous broadcasting in the public interest once was, the Revd Dr Sam Wells had the following to say:

"There used to be a profession called journalism. Today we are led by people who don't know what truth is. Journalism is becoming an adjunct of marketing, governed by algorithms. Real journalists, who believe the truth will set you free, are so rare they are better described as prophets," Revd Wells said.

And in gathering to honour Richard Lindley, it was only then that it was realised he had been a prophet. "And his faithful, dangerous, counter cultural, courageous message was this: the truth will set you free. Free indeed," the Revd Wells concluded.

How far we have come from the days of Richard Lindley is set out by Helen Lewis, a staff writer for the *Atlantic* magazine and former deputy editor of the *New Statesman*. For political journalism, one of the greatest distorting factors is the endless repetition of conventional wisdom, she writes.

"Jeremy Corbyn is useless, Donald Trump is a joke, Theresa May is the Iron Lady, Remain will win, the Liberal Democrats are finished, Nigel Farage has retired from politics. All of these seem true until suddenly they are not," Lewis emphasises.

For her the first sin of political journalism is indulging in a teleological view of history – assuming a fixed end point and then telling the story as if it were always heading for that point. "It is also the easiest to cure. Stop doing it," says Lewis.

She believes that it is not journalism's job to report that people are saying it's raining. "It's journalism's job to look out of the window," she adds.

Richard Tait, editor-in-chief of ITN and a senior regulator on the BBC Trust, notes that although the BBC was accused of biased general election coverage from all sides, there have been a long series of academic studies that have found no evidence of institutional bias, a view backed up by a more recent study by Ofcom, the communications regulator.

The BBC works hard at being impartial, even though it did not always succeed, he writes. "Where it fell short was more often in providing analysis, context and expertise and that there was need for more specialist reporting," Tait argues.

Ofcom wanted to see less of the "false equivalence" which gives equal weight to views with an unequal factual basis and urged the BBC to be bolder in its journalism and more determined to challenge the false.

For Tait this amounts to a perfect storm for the BBC with its regulator urging it to be less cautious, when even its current approach to impartiality has helped to provoke an existential crisis in relations with the Johnson government.

The current threats by the Government are "off the Richter scale" compared with previous routine bullying by governments, which usually fade as more important issues take over.

I highlight a question that appeared to come out of the blue four days before the general election vote, when a worker at a haulage company in the North East suddenly asked Boris Johnson live on Sky News when he was going to abolish the BBC licence fee.

In an election campaign dominated by the NHS and 'Getting Brexit Done' this was slightly odd. The future funding of the BBC had not been an issue and came in the afternoon of a day in which Johnson had committed his worst gaffe – refusing to look at a photograph of a four-year-old boy who had to sleep on the floor of a hospital because there was no bed for him. Johnson made things worse by pocketing the reporter's phone.

Whatever the origins, out came an attack on the BBC over free licence fees for the over-75s, an interest in decriminalising evasion of the licence fee, and a serious questioning of the long-term viability of the licence fee itself. It was the first public sign just how serious the Government's attacks on the BBC were likely to become.

Michael Gilson, former editor of both *The Scotsman* and the *Belfast Telegraph* hopes that with Boris Johnson, a former journalist in Downing Street, serious action will finally be taken to boost journalism.

The Government could blow the dust off the Cairncross Report it supported, he says. It may have avoided suggesting a windfall tax on the tech giants, but the report did call for the creation of a new Institute for Public Interest News that would work rather like the Arts Council.

One of the lessons of the general election was that journalism was not strong enough or sufficiently prized to counter the snake oil salesmen of politics, Gilson says. There will be a correction against the channels of news that merely confirm prejudices and journalism must be ready for that correction when it comes – "Ready to fulfil its simple, age-old task: telling people important things they did not know."

The truth will set you free

Richard Lindley was one of the great figures of the golden age of British broadcast journalism, first as an ITN correspondent and later as a BBC *Panorama* reporter. His funeral on the day before the December 2019 election at St Martin-in-the-Fields was attended by the director general of the BBC and editors and journalists from all parts of the UK media. This is the sermon by the Rev Sam Wells. The text is John 8: 26-32. Thought for the year?

There used to be a profession called journalism. Notice two words in that sentence. Have you ever noticed that journalism is an ism? Like socialism, Epicureanism, or… Anglicanism.

In other words it's something that requires commitment and conviction, and involves loyalty and solidarity. Law, accountancy, politics – those aren't isms; but journalism is. Likewise the word profession. It refers to a guild, of members who have training, apprenticeship, standards, integrity, and a desire to serve the public at cost to their own comfort or freedom. There used to be a profession called journalism. There used to be a man called Richard Lindley.

The word 'profession' and the discovery that journalism is an ism, a kind of faith, are ways of saying Richard Lindley was a person whom Aristotle would regard as a man of virtue. All the cardinal and theological virtues – justice, temperance, courage, prudence, faith, hope and love – fit Richard pretty well, but the one that stands out is courage. He talked about the fear of failure that spurred him on.

Thomas Aquinas says an important thing about courage. He says those who have no fear aren't courageous. Instead, courage means having fear but persisting anyway. That was Richard Lindley.

And what is it that took so much courage? Meeting a man like Saddam Hussein, yes. Facing horror in Bangladesh, yes. Being arrested in Angola, yes. Facing

Alzheimer's – yes. But one thing above all requires courage, from a journalist and from all of us. What requires courage most of all is to tell the truth.

What makes journalism an ism, a form of faith, what makes it a profession, a guild of honour, is this commitment above all: to tell the truth, come what may, whoever's embarrassed, or aggressive, or alienated, or wild with threats. You will know the truth, and the truth will set you free. That is the Hippocratic Oath of journalism. That was the creed of Richard Lindley.

The Christian faith is that there is truth, and that truth became flesh in Jesus, and the world is allergic to the truth, and so Jesus was crucified; but truth can't be suppressed, so Jesus rose from the dead, and the Spirit came to empower Jesus' followers to spread truth into all the world.

That Christianity, in the minds of many, ceased to be synonymous with truth, is a great tragedy. That people beyond the church speak the truth anyway, is part of the way God redeems the world despite the failures of the church. One person who spoke the truth in such a way was called Richard Lindley.

Eight months ago in this church a bunch of asylum-seekers played the disciples, and city slickers played the Sanhedrin, and a New York mogul played Pontius Pilate, as the congregation of St Martin's enacted the passion of Jesus, as it does every Palm Sunday.

At his trial, standing before Pontius Pilate, Jesus said, 'For this I came into the world, to testify to the truth.' Pilate replied, from exactly where I'm standing now, in a broad New York accent, 'What is truth?' … And everyone thought, 'You don't know, do you? You've got so mixed up with lies, manipulation and distortion, that you actually have no idea.'

In the first century AD, those who spoke the truth to people who controlled resources and information were called prophets. Today such people are called journalists.

There used to be a profession called journalism. Today, we're led by people who don't know what truth is. Journalism is becoming an adjunct of marketing, governed by algorithms. Real journalists, who believe the truth will set you free, are becoming so rare they're better described as prophets.

We've gathered to honour Richard Lindley, journalist. Only now do we realise he was a prophet. And his faithful, dangerous, countercultural, courageous message was this: the truth will set you free. Free indeed.

Note on the contributor

The Rev Dr Sam Wells has been the vicar of St Martin-in-the-Fields, in central London, since 2012. He is Visiting Professor of Christian Ethics at King's College, London. He is a member of the Multistakeholder Council that advises the G20 international forum.

Why political journalism keeps getting it wrong: From the Posh Man Problem to the war of facts against narrative, the deadly sins of covering politics

When I started at the *New Statesman* in December 2010, we were six months into Britain's first experience of coalition government since the 1940s, a surprisingly strong alliance between David Cameron's Conservatives and Nick Clegg's Liberal Democrats. Before I left in June 2019, we had two more general elections, a Scottish independence referendum and a referendum on our membership of the EU. In both the general elections I covered, as well as the 2015 Labour leadership contest and the US presidential election, the working assumption of most political journalists about the result was wrong. That is not only embarrassing; it has grave implications for our trade, warns Helen Lewis

Historians warn about 'the teleological view of history' – assuming a fixed endpoint and then telling the story as if it was always heading for that point. Something similar has happened, over and over again, in political journalism. In 2015, we assumed the Conservatives could not win an overall majority. The likeliest result, most journalists thought, was a Labour minority administration backed up by the SNP. That affected the questions we asked Ed Miliband: "Would you do a deal with the Scottish Nationalists? Would you give the SNP another referendum? How much money would you give to Scotland to get their votes?" And it also affected the Conservatives' 'squeeze' message to bolster their own support.

What happened feels like a version of the Hawthorne effect in science, where study participants alter their behaviour because they know they are being observed. By focusing so strongly on the possibility of a deal with the SNP, journalists made it look extremely likely. That, in turn, drove voter behaviour. It wasn't only journalists who assumed the wrong endpoint. In the years since, senior Tories have admitted the Conservative manifesto was written with the idea that some of its policies would have to be junked in a horse-trade with the Lib Dems.

Cut to election night 2015. The exit poll arrives – and it's an overall majority, albeit it a slim one, for David Cameron. All those questions about the SNP were not just redundant, but might have influenced the outcome. At the same time, insufficient consideration was given to what the Conservatives might do with a majority. The answer was an EU referendum, long demanded by a small but monomaniacal subset of the Conservative parliamentary party. Covering the build-up to that, once again political journalism struggled because it assumed the result – Remain – and worked backwards from there. In the course of the campaign, I can remember hardly any consideration being given to what form Brexit would take: there was no appetite for discussions of the merits of 'Norway plus' against a Canada-style trade deal. Leaving the EU was deemed unlikely to happen, and therefore not sufficiently interrogated. That has had enormous repercussions ever since.

Let's go across the Atlantic. There aren't many things Donald Trump and Jeremy Corbyn have in common, but here is one. Both were treated as joke candidates at the start of their campaigns. And joke candidates don't face the same level of scrutiny as front-runners – which is a problem when they turn out to be serious contenders. The seductive power of the conventional narrative is one of the most distorting forces in political journalism. Jeremy Corbyn is useless, Donald Trump is a joke, Theresa May is the Iron Lady, Remain will win, the Liberal Democrats are finished, Nigel Farage has retired from politics. All of these seem true, until – suddenly – they are not. For commentators and reporters on the left, that is particularly tricky terrain to navigate, because the printed press is dominated by the right, and therefore the consensus tends to be sympathetic to that point of view. For me, indulging in the teleological view of history is the first deadly sin of political journalism. It is also the easiest to cure – just stop doing it! Ask questions even if they seem odd or niche. Pin down politicians on under-considered scenarios. We must try to tune out what everyone else is obsessed with, and ask ourselves: what could happen that no one is talking about?

As there are traditionally seven deadly sins, here are six others. To draw them up, I talked to some of the political journalists whom I most respect, and who are trying to improve the quality of their trade.

Innumeracy

Most political journalists are arts and humanities graduates. That can lead to a lack of ease with economics as a policy area, with reports that involve figures, with real-terms and with parliamentary arithmetic – how many votes are needed for this to pass? It also leads to a lack of understanding in the way polls are reported. Most have a margin of error of three percentage points. All are an art as well as a science, taking the raw numbers and applying filters (such as likelihood to vote). Still, though, outlying polls are reported as news without being placed in context and moves of one or two percentage points are treated as significant.

The 'neutral amplifier' model

One of my favourite sayings about journalism is: "It's not journalism's job to report that people are saying it's raining. It's journalism's job to look out of the window." Too often, the words of a high-profile politician are repeated uncritically: "I will renegotiate the withdrawal agreement and get something better" ... "we will leave the single market but retain the same benefits". In other cases, a clearly partisan source is treated as (anonymous) gospel because the story is deemed too good to debunk – and in any case, the person briefing might then go to a rival outlet with it. Some journalists are seen by MPs and special advisers as reliable relays for spin who won't ask awkward questions. "We'll use [X] when we want projection," is how that dynamic is phrased. But the job of journalists is not to tell you what the Labour spokesman and 'sources close to Michael Gove' are saying. It's to evaluate their words and deliver them to readers or viewers in context. We need to look out of the window.

A related problem is the rise of journalists as personal brands. Twitter has created an arena where status – measured in follower numbers – is obvious even to outsiders. That has gamified political journalism. Reporters want to get full credit for their own stories, attract attention to themselves personally and (sometimes) buff their egos. Tweet early, tweet often and don't worry too much if you get something wrong, the thinking goes, because any attention is good.

The Confident Posh Man problem

This phrase was coined by a lobby journalist I know who self-defines as a Confident Posh Man. There are loads of them in Westminster, he observes. There are two obvious reasons: the first is lobby journalists, being based in the Commons, double up as fixers and lobbyists for their papers with senior politicians. If a media organisation wants a cabinet minister to speak at a conference, it's often the lobby correspondent's job to put in the request to the relevant special adviser. It would be a brave, or confident, news desk that sent someone with blue hair and visible tattoos.

The Commons is extremely formal, insisting on men wearing ties in the chamber, and is an intimidating place to work. Stella Creasy, the Labour MP, calls it "Hogwarts". The strange quirks – prayer cards, Pugin carpets, tearooms serving spotted dick – are less disorienting if you already attended a public school. The second reason is that news desks each send one to six correspondents, so there is no way to co-ordinate gender balance, let alone racial diversity, across the entire lobby. As a result, the lobby is very white and dominated by graduates and the privately educated. It has plenty of younger women in it, but the attrition rate is high after 30, because late nights, long days and unpredictable hours are hard to juggle with caring responsibilities. It was only in 2015 that *The Guardian* announced the first ever job share for political editors (although that has already ended).

No punishment for failure

Political journalism is often speculative, so there has to be latitude for predictions which prove incorrect. Sometimes that is taken as licence to write stories that are unfalsifiable, or will be correct – eventually. 'Theresa May on the brink as Tory MPs revolt' was true for nearly two years after the 2017 election before she finally resigned. One Sunday paper reported 48 letters expressing no-confidence in her leadership had gone into Graham Brady, chairman of the 1922 Committee, a year before they did so. ("An amazing scoop, if you look at it one way," said a writer for another organisation, dryly.) Among the journalists I spoke to, there was a general acceptance some of their colleagues treated political journalism as entertainment. A story could be just that. At outlets such as the *Financial Times* and Bloomberg, which cater to a specialist audience who may make investment decisions based on their coverage, there are heavy sanctions for getting it wrong. Elsewhere, attitudes are more relaxed.

99-1 as balance

Many of the problems I've described are more acute on newspapers and websites, because of the time pressures and focus on headlines. This one is worse in broadcasters, which have a duty under regulatory rules to be impartial. After commissioning an expert report, the BBC has ruled climate change is a scientific fact and so the starting point for discussions is no longer 'is it real or not?' A briefing note sent to staff in September 2018 told staff: "You do not need a 'denier' to balance the debate." Yet during the EU Referendum campaign, I heard frequent complaints that the economic risks of leaving the EU – the subject of broad agreement by 99 per cent of economists, trade experts and scientists – were treated as impossible to rule on. One economist, usually Patrick Minford of Cardiff University, would represent the small 'it's fine' camp. One economist would represent the entire rest of the profession. But viewers and listeners would have no idea that one spoke for a much larger group than the other.

The view from Versailles

As humans, we find people more interesting than policies. But that has huge distorting effects. The best political journalists use people to tell their stories, reducing an abstract clash of ideas to a human scale. The worst ones treat existential questions as props for a Punch and Judy show. It was this tendency which led the EU Referendum campaign to be covered as a contest between 'Dave and Boris'. What can we do about this, I asked one journalist I respect. His answer surprised me. "People will read about clashes," he said. "They won't read about the dynamics between two theories." Political journalism was "not like a murder. It's like two sides of a debate, but you've decided what the debate is, and what the sides are. If you don't have the confidence to do that, you have nothing."

His answer, he said, was to 'create people' – that is, to build up politicians as emblems of a particular viewpoint. Middle-of-the-road MPs have traditionally been reluctant to talk to journalists. The whips don't like it; such MPs worry it will harm their careers. The 'awkward squad' – the fringes of the party – behave differently. "Jacob Rees-Mogg exists because he picks up the phone to journalists," he told me. But what that means is political shows where Anna Soubry debates John Redwood, forever. My unnamed source encouraged a moderate Tory MP to do more broadcast interviews and to present himself as the spokesman for the broad centre of his party. It was an act of chutzpah but perhaps a necessary one. "All our stories are told through other people's mouths," my source said. "Is creating someone to deliver those quotes overstepping the mark?" He thought not. And the more I've thought about it, the more I agree with him. Journalists "create" public figures all the time. We decide which YouTuber to interview, which athlete to put on the front page, and which politicians are at the top of our mental Rolodex. We are, quite rightly, beginning to reckon with the lack of race, class and gender diversity in political journalism, and to expand our pool of sources. Why shouldn't that apply on ideological grounds too?

There is another dark side to the view from Versailles, and it is this. Too often, I think, journalists identify one type of person with 'true Britons'. We talk about Labour's 'heartlands' in working-class northern English regions, when the party is now strongest in multi-ethnic big cities. Asked to reflect on Labour's loss of votes in the European elections, Richard Tice, chair of the Brexit Party, said: "This has happened because they haven't listened to their core heartlands, they've listened to people in Islington." But Labour has two Westminster seats in the Islington region, each with a thumping majority. So where is the party's heartland now?

Because political journalists are stuck in the Commons and on Twitter – real world and digital versions of Versailles – they are prone to panic about not representing 'real people'. But who gets depicted as the authentic voice of unheard Britain is governed by implicit assumptions that are grim when exposed to the light. Why are the views of a retired steelworker in Grimsby about 'where the country has gone wrong' more important than those of a second-generation Nigerian-British nurse in Plaistow? Citizenship is supposed to transcend personal identity, and yet we still indulge an idea of the '*volk*'. This tendency applies equally in America, where retired steelworkers in Pennsylvania were held up as the Great Unheard, but the same epithet was not bestowed on black voters in Detroit. The scattered successes of the far right across Europe are deemed to tell us something about what 'real people' are thinking, in the way the more quiet triumphs of Green politicians are not. Across Europe, the story of the latest EU elections was the rise of environmentalist parties. But somehow, their voters aren't held up as 'real people' whose real concerns must be heeded by the main parties. Why not?

Political journalism is incredibly difficult. It involves cultivating a source, sometimes over years, with the knowledge that a single rogue story could result in them freezing you out altogether. Party leaderships can be uncooperative, refusing to submit to print interviews or press conferences. In the age of Twitter and rolling news, speed is highly prized. Political journalists work long, anti-social hours, in a building full of mice. They get trolled on Twitter. At least one, the BBC's political editor Laura Kuenssberg, has needed bodyguards just to enable her to do her job. On print titles, they answer to news desks who want a story that is new, exclusive and can be summed up in a single sentence. Trying to mash the complexity of reality into that format is incredibly tough.

On television and radio, they struggle to navigate their way through rules on impartiality in a hyper-partisan environment where both sides constantly complain about bias. They are expected to understand a dizzying array of jargon, and to have the chutzpah to tell a cabinet minister, live and in real time, that they are talking bollocks. That takes serious confidence and expertise. They deal with liars, self-promoters and sources who are actively trying to manipulate them. There is excellent political journalism out there. And god, do we need it now more than ever.

Note on the contributor

Helen Lewis is a staff writer at the Atlantic, and a former deputy editor of the New Statesman, where this article originally appeared.

Impartiality's last stand?

The BBC's coverage of the election campaign infuriated its enemies and exasperated some of its friends. Richard Tait says it needs to be bolder in its journalism if it is to survive some dangerous times ahead

For nearly 100 years the key defining characteristic of BBC journalism has been its commitment to impartiality – today it is not hard to find people who think as a concept impartiality has passed its sell-by date.

The BBC faces a perfect storm and impartiality is at its epicentre. In the aftermath of the general election the political parties, winners and losers alike, united in attacking its coverage; the Government, with a big parliamentary majority, openly threatens its funding and its independence; the Prime Minister's chief adviser apparently supports a policy of "undermining of the BBC's credibility" (Mason, 2020).

And, at the same time, the BBC seems dangerously short of friends: its director general admits public perceptions of the BBC's impartiality have weakened (BBC, 2019a:8); the BBC's regulator, in an unprecedented intervention, tells it to be bolder in its journalism and reports public discontent with its lack of challenge and 'false equivalence' between truth and lies (Ofcom, 2019b: 3-4).

The longest election campaign in history

In part, this is the fallout of the political crisis which began with the referendum in 2016. If it has sometimes felt like one interminable election campaign since then, that is because in some senses, it has been.

Politics has dominated the news agenda with the (mainly) binary issues over Brexit. The broadcasters have been in something approaching election mode for most of this period. That matters because the way impartiality is interpreted in election periods is distinctive in a number of ways.

First, the broadcasters aim for a broad equality in time between Conservative and Labour, meaning many stories are 'on the one hand, on the other hand'. Second, politics dominates the news agenda and crowds out other stories. Third, coverage of the political 'process' dominates, leaving less time for analysis. The big loser is something which in normal circumstances the BBC is quite good at – specialist journalism

Analysis by Loughborough University shows that nearly a third of the campaign coverage in 2017 was process rather than policy (Deacon, Downey, Smith, Stanyer and Wring, 2017). It had been a similar story in the 2016 referendum (Deacon and Wring, 2017). The Loughborough team's analysis in their chapter for this book showed the 2019 election equally dominated by process and Brexit – but "even when Brexit was reported, there was a lack of policy focused analysis as to what implementation might mean".

Analysis for Ofcom by my colleagues at Cardiff University in the summer of 2019 came to similar conclusions about the BBCs coverage outside the election periods. The Cardiff research posed some uncomfortable questions: "What is the range of political actors that appear in output outside of election time? How far should coverage of political, economic and social affairs be about events rather than policy issues? How regularly does the BBC appropriately challenge claims by politicians in its routine coverage?" (Cushion, 2019).

When the Cardiff team looked at the 2019 election itself, in a chapter for this book, they found little space for experts to comment on the credibility of the politicians' claims: "In other words, broadcasters referee a contest in which politicians argue between themselves, with only limited external scrutiny."

The story which got away

It is usually really hard to see what does *not* get covered – but one story which *nearly* got into the main election bulletins caught my eye as evidence, perhaps, of how high the bar had been set for specialist reporting.

On November 13, 2019 Boris Johnson's election photo opportunity was at an electric taxi factory in the Midlands, making a speech about Britain leading in this technology revolution (Hutton, 2019). Overnight it had emerged that Elon Musk, the boss of Tesla, had announced at an event in Germany he would set up his huge European operation, both its 'Gigafactory' (making batteries and electric powertrains) and its technology campus, in Berlin. He had talked in the past of placing one or both in the UK, but he said Brexit made it too risky (Fowler, 2019).

The BBC's economics editor, Faisal Islam, knew the story backwards and that a key problem was the issue of 'rules of origin' for components (something we are all likely to hear more about this year). He produced a really good piece for the *Six O'Clock News* on Radio 4 (BBC 2019b), but it did not make the biggest bulletins – *The World Tonight* on Radio 4 or *News at Ten* on BBC1. It was a major business story by one of the BBC's very best specialist reporters – with significance for the arguments about Brexit and a link to the day's election events. For a television version, there would have been entertaining video of Musk making the announcement, impromptu, to the astonishment and delight of his German audience (You Tube, 2019) and the cars are pretty cool.

It was a busy news day, but *The World Tonight* found space for 20 minutes on the Trump impeachment (BBC, 2019c) and the BBC *News at Ten* was able to fit in a nicely produced film about deep sea mining of cobalt for electric car batteries off the coast of Spain (BBC, 2019d).

'Arguments between the top politicians'

The debate about the right balance in coverage is scarcely new. When the BBC was challenged in November 2016 over the lack of analysis in the 2016 referendum campaign, its head of political news, Katy Seale, told the NewsXchange conference: "I accept that and I think we should do more and we try and do more, in the end, it's just a bit boring. The more exciting stuff is the arguments between the top politicians…and in the end I don't think that's going to change" (NewsXchange, 2016). The risk in that approach is that what suffers is specialist journalism.

The nature of modern campaigning, with the parties abandoning press conferences, where their proposals were examined in detail, for photo opportunities and social media, means there is less opportunity than ever for ensuring enough analysis.

It has been all the more a problem because the UK electorate did not start this process with a firm bedrock of knowledge about the issues: a survey in 2015 showed the UK public second from the bottom of the then 28 member states in knowledge about the EU, with just one on four able to answer correctly three basic questions (Hix, 2015).

The need for analysis will not go away now Brexit is 'done' – as many of the key concepts and issues in the negotiations are scarcely familiar territory. If anything, as audiences wrestle with rules of origin, cumulation, tariff quotas and passporting, equivalence and mutual recognition, there will need to be a lot more specialist analysis, even at the price of cutting back a little on the 'arguments between the top politicians'.

A short history of impartiality

To understand how the country's most important journalistic institution has got into this situation you do need a quick dive into recent history and, in particular, the way the BBC has tried to define and practice impartial journalism.

After the disaster of the Hutton report in 2004, the BBC Board, first the Governors and then the Trust, made impartiality a priority (BBC, 2004). An external review in 2007 came up with a key finding – that impartiality was no longer simply a seesaw between two positions but a wagon wheel, reflecting a wide range of views like the spokes of a wheel. Audience research also established the public's view – that BBC impartiality was very important and that if the BBC did not always achieve it that was a reason for the BBC to try harder rather than abandon its principles (BBC, 2007).

The BBC also started commissioning independent reviews of its coverage of hotly contested areas, such as the EU (BBC, 2005) and Israel (BBC, 2006). The reviews had independent panels or single reviewers, relied on academic content analysis and audience research. They went on to cover a really wide range of topics: devolution (BBC, 2007 and 2016a); science (BBC, 2011); rural affairs (2013a); and statistics (BBC, 2017).

What is striking about them as a body of work is how consistent their findings were. They found no evidence of the institutional bias alleged by some politicians and lobbying groups – the BBC worked hard to try always to be impartial although it did not always succeed. Where it fell short was more often in providing analysis, context and expertise and that there was need for more specialist reporting.

The reviews did result in some positive changes –particularly in specialist journalism. The BBC appointed a Europe editor, a Middle East editor and a science editor; there was a measurable improvement in reporting devolution; the BBC launched Reality Check.

The abolition of the BBC Trust and its replacement in 2017 by a unitary board running the BBC with Ofcom as regulator meant for the first time, the BBC's impartiality had an external judge. The cycle of detailed impartiality reviews seem to have died with the Trust, but on October 24, 2019, just before the election, Ofcom published a review of the BBC's journalism (Ofcom. 2019b).

It was ignored in the political mayhem of that week, but its verdict was truly jaw-dropping to anyone, who like me, had spent much of their professional life dealing with cautious, even restrictive, external regulators. Ofcom's main conclusion was that BBC journalism did not have to be restrained – on the contrary, it had to be bolder in a challenging, polarised political climate:

> "*Broadcasting rules do not require the BBC or other broadcasters to be absolutely neutral on every issue within news and current affairs, but they must be duly impartial. This means journalists should take context into account when considering how to achieve due impartiality. They should feel able to challenge controversial viewpoints that have little support or are not backed up by facts, making this clear to viewers, listeners and readers. Our research shows that audiences have respect for the calibre of the BBC's journalism and expect its reporters to investigate, analyse and explain events. This should give the BBC confidence to be bolder in its approach*" (Ofcom, 2019b: 4).

Equally important, Ofcom went on to stress it had found no evidence of the institutional bias alleged by critics of the BBC. It had rejected every complaint about BBC impartiality, including a massive complaint by a group of Eurosceptic politicians about 75 hours of *Today* programme coverage of Brexit issues in 2017 and 2018 (Ofcom, 2019a).

'False equivalence'

What makes the current situation really dangerous is that public discontent with the BBC over impartiality has spread beyond the usual suspects. Anyone who has worked as an editor in broadcast news, or been a regulator (and for my sins I have been both), knows that on the extremes of any controversy are people who will never be satisfied with any form of journalism except slavish endorsement of their views.

But the political crisis which began with the EU Referendum has polarised public opinion in a way not seen in the UK since the miners' strike. And discontent with the way the BBC has covered the crisis is alienating some of those who would normally be its defenders.

Ofcom still found strong support for the idea of the BBC and the principle of impartial accurate journalism – but also reported a desire for more analysis, more challenge and less of the 'false equivalence', where equal weight was given in a debate to views with an unequal factual basis. Ofcom agreed with them, arguing that "Giving 50:50 airtime to opposing views can lead to false equivalence, as opposed to due impartiality" (Ofcom, 2019: 15).

The perfect storm for the BBC is that its regulator is encouraging it to be less cautious when even its current approach to impartiality has helped provoke an existential crisis in its relationship with the Johnson government. The current threats – to cut the BBC's income, to review/abolish the licence fee, to sack the director general if she or he not to the government's taste – are off the Richter scale of routine government bullying which usually fades as more important issues take priority.

I hope I am wrong, but the suspicion that this time something else is going on was reinforced by the discovery of a September 2004 blog by the New Frontiers Foundation where Dominic Cummings was director. It said: "There are three structural things that the right needs to happen in terms of communications... 1) the undermining of the BBC's credibility; 2) the creation of a Fox News equivalent / talk radio shows / bloggers etc to shift the centre of gravity; 3) the end of the ban on TV political advertising" (Mason, 2020).

'Don't let it happen'

Anyone who doubts where this might be heading need only look across the Atlantic where the 'undermining' of the credibility of honest journalism is well advanced. Donald Trump's vilification of the 'mainstream media' as 'fake news' has so polarised public opinion in the US that fact-based reporting by CNN, ABC, CBS and NBC is now denounced by the government and its many supporters as opposition propaganda.

More than a third of Americans no longer trust the news to tell the truth (Talcott, 2019). And Fox News itself (which I remember when it started, 24 years ago, and for many years after, as partisan, but also capable of good hard news reporting) is now apparently willing to provide an uncritical platform for the President's views. For a horrible, Orwellian, glimpse of that future, take a look, for example, at the President's nearly hour-long phone call to *Fox and Friends*, his favourite breakfast show, on November 22, 2019 (Fox 2019).

For more than 50 minutes, with minimal interruptions, Donald Trump insulted his current opponents, alleged Barack Obama had spied on him and repeated the totally discredited conspiracy theory that the Ukrainians, not the Russians, had hacked the Democrats.

The *New York Times* produced an exhaustive list of inaccuracies and exaggerations (Qiu, 2019). It is 13 minutes into the 'interview' before any of the three Fox presenters, fronting after all, one of the top news shows of one of the most powerful news organisations in the world, asks anything other than a soft or leading question and there was no serious attempt at any stage to challenge any of the President's most outrageous claims.

This is not the American tradition of independent, fact-based, journalism and is equally far from what British broadcast news has always been, and, for the present at least, continues to be. Nor is it a sign of a healthy democracy.

The enemies of the BBC claim to want to cripple it and undermine its journalism because it is not impartial and/or that impartiality no longer matters – the reality is they want to diminish or destroy it because, with all its faults, the BBC overall *is* still impartial; and impartial, fact-based journalism matters now more than ever.

'Orwellian' can be an over-used term, but on this occasion I think it is justified. The BBC can be an exasperating organisation – George Orwell himself, who worked for it, called it 'somewhere halfway between a girls' school and a lunatic asylum'. But right now it needs all the friends it can muster – and it needs to be true to the words beside Orwell's statue, which after a customary BBC wobble, was installed at New Broadcasting House in 2017: "If liberty means anything at all it means the right to tell people what they do not want to hear" (Orwell, 1945: 107).

As Orwell wrote in his last letter about how to avoid the world of 1984: "The moral to be drawn from this dangerous nightmare situation is a simple one: don't let it happen. It depends on you" (Orwell, 1949).

References

BBC (2004) The BBC's Journalism after Hutton: Report of the Neil Review Team: London, BBC. Available online at http://downloads.bbc.co.uk/aboutthebbc/insidethebbc/howwework/reports/pdf/neil_report.pdf, accessed 27 January 2020.

BBC (2005) BBC News Coverage of the European Union: Independent Panel Report. London: BBC. Available online at http://downloads.bbc.co.uk/bbctrust/assets/files/pdf/our_work/govs/independentpanelreport.pdf, accessed 27 January 2020.

BBC (2006) Report of the Independent Panel for the BBC Governors on Impartiality of BBC Coverage of the Israeli-Palestinian Conflict, London: BBC. Available online at http://downloads.bbc.co.uk/bbctrust/assets/files/pdf/our_work/govs/panel_report_final.pdf, accessed 27 January 2020

BBC (2007) From Seesaw to Waggon Wheel: safeguarding impartiality in the 21st century. London: BBC. Available online at http://news.bbc.co.uk/1/shared/bsp/hi/pdfs/18_06_07impartialitybbc.pdf, accessed 27 January 2020.

BBC (2008) The BBC Trust Impartiality Report: BBC Network News and Current Affairs Coverage of the Four Nations. London: BBC. Available online at http://downloads.bbc.co.uk/bbctrust/assets/files/pdf/review_report_research/impartiality/uk_nations_impartiality.pdf, accessed 27 January 2020.

BBC (2011) BBC Trust Review of the Impartiality and Accuracy of the BBC's Coverage of Science, London: BBC. Available online at https://downloads.bbc.co.uk/bbctrust/assets/files/pdf/our_work/science_impartiality/science_impartiality.pdf, accessed 27 January 2020.

BBC (2013a) BBC Trust Review of Impartiality: BBC Coverage of Rural Affairs in the UK, London: BBC. Available online at http://downloads.bbc.co.uk/bbctrust/assets/files/pdf/our_work/rural_impartiality/rural_impartiality.pdf, accessed 27 January 2020.

BBC (2016a) BBC Trust Impartiality Review: Network news and current affairs coverage of the four UK nations: 2015 and 2016 follow- up to 2008 review, London: BBC. Available online at http://downloads.bbc.co.uk/bbctrust/assets/files/pdf/review_report_research/impartiality/2016/trust_conclusions.pdf, accessed 27 January 2020.

BBC (2016b) BBC Trust Impartiality Review: Making Sense of Statistics, London: BBC. Available online at http://downloads.bbc.co.uk/bbctrust/assets/files/pdf/our_work/stats_impartiality/2017/trust_conclusions_follow_up.pdf, accessed 27 January 2020

BBC (2019a) BBC Annual Plan, 2019-2020, London: BBC. Available online at http://downloads.bbc.co.uk/aboutthebbc/reports/annualplan/annualplan_2019-20.pdf, accessed 27 January 2020.

BBC (2019b) Six O'Clock News, 13 November 2019. Available online at https://www.bbc.co.uk/programmes/m000b4xd, accessed 2 February 2020.

BBC (2019c) The World Tonight, 13 November 2019. Available online at https://www.bbc.co.uk/programmes/m000b4xq, accessed 2 February 2020.

BBC (2019d) BBC News: Electric car future may depend on deep-sea diving. 13 November 2019. Available online at https://www.bbc.co.uk/news/science-environment-49759626, accessed 2 February 2020

Cushion, Stephen (2019) The Range and Depth of BBC News and Current Affairs: A Content Analysis Summary Report. Available online at https://www.ofcom.org.uk/__data/assets/pdf_file/0016/174022/bbc-news-review-content-analysis-summary-report.pdf, accessed 31 January 2020.

Deacon, David and Wring Dominic, (2017) One party, two issues: UK news media reporting of the EU Referendum Campaign, Mair, John, Clark, Tor, Fowler, Neil, Snoddy, Raymond and Tait, Richard (eds), Brexit Trump and the Media: Bury St. Edmunds:Abramis pp 36-44

Deacon, David, Downey, John, Smith, David, Stanyer, James and Wring, Dominic (2017, Two parts policy, one part process: News media coverage of the 2017 election, Mair, John, Clark, Tor, Fowler, Neil, Snoddy, Raymond and Tait, Richard (eds), Brexit, Trump and the Media (Bury St Edmunds: Abramis) pp 367-371.

Fowler, Steve (2019) Tesla Gigafactory Europe to be built in Germany, not UK, as Elon Musk blames Brexit uncertainty, Auto Express, 14 November 2019. Available online at https://www.autoexpress.co.uk/tesla/108395/tesla-gigafactory-europe-to-be-built-in-germany-not-uk-as-elon-musk-blames-brexit, accessed 2 February.

Fox News (2019) Trump calls into 'Fox & Friends' amid impeachment probe, upcoming FISA report, 22 November 2019.
Available online at https://www.youtube.com/watch?v=WNqKhRcpktU, accessed 31 January 2020.

Groves, Jason and Revoir, Paul, Downing Street threat to BBC: pick the right boss to replace Lord Hall as director general… or we'll fire them, Daily Mail, 21 January 2020. Available online at https://www.dailymail.co.uk/news/article-7913609/Downing-Street-threat-BBC-Pick-right-boss-replace-Lord-Hall-fire-them.html, accessed 27 January 2010.

Hix, S (2005) Brits know less about the EU than anyone else. LSE Blog, 5 December 2015. Available online at https://blogs.lse.ac.uk/politicsandpolicy/brits-know-less-about-the-eu-than-anyone-else/, accessed 31 January 2020

Hutton, Robert (2019) Electric Cars and Floods Stall Johnson's UK Election Drive, Bloomberg 13 November 2019. Available online at https://www.bloomberg.com/news/articles/2019-11-13/electric-cars-and-floods-stall-johnson-s-u-k-election-drive, accessed 2 February 2020.

Mason, Rowena (2020) Dominic Cummings think tank called for 'end of BBC in current form', The Guardian, 21 January 2020. Available online at https://www.theguardian.com/politics/2020/jan/21/dominic-cummings-thinktank-called-for-end-of-bbc-in-current-form, accessed 27 January 2020.

NewsXchange (2016). Are We Out of Touch? Available online at https://vimeo.com/showcase/4459104/video/207267465, accessed 3 February 2020

Ofcom (2019a) Ofcom Broadcast and On Demand Bulletin, 372, 11 February. London: Ofcom. Available online at https://www.ofcom.org.uk/__data/assets/pdf_file/0028/136585/Issue-372-of-Ofcoms-Broadcast-and-On-Demand-Bulletin.pdf, pp 23-30, accessed 28 January 2020.

Ofcom (2019b) Review of BBC news and current affairs, London: Ofcom. Available online at https://www.ofcom.org.uk/tv-radio-and-on-demand/information-for-industry/bbc-operating-framework/performance/review-bbc-news-current-affairs. Accessed 27 January 2020.

Orwell, George (1948) Statement on 1984, June 1949. Available online at https://gatwickcitytimes.wordpress.com/2017/09/08/september-8-2017-dont-let-it-happen-it-depends-on-you-george-orwells-last-known-published-words-statement-on-nineteen-eighty-four-june-1949/, accessed 31 January 2020.

Orwell, George (1945) Animal Farm. London: Penguin 1987.

Qiu, Linda (2019) Trump's Long List of Inaccurate Statements on 'Fox and Friends',

New York Times, 22 November 2017. Available online at https://www.nytimes.com/2019/11/22/us/politics/trump-fox-and-friends-fact-check.html, accessed 2 February 2020.

Talcott, Shelby (2019) Almost One Third of Americans Don't trust the Media: Poll, The National Interest, 21 November 2019. Available online at https://nationalinterest.org/blog/buzz/almost-one-third-americans-dont-trust-media-poll-98697, accessed 2 February 2020.

You Tube (2019) Elon Musk announces Berlin Gigafactory. 12 November 2019. Available online at https://www.youtube.com/watch?v=RoMdS2zIhqw, accessed 31 January 2020

Note on the contributor

Richard Tait CBE is Professor of Journalism at the School of Journalism, Media and Cultural Studies, Cardiff. From 2003 to 2012 he was Director of the School's Centre for Journalism. He was Editor of *Newsnight* from 1985 to 1987, Editor of *Channel 4 News* from 1987 to 1995 and Editor-in-Chief of ITN from 1995 to 2002. He was a member of the 2004 Neil Review of the BBC's journalism after Hutton. He was a BBC Governor and chair of the Governors' Programme Complaints Committee from 2004 to 2006, and a BBC Trustee and chair of the Trust's Editorial Standards Committee from 2006 to 2010. He is a fellow of the Society of Editors and the Royal Television Society, a Trustee of the Disasters Emergency Committee and a Board member (and former Treasurer) of the International News Safety Institute.

The gaffes that failed to unseat Boris

The prime minister made what seemed to be serious errors of judgment and refused to take part in detailed one-to-one interviews – yet he still won the 2019 election. Raymond Snoddy wonders why

Monday December 9, 2019 was a perfectly ordinary day in the general election campaign – if anything could be considered ordinary about the campaign - just four days before the vote on December 12.

The Conservative leader Boris Johnson was in the north east of England, chasing traditional Labour voters who had voted for Brexit to try to persuade them to vote Tory for the first time with the slogan 'Get Brexit Done'. It turned out that the strategy was successful beyond most people expectations, though Johnson did not know it at the time.

However, in what could have turned out to be a fatal blow to the campaign, Johnson was unexpectedly confronted with a photograph of four-year-old Jack Williment-Barr, suffering from suspected pneumonia. The child had been forced to sleep on the floor of Leeds General Infirmary covered in coats because there was no bed for him. It took more than 13 hours for Jack to finally get a bed.

A sick child on a hospital floor in the run up to a general election vote could hardly have been more politically toxic. The story by *Yorkshire Evening Post* reporter Dan Sheridan, complete with picture, had gone on the internet and been followed up by the *Daily Mirror*, which splashed with the story that morning, dominating that day's campaigning.

The story was seen as so serious that Health Secretary Matt Hancock was despatched to the Leeds hospital for an unscheduled visit to voice his concern. In what may have been a bit of a deflection tactic, one of Mr Hancock's aides even claimed he had been punched by a Labour-supporting protester outside the hospital. Analysis of videos of the incident showed it was 'fake news' and that the aide had accidentally walked into the arm of a protester.

The story took on a life of its own when a local political reporter for ITN, Joe Pike, repeatedly tried in an underground car park to confront Johnson with the picture of the boy on his mobile phone. Johnson would not look at the picture and, out of sight of the ITN camera, he took Pike's phone and put it in his pocket. Pike said to Johnson: "You refused to look at the photo. You've taken my phone and put it in your pocket, Prime Minister. His mother says the NHS is in crisis, what's your response?"

Johnson then took the phone out of his pocket and looked at the picture. "I'm sorry. It's a terrible, terrible photo, and I apologise obviously to the family, and all those who have had terrible experiences in the NHS, but what we are doing is supporting the NHS and on the whole I think patients in the NHS have a much, much better experience than this poor kid has had," said Johnson. He later apologised for taking the journalist's phone.

By any standards, not only trying to avoid a picture but actually taking a reporter's phone, was extraordinary behaviour, not least by a prime minister. Nothing quite like it has ever happened before.

A matching gaffe

As a gaffe it more than matched then Prime Minister Gordon Brown's description in the 2010 election campaign of Labour supporter Gillian Duffy as "that bigoted woman." The remark had been accidentally picked up by a Sky News microphone and led to an afternoon of grovelling apologies by Brown.

Boris Johnson then had an interesting afternoon in the Sunderland area that led to the story moving on from the NHS and the effects of austerity 'to the future of the BBC, its funding and licence fee. BBC funding and the licence fee had not been an issue in the election campaign and seemed secondary to the funding crisis facing the NHS and the main theme, to Get Brexit Done'.

There an employee at Fergusons haulage company in what was then the Labour stronghold of Washington, Tyne and Wear, asked Johnson: "Why don't you abolish the TV licence, please?"

The Prime Minister, being covered at the time live on Sky News asked: "For everybody?"

The Ferguson's employee replied: "Yes" – that was what he did mean.

Johnson appeared slightly surprised before replying that he was not going to make such an unfunded commitment so late in the campaign. "What I certainly think is that the BBC should cough up and pay for the licences for the over-75s as they promised to do. At this stage we are not planning to get rid of all TV licences, although I am certainly looking at it," he said.

The Prime Minister noted he was under enormous pressure "not to extemporise on the hoof" but added that you have to ask yourself whether that kind of approach to funding a media organisation made sense in the long term, given the way other organisations manage to fund themselves.

"The system of funding by what is effectively a tax on everybody that has a TV, it bears reflection, let me put it that way. How long can you justify a system whereby everybody who has a TV has to pay for a particular segment of TV? That is the question," Johnson explained.

After the exchange it was revealed that the future of the television licence was indeed under consideration in Downing Street and that the Prime Minister's main advisor, Dominic Cummings, was a long-term opponent of the licence fee.

No. 10 admitted that it was looking at the possibility of funding the BBC by a voluntary subscription or, at the very least, of decriminalising licence fee evasion, which was likely to have a similar effect.

In February, Culture Secretary Baroness Nicky Morgan announced an eight-week public consultation on decriminalisation and added that the licence fee could be abolished from 2027. The Culture Secretary, who now sits in the House of Lords, said that she was "open-minded" about how to fund the BBC from that point onwards.

A question out of the blue?

Did the question to the Prime Minister come out of the blue, and was the carefully worded, thought out response to it, clearly with more to come after the election, coincidental? Perhaps, but at the very least Johnson may have spotted an opportunity. Certainly the attack on the BBC licence fee quickly dominated the newspaper headlines and broadcasting running orders that day, turning the story of the four-year-old on the floor of a Leeds hospital into old news.

In his supposedly off-the-cuff remarks Johnson also told the BBC to "cough up" and pay the free licence fees for the over-75s "as they had promised to do."

The BBC had promised no such thing. When then Chancellor George Osborne tried to force the BBC to take on the full obligation of the over 75s, previously funded by government, the Corporation warned privately that this would mean the closure of BBC 2, the BBC News channel, all BBC local radio stations and the national radio services for Scotland, Wales and Northern Ireland.

The Government backed down and the compromise agreement meant that the transfer of responsibilities for the free licences would be phased in between 2016 and 2020.

It was a poisoned chalice. The BBC was explicitly given the freedom to decide what to do. Rather cunningly it would be the BBC rather than the Government that would face unpopularity if the Corporation ended the concession. Paying all of the free licences for the over 75s, many of whom are relatively well off, would cost the BBC around £750m a year, a sum that would rise to £1bn a year by the end of the decade because of an ageing population. Such a course, accounting for more than 20 per cent of the BBC's total budget, would inevitably mean significant cuts to BBC services.

After a public consultation Sir David Clementi, the BBC chairman, announced "a difficult but fair" decision to continue free licences for the over 75s who are on pension support, but the rest would have to pay. Even that will cost the BBC £250m a year, and possibly even more, if the licence fee issue encourages more over 75s to apply for pension support.

A sign of the future came in the January 2020 announcement that 450 jobs were going to be lost in BBC News, including the closure of the award-winning Victoria Derbyshire television programme.

The aim is to move to a more centralised 'story-led' production model to avoid duplication, a system considered more relevant for an online digital age.

Modernisation was one aspect of the change but the main imperative came from the need for BBC News to save £80m by 2022.

The decision to look again at decriminalising the licence fee and turn non-payment into a civil debt seems odd because then Prime Minister David Cameron in 2015 set up an inquiry into the issue and called in leading criminal barrister David Perry QC to investigate. Perry decided that "in the overall public interest" the current system should be maintained, although he did ask both for more research on why a disproportionate number of women come before the courts and easier ways to stagger licence fee payments

The lawyer noted that frequent claims that the system clogged up magistrates courts – still being repeated today – were untrue. Magistrates dealt with non-payment fines in batches and they accounted for only 0.3 per cent of court time. Perry also noted that decriminalisation would inevitably lead to an increase in evasion, something that the BBC estimates could cost up to £200m a year.

As for the licence fee, it is guaranteed under the BBC's current Royal Charter until 2027. There is a mid-term review in 2022, by coincidence the BBC's centenary year, although that is seen as an opportunity to look at the level of licence fee, currently £154.50, although it will rise in line with inflation to £157.50 from April.

The BBC will try to make a case for more. Given the scale of the competition it faces from the tech giants of California. Johnson might just go for a crowd pleaser and try to reduce the licence fee, although that would be controversial.

Even more controversial, and something that would lead to a legal challenge, would be any attempt by the Government to try use its strong majority to try to overturn the Royal Charter midway through its life and replace the licence fee with a subscription system. There is now no indication such a thing will happen before 2027.

The structural problems that the BBC is facing – or could soon face – are only part of "the Boris Johnson problem." There were Conservative allegations of bias against the BBC both in the run-up to Brexit and from the general election campaign itself.

The pursuit of Boris Johnson

Considerable bitterness arose from the BBC's vigorous pursuit of a Boris Johnson interview with Andrew Neil, the BBC's star interviewer – an ordeal that all the leaders of the major parties had already endured. As the clock ticked down to the general election and there was no sign of Boris, at least as far as an Andrew Neil was concerned, the forensic interviewer launched what amounted to an on-air attack on the Prime Minister.

Neil, once Johnson's boss when the future Prime Minister was editor of *The Spectator*, did not pull his punches. He told his audience such an interview was a matter of trust. "The theme running through our questions is trust, and why at so many times in his career in politics and journalism, critics and sometimes even those close to him, have deemed him to be untrustworthy," Neil said on live television.

The former *Sunday Times* editor listed a number of disputed Johnson's policy proposals from the 50,000 new nurses to the 40 new hospitals and the extra £34bn for the NHS and asked whether Johnson could be trusted to deliver on his promises. Neil did not get his interview, nor did ITV's Julie Etchingham who had also interviewed the other major party leaders.

Channel 4 also incited the ire of Johnson when they 'empty-chaired' him, along with Brexit Party leader Nigel Farage, with a block of ice when he failed to turn up to a Leaders' debate on climate change. Instead, Johnson sent former environment secretary Michael Gove, now Chancellor of the Duchy of Lancaster, and Boris's father Stanley. Neither was acceptable to the broadcaster.

The Conservatives complained to regulator Ofcom that the melting block of ice broke broadcasting impartiality rules and cited what they saw as a widespread pattern of anti-Tory bias at the channel, including previous criticisms of Boris Johnson by Dorothy Byrne, Channel 4's head of news. Ofcom ruled that Channel 4 had not broken broadcast impartiality rules because Conservative views had been represented in the programme but noted it might have taken a different view if the block of ice had been carved into a Boris Johnson likeness. Afterwards, anonymous Conservative sources hinted that the Government might consider reviewing Channel 4's licence.

BBC bears the brunt

It was the BBC however that bore the brunt of the Johnson Government's attacks in what looked like an orchestrated pattern. Non-appearance at crucial interviews was one thing but Johnson also banned all his ministers from appearing on Radio 4's flagship *Today* programme where they used to command the 8.10am main political slot but faced vigorous questioning. Though Johnson did turn up in January 2020 for what was seen as a 'soft' interview with BBC Breakfast's Dan Walker. There was another much, much softer interview with Facebook – where Johnson was asked what shampoo he used.

Sarah Sands, departing editor of the *Today* programme, accused Downing Street of deploying "Trumpian" tactics in banning ministers from appearing on the programme and accused the Government of using its majority to "put the foot on the windpipe of the BBC." The ban looked as if it has been extended to *Newsnight*, too, after Downing Street took exception to the appointment of Lewis Goodall, an allegedly 'anti-Johnson' journalist as policy editor of the programme.

There have always been rows between the BBC and politicians of all parties across the years but the current depth and range of the animosity appears unprecedented.

The out-going director general of the BBC, Lord Tony Hall, rejected all claims of bias in the Corporation's election coverage and insisted the BBC had the public's trust.

"Yes, of course we faced some criticism. That is to be expected as the national broadcaster. Where we can and need to improve we will. But the fact that criticism came from all sides of the political divide shows to me that we were doing our job without fear or favour," Lord Hall wrote in an article in the *Daily Telegraph*.

Whether the Prime Minister will pay much attention to such an argument is problematical. Are the current attacks on the BBC just the normal cut and thrust of general election politics? After all, apart from ministers not turning up to the *Today* programme little of a concrete nature has actually happened?

The record going forward will answer that question, but the portents are not good. Decriminalisation of the licence fee could have a devastating impact on BBC finances, perhaps even more than the BBC currently estimates, if over time the word spreads that if you don't pay your licence fee nothing happens.

In the meantime, for anyone who values public service broadcasting, it would be wise to assume that an unprecedented degree of malice is informing the Johnson government's attitude to the BBC. Great and irreparable damage could be the result, whether deliberate or not.

The last week of the election campaign ended as it began – with another world-class Johnson gaffe.

On the eve of voting Boris Johnson hid in an industrial fridge to avoid Jonathan Swain, a reporter from ITV's *Good Morning Britain,* who was live on air. The reported shouted: "Morning Prime Minister, will you come on *Good Morning Britain*? Will you deliver on your promise to speak to Piers Morgan and Susanna Reed?"

Johnson then walked into the industrial container-sized fridge to escape and answer came their none. The Prime Minister's behaviour was as bizarre as when he pocketed the reporter's phone to avoid looking at that plight of the sick child.

If any of the gaffes, or his unwillingness to face serious questioning about his record or policies, had any effect on the electorate it was difficult to discern, as Boris Johnson came out of the fridge to win an 80-seat majority and push on with getting Brexit done.

Note on the contributor

Raymond Snoddy has been a journalist all his working life on local and regional newspapers and on the *Financial Times* and *The Times*, for many years specialising in the media. He has also presented a number of television series including *Hard News* for Channel 4 and the accountability programme *News Watch* for the BBC. He is a co-editor of this book.

A lesson for our new PM: funding the 'dying beasts' will not save the future of journalism

With a journalist in 10 Downing Street, this should be the moment for action to save journalism at the regional level, but it is a time to be bold and not merely repeat the mistakes of the past, says former newspaper editor Michael Gilson

For the first time in 35 years the General Election passed me by. I voted but, no longer a newspaper editor, I had the luxury of opting out of thinking too much about it. No more worrying about weighing up column inches, planning reporting at counts, fielding complaints of bias. My radio was retuned from Radio 4 to Radio 3.

It was a relief to be disengaged from an election campaign that was lamentably low on vision and foregrounded how easily traditional media could be bypassed, even from the distance of the last poll just two years ago. The BBC being forced into its traditional role of Aunt Sally was too predictable even to get worked up about and a quick survey amid the wreckage of the local press revealed little to derail campaigns beyond perhaps, temporarily, the Yorkshire Evening Post's 'boy sleeping on the floor of A&E' story.

But journalism never really leaves you and so thoughts about its future did come quickly after. If it remains in the bloodstream what would a former journalist now heading a government with a big majority do about the parlous state of our industry? Does our Prime Minister care enough about the ever-growing democratic deficit in huge swathes of the UK, caused by the decline of traditionally-funded journalism, to do anything about it? The early signs, a despotic hint of a punishment beating for the 'liberal' Beeb over de-criminalisation of non-payment of the licence fee, did not augur well.

The state of journalism will not be in the intray of Boris Johnson's top ten most pressing matters but it is clear some kind of Government intervention, or even just a little bit of attention, is going to be needed before long to address the drift into irrelevance of vast areas of the media. Competing for low common denominator clicks amid the white noise online is never going to convince people that the demise of some forms of journalism is worth caring about. Take an hour to browse through a random selection of regional press websites if you really want to depress yourselves. In the circumstances the Government could even do worse than blowing the dust off the Government-backed Cairncross Report, released in February last year examining what a sustainable future for journalism might look like. Maybe our former journalist PM could call up a cross section of his former industry pals to look at how some of the report, too modest but with some good starting points, could be implemented. I won't be holding my breath.

Cairncross was lily-livered on what to do about the Vampire squids of Google and Facebook hoovering up a huge percentage of the global advertising spend while feeding off journalism that has been invested in by others. No windfall tax proposal can be found in its largely unread pages but at least it suggests a regulator to oversee social media platforms sites to ensure the 'news' they carry is trustworthy, even if initially it would only assess how well these sites are performing. If systematic and consistent problems are found, the report warns, 'it may be necessary to impose stricter provisions'. I imagine Mark Zuckerberg cowering behind the sofa as I write.

But there are proposals that pique the interest. The report calls for a new Institute for Public Interest News which could work in a similar way to the Arts Council, channelling public and private funding to 'those parts of the industry it deemed most worthy of support'. Possible tax relief for publishers is mentioned as is a possible extension to the BBC-funded Local Democracy Reporting Service.

But if we are to revive the debate it is at this junction we will be in danger of taking the wrong turn. To illustrate it's worth remembering that, just before Cairncross limped out of the starting blocks last year, a group of regional publishers already had the begging bowl out, calling for 1,500 (yup that figure is right) more Local Democracy Reporters to be funded by, well, not them.

On this score I was intrigued by an interview the chief executive of Newsquest, Henry Faure Walker, gave to Raymond Snoddy, for InPublishing magazine, in February last year. One sentence jumped from the page and hit me like a comedy boxing glove on a spring.

Said Faure Walker: "Journalism is becoming an increasingly unprofitable activity so you need to incentivise publishers to do journalism."

I'll leave the quote where it surely deserves to be; sitting in a paragraph all of its own. Forgetting the grammar which would have had a sub-editor, if there were any left, weeping real tears, it is the sentiment which, only a few years back, would surely have been accompanied by the clunking sound of collective journalist jaws hitting the floor. In other news Mr Heinz has today announced that, while he is OK still manufacturing the tin, he can no longer afford to supply the beans.

The chief executive did tell Snoddy Newsquest was in it for the long term, did not 'flip' titles like a private equity company, had to live with the consequences of its actions and wanted a proper debate about the future of quality journalism. He echoed calls for the Beeb to stump up the cash for those 1,500 journalists to cover local courts and councils, somewhat mystifyingly adding that the money would not help Newsquest profits but only journalism itself.

At this point the new Government should be drawing its red line. For Boris Johnson need only pop along to the Treasury to have the financial wonks tell him you don't throw good money after bad. Frankly the debate about how we support public service journalism has to move way beyond the concept of propping up the dying beasts of the newspaper industry. They cannot be blamed for the perilous state of journalism but their decades-long myopia, chasing of eye watering margins, payment to their top echelons of staggering salaries while the grunts toiled on low pay, has been a contributing factor. There is evidence that the employment of Local Democracy Reporters in local patches has allowed the non-replacement of staff in newsrooms.

I have huge respect for my former colleagues still working, sometimes against incredible odds, to produce great examples of journalism on the ground, especially at the local level where, of course, we all live. However the future does not belong to the companies that currently employ them.

At this point my mind keeps going back to the Institute for Public Interest News (IPIN?) awarding public and private (donations, foundations, bequests) monies to 'those parts of the industry deemed most worthy of support'. There is the kernel of good idea here but we must redefine 'industry' in the widest possible terms so that funding is really investment not bail out.

Here's one possibility. Up and down the country there are excellent schools of journalism at our universities run by first-class tutors imbibing their students with a public service journalism ethos, enthusing them to go out and be what all good reporters should be; troublemakers to those in power. The fire in the belly of those students is soon doused as they embark on careers in digital marketing.

Why not fund these universities to set up Centres for Public Service Journalism in their regions running websites publishing real stuff that challenges, sheds light, reveals, investigates, tells local communities what is really going on where they live? Bring in real journalist talent to guide and help. Place the Local Democracy Reporters in these university newsrooms too. Train those new journalists for a future out on their own or in groups of troublemakers (gangs?) doing the same thing. I'm pretty sure that soon other universities and centres of higher learning would sit up and take interest should the project prove successful.

Think there would be no support for this sort of thing? In the last couple of years I have spent a lot of time with local authorities, NHS trusts, development bodies and politicians (on the dark side as I still say) and can report there is a genuine concern about the lack of media coverage concerning their activities at a regional and local level. Some politicians have even pined for the days when they used to 'get a good kicking from the press' for it meant what they were doing was important.

I have been in conversations in which various bodies have wondered privately about public funding for some form of local journalism, perhaps placing a newsroom structure in a 'blind trust' with a board containing experienced journalists and academics to avoid any sense of control from funding organisations which should often, of course, be the subject of the said newsroom's investigative gaze. I can hear the howls of outrage from journalists about state-sponsored control, indeed feel a little queasy myself, but, if it does anything, it serves to show how concerned many are about the democratic deficit in their patches. If there is no communication or engagement with communities, they make policy in a vacuum. The more advanced thinkers in the public sector recognise this is a bad thing. In any case might this model be better than what many communities are being presented with right now?

The trouble with all of this is that the debate needs to be had outside of the narrow confines of the journalism 'industry' we have at present otherwise it will simply be filled with the kind of special pleading the chief executive of Newsquest made in his interview. It will get us nowhere. The truth is this business is too important to be left to the business. Despite the earlier analogy, journalism was never the equivalent of cooking beans in tomato sauce to fill a can, even though there were plenty of those in charge back in the day who believed just that.

The General Election taught us many things. One was that journalism is not strong enough, nor, more importantly, sufficiently prized, to counter the snake oil salesmen of politics nor correct with facts the tidal waves of prejudice and misinformation coming at us through our mobile phones. In a way that lesson is timely and could, just could, force a radical rethink of what we mean by journalism and how it should be funded.

As with all societal trends the current technological determinism that gives us channels to confirm our prejudices, bolster our narcissism, protect us from challenge will be the subject of a correction. Journalism must be ready for that correction, ready to fulfil its simple, age-old task: telling people important things they didn't know. A lot of impetus for the debate will depend on the former journalist now in Number 10. In the next few years we will find out just what kind of hack he really is.

Note on the contributor

Michael Gilson is the former editor of, among others, The Scotsman, Belfast Telegraph and The News, Portsmouth. He is an Associate Fellow of the School of Media, Film and Music, University of Sussex. He has a Master's degree in Garden and Landscape History from the Institute of Historical Research, University of London.

Postscript

Election 2019 – a grey and characterless contest

The winter election – with its angry tone and interview-shy leading politicians – had Channel 4 News anchor Jon Snow feeling nostalgic for lively elections of the past, and he's seen a few

It was the election nobody wanted, but everyone needed. In the dozen or more general elections I have worked on, this was the most rancorous, characterless, and abusive I can remember. It was also, intriguingly, the election in which politicians least wanted to be seriously interrogated.

The dominance of the social network ensured a level of nastiness that had not previously been particularly prevalent. At the same time political parties and their candidates utilised it to the full. It seemed at times they preferred their own unmediated campaign words above face-to-face contact with the voters, and particularly the media.

Thanks to the 2016 Brexit Referendum, in which there was less than four per cent separating those who voted to Remain, and those who voted to Leave, it remained the dominant issue of the 2019 General Election. Britain went to the polls more divided than at any time in living memory. The bile and argument dominated not only the election campaign, but seriously infected the discourse on the social network.

Boris Johnson and Jeremy Corbyn set the tone of the campaign – neither of them particularly keen to be interrogated by the media. As Johnson was already ensconced in Downing Street, there were few if any chances to catch him on the doorstep leaving home. For Corbyn, running the gauntlet of the waiting press at his home became a regular endurance. His determination never to answer a question at his garden gate made grumpy television, and tedious photos. For the early news broadcasts of the day, those unhappy images were often all the media had to play with.

The nostalgia of elections past

This lack of access found many reporters, me included, yearning for the old days of the morning press conferences. Up until the 2015 General Election, starting at 8.30 each morning, the major parties would in turn stage 40-minute-long news conferences starring major party figures. It was an opportunity for a wide cross section of journalists to have direct access to senior politicians on a subject chosen by the parties – questions on other key issues were also permitted. Unlucky was the reporter if he or she did not manage to pose a question. Needless to say, there were similar opportunities for the media in Scotland, Wales and Northern Ireland. The absolute avoidance of such daily access was the mark of this general election.

Whether trudging the streets, traipsing to distant UK destinations, reporting the election out on the road, or anchoring news programmes in the studio, for interviews, the media in the main had to make do with junior frontbenchers and former politicians. An additional limitation was that even before the campaign had begun, Mr Johnson had expelled a dozen or more of his most articulate Tory MPs – Dominic Grieve, David Gauke, Philip Hammond, Amber Rudd and others. Thus, in the search for interviewees to advocate for the Conservative Party, these people could no longer be regarded as 'current mainstream' Tory politicians despite having served in high positions in Conservative cabinets.

This was the general election with the least media access to the top candidates contesting it. For TV debates, if a party refused to participate, it often provided other parties with an excuse not to participate either. The refusal to appear, as a political strategy, has set in.

Outcome never in doubt

In short, the 2019 General Election added up to what was to prove a grey, characterless contest. The question was rarely about who would win. Few believed Labour under Corbyn had the slightest chance. The only question was whether any of the smaller parties would do anything to dent the Tory lead. There were those who believed the Liberal Democrats might win up to 60 seats. In the end they secured eleven – one less than last time. There was an awareness there was 'something' stirring in some of Labour's northern seats, but few were precise about what.

Many people who were simply fed up with the whole Brexit saga – whatever their views on the issues – simply wanted to rid themselves of the issue. Hence Boris Johnson's 'get Brexit Done' slogan picked up immediate traction, whilst other parties were still talking about a second referendum. The divided messages on the issue from Labour intensified, as did the Liberal Democrats in their pro-remain campaigning. In England, neither pro-remain, nor pro-second referendum campaigns picked up any noticeable amount during the campaign. If anything, they lost their advocates a good number of votes. That cost both Labour and Liberal Democrats dearly.

Views from around the kingdom

The SNP had a spectacular election in Scotland whipping seats off all other comers – including that of the Liberal Democrat leader Jo Swinson. Not for the first time, Nicola Sturgeon ran an assured campaign and set hares running as to the future of the Union. Spending a week in both Scotland and Northern Ireland during the campaign I found palpable evidence of change. In Scotland the independence movement was consolidating. In Northern Ireland there was a tangible shift, spurred by Brexit, to think seriously about eventual union with the South. Even in Wales where I also spent time, there was a questioning around what Brexit meant for their constitutional future.

The massive 80 seat majority for the Conservatives had the effect of somehow fixing the Brexit damage for a bit. But everybody knew a very tricky period for the United Kingdom lay ahead, centred on huge negotiating challenges with Brussels and a soothing of nerves at home. In addition, so much more seemed to be open for re-thinking; the future of the Union, the very governance of the country and, not least, electoral reform.

Note on the contributor

Jon Snow is the presenter of Channel 4 News. He joined ITN in 1976 reporting from Africa, the Middle East and Europe. He served as Washington Correspondent 1983-1987, Diplomatic correspondent 1987-1989 and has been the main anchor of Channel 4 News since 1989.

Lightning Source UK Ltd.
Milton Keynes UK
UKHW021246200320
360667UK00003B/49

9 781845 497644